MURDER DOG
THE INTERVIEWS VOLUME ONE

FOUNDED BY Black Bone Dog
EDITED BY Black Dog Bone & Paul Stewart

PUBLISHED BY

Murder Dog The Interviews Vol. 1
2015 © Copyright at Murder Dog / Rain Face Eye
Over The Edge Publishing

ISBN - 978-0-9964238-2-3
Cover & Design by Michael Ziobrowski for X Is The Weapon

All rights reserved. No part of this book may be reproduced or transmitted in any form or by any means, electronic or mechanical, including photocopying, recording, or by information storage and retrieval systems, without the written permission of the publisher, except by a reviewer who may quote brief passages in a review. Printed in the United States of America.

overtheedgebooks.com

CONTENTS

THANK YOU   4
INTERVIEWS   5

BG 6
JACKA 10
TOO SHORT 16
C MURDER 19
BUN B 22
DJ SCREW 26
EC ILLA 27
OUTLAWZ 30
FREDDIE GIBBS 32
SANTIGOLD 36
RBL 39
INSANE CLOWN POSSE 41
JT THE BIGGA FIGGA 50
MOB FIGAZ 53
LIL WAYNE 54
BAD AZZ 56
ZION I 58
YUKMOUTH 61
HI TEK 66
E 40 69
WHORIDAS 75
BIG MOE 77
TECH N9NE 80
ICE CUBE 84
BEANIE SIGEL 87
ACE HOOD 90
FAT KILLAZ 93
BABY OF BIG TYMERS 96
GORILLA ZOE 98
JAY ROCK 100
GUCCI MANE 103
DROOP-E 106
LIL FLIP 108
KRIZZ KALIKO 110
MASTAMIND 115
HOOD STARZ 118
PASTOR TROY 120
CHUCK BROWN 123
YOUNG JEEZY 127
TURF TALK 132
TWIZTID 137
AL KAPONE 140
MESSY MARV 145
SHAWTY LO 148
JAYO FELONY 150
TELA 153
LORD INFAMOUS 155
YG 158
FIN 162

COVER PHOTO:
TECH 9 BY MARCUS HANSHEN

THANK YOU

FOR MARY DOWNS.
THIS BOOK AND ALL THE MURDER DOG BOOKS ARE FOR YOU. WITHOUT YOU THERE WOULD BE NO MURDER DOG. THANK YOU FOR EVERYTHING.

TO EVERYONE WHO DID INTERVIEWS FOR MURDER DOG, AND EVERYONE WHO CONTRIBUTED TO MURDER DOG. THANK YOU SO MUCH. I LOVE YOU.

SCOTT BEJDA, DAVID FRIEDMAN, DAIKA BRAY, BRAD SADLER, MATT SONZALA, ALLEN GORDON, J.DOGG, LOU NUT, FLAGGS, GEZUS ZAIRE, COURTNEY OMEGA, TED WILLIAMS, CHARLIE BRAXTON, RICK THORNE, BRIAN BARTHOLOMEW, DAVE KATZ, GREG DAVENPORT, NANDA PABA, RICHARD D, AL KAPONE, NIKI GATEWOOD, ADELL HENDERSON, KEITA JONES, PAUL ARNOLD, SOREN BAKER, X-RAIDED, DOLLAR BILL KELVIN, ROOT DOCTOR, CHIEF HYDRO, RICHARD HENDERSON, JAVON ADAMS, MJ RASOOL, BEN LEWIS, DOUBLE E, JD HILL, RAY RAY AKA RED BIRD, GARWYNE JONES, MADUMA SALIKA, KEVIN SHORT, WENDY DAY, JIM DOWNS, RENE MORALES, BRIAN LASSITER. PK, DIRTY J, V TOWN.

ALSO THANK YOU TO MATT SONZALA, ANDREW NOSNITSKY, PAUL STEWART, FOR HELPING TO MAKE MURDER DOG BOOKS HAPPEN.

INTERVIEWS

INTERVIEW WITH BG

BY BLACK DOG BONE • PHOTO BY MARCUS HANSCHEN

Last time I met you in New Orleans you hadn't signed the deal with Universal yet. What's been happening since that time?
At that time we were just doin our independent thing, it was just straight Cash Money Records. We were layin our hustle down, doin our Hot Boy thing, doin the BG thing, Juvenile, Big Tymers. We been doin this for so long, a lotta major companies was lookin at us, before you know it when we had somethin on the table that was sweet, we jumped on top of it and here we are today.

Did you think Cash Money would sign a major deal like you did?
We wasn't tryin to rush it or nothing, we just was waitin our time...and our time came. We knew it was gonna happen for us eventually cause we had what it took. We knew what the world wanted and we knew can't nobody give it to the world like we could give it to the world—rough, rugged and raw.

Before you signed with Universal you had one album out?
No, I had three records out. When I met you I was on that It's All On U Vol. 2, but before that I had Chopper City and I had It's All On U Vol 1.

All your albums were released on Cash Money Records?
Straight Cash Money Records.

Which of your albums did the best?
The one I like the most was Chopper City. That was my second one, with all the bullets on the cover. That was my favorite outta all the albums I had done. That's a classic. It's just raw, man. I can still listen to that to this day. I listened to a song on that the other day, word for word just listened to it, and I didn't know I was spittin on that song like that.

Why did you like that one the best?
All my albums musically was tight cause I got the best producer in the world, Manny Fresh. But Chopper City, it was just real life situations—shit people could relate to, shit I could relate to. I bump it myself and just be feelin myself. I gotta do another album like that man, that one there a classic. This new album I got, Chopper City In The Ghetto, it's off the hook. I give myself 100% on this one here, but that Chopper City was the shit.

Which one did your fans like the most?
They liked all of 'em, they related to all of 'em. They gave me my props on everything I ever done cause I gave it to 'em correct, I gave it to 'em how they wanted it. They ain't gonna accept me no other way but thugged out, cause that's me all year round, all day long, it's just in my nature to be real. I came real on all my records, they respect me for that and they took it and accepted it.

How old were you when your first record came out?
When I dropped my first record I was 13-14. I was young.

You were in school at that time?
I was goin to school, but I was young in the hood, doin shit I ain't had no business doin—gettin suspended, gettin expelled, just violent man, doin all kinds of stupid shit, you dig?

How did you connect with Cash Money Records?
It's like this here: I been down with Baby and Slim, they been down with me since day 1. They knew me since I was 8 years old, I grew up under them, all us from out the same neighborhood. They heard that I rapped, they came to me, told me to spit somethin to 'em in a barbershop, I spit for 'em, and all I can say is the rest history. Two weeks later I was in the studio layin it down. They was like, man we got to have this lil nigga here.

> "I BEEN DOWN WITH BABY AND SLIM, THEY BEEN DOWN WITH ME SINCE DAY 1. THEY KNEW ME SINCE I WAS 8 YEARS OLD, I GREW UP UNDER THEM, ALL US FROM OUT THE SAME NEIGHBORHOOD."

This lil nigga here the future man.

Who else was on the label when you came in?
It was UNLV, Pimp Daddy, G-Slimm, Ms. Tee, PMW. It was a few artists on the label. That was '92.

At that time Juvenile and Lil Wayne weren't part of the label? When did the Hot Boys come together?
Right, I'm part of the Hot Boys. I was already there. Lil Wayne came. At first it was me and Lil Wayne, we was a group called The BG's. A little altercation happened with him and his family and they pulled him away, so I went solo as The BG. I done my solo thing, then situations got better, Lil Wayne came back. Then Juvenile came and Lil Turk came. All us solo artists, we just formed the group, The Hot Boys. We a group, and plus we branch off and do our solo thang.

What made you want to write lyrics?
I felt that within myself and I just wanted to do the best I could with it. I always loved to write. It's like that's my callin right there. I like to express myself.

Was there something that influenced you to take that path?
It's just in my heart. I been doin it since I was like 9-10 years old. Elementary school I started freestylin, beatin on the desk, gettin put outta class. Then middle school I'm all beatin on the desks and in the hallways givin concerts, freestylin. Then I just went to writin and I got tighter and tighter, and here I am today.

What did your parents have to say about all that? They were behind you?
All I got is my mama and my aunty. My mama at first was like, you can rap I don't care, but she didn't think it was gonna turn out like it turned out. She didn't think it was gonna be this serious. Now I'm comin home with the bread, payin the bills, breakin it off—it's all gravy.

At the time you were starting to rap, Bounce was the big thing in New Orleans. What made you go in that direction instead of doing Bounce?
Bounce, that ain't my style. Bounce down here, that's like pussy poppin music. That gets the crowd. That ain't nothing, but you just chantin through a whole song. You just sayin the same things over and over. I always been a lyricist, I always wanted to come real with it. Bounce just never was my thing. I listened to it from local artists and shit, but as far as me doin it myself I just was off that straight Gangsta shit. With the life I was living Bounce Music just didn't fit. I don't even know how to rap Bounce. I always kept it real and represented the streets. I always done Gangsta Rap.

The Cash Money sound has a little Bounce in the beats, but the lyrics are straight Gangsta.
All Gangsta. Fresh just do his own thing, he got his own sound. The way he do our tracks, you could ride to it, you could be in the club with it, it's for all areas of the game. He lock down all areas, he lock down all locations. You could be in your ride, you could be in your house, you could be chillin with your bitch, you could be in the club—you just gonna feel that shit. It's just got that

sound that make a nigga bounce to it.

Why did you have to go to jail a while back?
When I was a juvenile I had caught a gun charge and a crack charge and a weed charge. I was on probation and I violated my probation, they tried to give me some time, I come up from under that. Then I went back to jail for some marijuana and some valiums, they locked me down for a minute. I coughed up a few dollars and now I'm back out.

It was the time you signed the deal with Universal?
We had just signed the deal. After we signed the deal I went to jail like a month and a half later. We had shot the Big Tymers video, shot the Juvenile video, and a week before I was supposed to shoot my video for my single on this album here I went to jail.

I know your record was scheduled to drop in November or December of '98....
I wasn't there, they had to set it back.

In your new album you talk about a problem with drugs.
I was just layin it down, keepin it real with myself, puttin myself in different situations, shit I done been through. You dig? I'm young, but I done did a lot in my time. Like the shit I rap about on my song "Made Man", I done been through it all. I'm just puttin it on wax, keepin it all the way street.

What made you get out of drugs?
My future. If I woulda kept doin what I was doin I was gonna run into a brick wall, cause the shit I was doin was definitely gonna lead to destruction. I had a way out and I took this Rap thing as my way out.

When you were into drugs did Baby and Slim try to stop you?
Oh yeah, most definitely. They was against that 100%. They tried to help me every which way they could, but I wanted to be my own lil man.

One day you just decided to stop?
Yeah, I went to jail, then come home and ain't done it since.

Being in jail woke you up?
It woke me up in a major way. When I was in there I had time to think, I had nothin but time. I was locked up for about seven months.

You got into drugs heavy as a kid?
Growin up in a drug infested neighborhood, growin up in the ghetto without a father. Nine times outta ten you gonna branch off into that gangsta life. I'm lookin up to niggaz older than me, all they doin is sellin drugs and totin guns and gettin loaded and shit. That all I see, that's all my surroundings was. Where I'm from that's the thing to do. But Baby and Slim, they just showed me a different look on life. You dig?

What neighborhood are the Cash Money artists from?
Uptown—Magnolia Projects, Valise and Magonolia. Just from Martin Luther King all the way back.

Where's you father?
My daddy was killed. Somebody kicked his door in, tried to rob him, and he ain't wanna give it up. They shot him in the head and the chest and shit. I was like 12 when it happened.

You were at the house?
No, I had just left. It coulda been both of us.

You have other kids in your family?
I got a little brother. It's just me, my mama and my lil brother.

He raps too?
Yeah, he been tryin to do a little something. You might hear him on my next album.

Your dad getting killed must have affected you a lot.
That took a lot away from me, you heard me? Me and my daddy was real close.

At that time you were rapping?
I was doin my lil freestyle thing back in school and shit. But I wasn't into it like I'm into it now.

I heard you had some other songs that were supposed to go on your album that were real tight, but never made it in.
Yeah, they pulled part of it. They pulled a song called "187" off the album. They pulled a song called "Comin Round No More" featurin my dog Juvenile. And they pulled another song called "Rollin Raw". And I think they pulled one more. They pulled four songs.

What are you planning to do with the songs they didn't put out?
I'm gonna still use 'em. You might even look for some of them on the new Hot Boys album. They was super tight.

That's what I heard. Why did they pull them?
I'm not quite sure what the reason was, but they say lyrically it was too hard for Universal. I had to replace 'em with four new songs.

How would you compare your new album to the previous ones?
This album here, lyrically I'm more mature. Fresh with the production is just A-1. I just got a whole variety of shit, it's just unexplainable—the album on fire. You just got to listen to it, it's just me, I'm representin BG, I'm lettin you know that shit real. It's all the way street, all the way ghetto. It's gonna be major. I know this. We knockin doors down, we comin through like an army. We comin through, get out the way or be prepared to do what you gotta do. If you ain't gonna roll with us then you gonna get rolled through. Situation's real, we keepin it real, we keepin it all the way streets, all the way ghetto, how it's supposed to be done. My clique is the best clique in the industry right now, we can't be faded.

When do you write your lyrics?
I don't like comin in the studio with no raps. Once I go in the studio, I hear what Fresh did, I get the title together and I go from there. Once I get the title, and whatever concept, I put myself in that situations, visualize it, and I just put it on paper, put it on a track and there it is.

Do you write your lyrics down?
My thought process, I give myself an A when it comes down to thinkin. I know how to think. All I gotta do is just reminisce on my past and look at what's goin on around me. When it comes down to flossin on a song, I can just look around in my clique and write about that all day, cause that's all we do is get our shine on, floss and shit. Then if I want to thug with it, all I gotta do is think back and I still be on the block down there every day runnin with my old dogs and shit. Whatever topic it is I can cover it cause I done been there, I done done that.

First you hear the beat?
Yeah. I write before I get in there, but I do it better when I hear the track. I go from there. Once the track get done I do my thing. I don't take me no two days to write to no track. Once I hear the beat I'm right there get my pen, get my pad and go to work, doin what I do best.

You've been writing since you were 12-13 years old. How much has your writing changed since you started?
My pen and pad done matured since I was young. I was tight then, I always been tight, but as you get older you get wiser. I can come from different angles now and capture different topics and put myself in different situations and give it to you.

Who influenced you when you were growing up?

I was on that Pac. I was on that Eightball & MJG. Before that I was on that Scarface and Geto Boys. All that street shit, man, that shit that have a nigga buck.

What have you been listening to lately?
Lately I been bangin that Jay-Z. I'm diggin that. And I been bangin that fuckin DMX. And I been bangin that fuckin Juvenile. That nigga is raw. Juvenile just done bust the doors open for Cash Money. That "Ha" single is hot as a muthafucka.

Did you that that single would blow up the way it did?
I knew that it was a major single. The hook was catchin, I knew it was gonna be big, but that muthafucka just done took all the way off. Sky's the limit for that muthafucka.

You need that one hit single to break through.
All our songs be hits. We ain't just no one song a album. Everything be a hit, man. You could take any one song of the album and make it a single. On my album we had a hard time pickin the single, we didn't know which one to roll with cause all them muthafuckas was tight. We just gonna roll with this, then we gonna roll with that, then roll with that. That's how we done it.

How many singles are you doing?
Three. The first one's "Cash Money Is An Army". That's one of my solo songs off my project. It's just lettin you know that Juvenile and Big Tymers, that ain't even half of it. Cash Money ain't finished. We comin through this muthafucka like an army. You know when an army go to war it's either kill or be killed, that's how we comin through shuttin shit down. It's a force. Then my second single's "Made Man" featurin Baby from the Big Tymers. Just talkin about where I done come from, what I done been through, where I'm at now. I just figure I'm a made man now. I been through all a juvenile could go through. I'm at the point where I can just lay back and get my money right and just chill—raise my little girl.

You have a daughter?
Yeah, I got a little girl. 16 months old. Kristiana.

You're married?
No, I ain't married! I'm single. A baby from a baby, that's all that was.

> "MY PEN AND PAD DONE MATURED SINCE I WAS YOUNG. I WAS TIGHT THEN, I ALWAYS BEEN TIGHT, BUT AS YOU GET OLDER, YOU GET WISER."

What are you doing in LA?
I'm out here shootin my video, doin a lotta publicity stuff, just doin what it take to be successful—I'm just hustlin right now in LA, Rap hustlin. I'm shootin a video for the first single off the album, it's called "Cash Money Is A Army".

You probably meet a lot of famous rappers when you're in LA?
I met a lotta stars. I done met E-40, I met Mack 10, Missy Elliot, I done met Wyclef, I met Brandy. I met a whole lotta stars. In the studio, in restaurants, in the hotel. In LA you bound to meet anybody.

What were you doing with E-40?
I just done a song on his Charlie Hustle album. I don't know how it came together, Baby called, said look we got to get down to the studio, lay something down with E-40. Yeah, we ready, we were born ready, let's go do this. And we went down there. It was super tight.

How do you feel about the way your career has been going? There are millions of rappers, but very few people reach the level you've reached.
I feel that we're blessed. Not just that—hard work, dedication. We've been doin this for so long. We ain't no rookies, we veterans, we been doin this. We was overdue for this anyway. It's our time to shine and we gonna get our shine on.

JACKA INTERVIEW

INTERVIEW BY BLACK DOG BONE • PHOTO BY MARCUS HANSHEN

Get It In

Oh man—The Inkredibles did that beat. That's the song I did with Paul Wall. When I first heard that beat I was like "That's a big beat!!" The average muthafucka might listen to that and not really get it at first. But I know once they listen and keep comin back to this shit they're gonna realize how big some of these beats is and the reason why I picked them. I'm like, "I don't give a fuck what tempo this is, I'm doin it. I love the sound."

The tempo on some of the songs you did on "Tear Gas" are strange. At first you wonder why Jacka would pick certain beats, but after listening for a while it makes sense. With your records you really have to spend time with them—it's a lot of new styles and sounds.

A lot of people I talk to say the same things you're saying about this album. They know how to listen and what to listen for. Even "Jack Artist" people still tell me that's their favorite shit. At first they didn't realize, they slept on it and found out about it later. You don't feel nothing when your first hear it.

When you sent the tracks for the Murder Dog "Best of the Best" compilation, we didn't know where to place your track and Hussalah's. That's why we put you at the end of the album, because what you're doing is so unusual. It's hard to fit you in with other Rap. Sometimes I don't even know if you are a rapper! What you're doing is unique.

I know how to do a lotta different shit and I'm really tryin to showcase it. I don't want them to just label me a certain way. I wanna keep them guessing, no tellin what he gonna do.

You have such a unique style that I'm starting to hear people that sound like The Jacka. That's a compliment.

Yeah, I've been noticing that too.

What's Your Zodiac

I thought it was gonna be funny because you know when somebody asks a girl what's her sign, it's like a corny line. I thought it would be funny, but then the beat was so good it started making me think. What I thought was, a real rapper needs to be on this beat. So I went and got Phil The Agony, he's in the group Strong Arm Steady with him, Krondon and Mitchy Slick. I knew that boy would destroy this. He would murder this beat because he know how to rap. He's from LA too. He got on it and set the pace. He really said some shit that you gonna love. If you like Rap and muthafucka's comin dope, you gonna like that song. You might think it's a song for girls; it might be but, it's for everybody. The beat is ridiculous, and the wordplay and the rhyme skills on the song—it makes a lotta sense.

I'm glad that you're working with these new artists from LA. There are a lot of good new artists coming from LA—Glasses Malone, Nipsey Hussle, Jay Rock. For a long time the Bay and LA weren't working together much. It's good to see we are working together.

At the end of the day we all from California. Whether you from LA, the Bay, the Central Valley, up North, it don't matter. We all got that in common and we all should have a certain vibe. We need to stick together and everybody need to know about each other. It's so spread out out here, it ain't like New York where you can hear a lotta guys. We gotta hold our shit together. Glasses Malone and all them started a little movement called One West. That's a movement from Southern California to Northern California.

"Tear Gas" is definitely a California album. The whole feel is California. It's a great summertime album also.

It is, that's why I wanted it to come out in the summertime. It all worked out perfectly. People who have this album are really gonna have a good summer. In the future when you think back on 2009 summertime, I want you to think about "Tear Gas". I want you to think about The Jack.

When I get an album I like I might keep playing it for a month. It captures that time for me. Right now I'm playing "Tear Gas" and DJ Diplo's "Major Laser" album; both are super classics. What is the concept behind the title "Tear Gas" and the cover image?

Even though it's a summertime album, when you actually hear what's being said on the songs you understand that it's serious. More serious than anything. That's why I couldn't leave the concept "Tear Gas" behind, because that's what it is. And it's settin me up for the next thing I have. It's still war, no matter what. We have a Black president, that's cool. But we still poor, we still strugglin on the streets. The title "Tear Gas" just covers all of that. And it's history too. We not goin out, when you see those soldiers on the cover, they're reppin the people. They ready to kill. They're not all decked out in military fatigues or nothing—everybody's in regular street clothes because it's a war on the streets. People know about that shit. You wonder when is it all gonna explode? We're showing militancy on that cover. We're not showin no violence. When you open the CD cover you see drugs on the floor, I'm on the news wanted, and the police are tryin to kick the door down. It's a war on the people by the police. They don't really publicize that, so it's up to us to do it.

No matter what subject you take on, there's always a melancholy sound in your voice. The underlying feeling is sadness, a feeling of loss. Everybody in Rap is trying to be gangsta and hard, and they never show the other side. In your album you show all sides.

A lot of them don't deal with the other side.

> "I'M WORRIED ABOUT GOING TO JAIL. YOU'RE NOT SUPPOSED TO SHOW THAT SIDE. I CAN'T RIDE AROUND BECAUSE WHEN I COME UP NEXT TO A CAR FULL OF NIGGAZ 4-DEEP, YOU NOT LOOKIN AT EACH OTHER SAYING "WHAT'S HAPPENING, HOW YOU DOIN?" I'M LOOKIN LIKE "WHO THE FUCK IS YOU?" AND YOU'RE LIKE "WHO THE FUCK IS ME?""

They probably just is gangstas and there ain't no other side. Really when you're on the streets one thing they teach you is never to show no emotion. Show anger or violence, that's the only emotion you can show. Don't show: This shit is getting to me; I'm doin all this shit and it's weighing me down; I'm worried about something happening to me; I'm worried about going to jail. You're not supposed to show that side. I can't ride around because when I come up next to a car full of niggaz 4-deep, you not lookin at each other saying "what's happening, how you doin?" I'm lookin like "who the fuck is you?" and you're like "who the fuck is me?" It ain't a good feeling. When you in the streets out here it ain't friendly. Not for us. Not here in California, maybe somewhere else. Here if you look in a car and say "what's up?" they're gonna say "what the fuck you mean, what's up??" It ain't easy. Rappers is showing some type of unity with each other, but that's because it's our business to deal with each other. Muthafuckas in the streets though, they don't give a fuck about nothing. Look what they go through. Look at everything they have to deal with every fuckin day. The way you gotta survive is harder. You supposed to do better than your parents, but it's at the point where the kids are doin worse than there parents. It shouldn't be like that but it is. "Tear Gas" is tryin to tie it all up and make sense. Make people understand it at the end of the day. It might take you 3 days or 3 years, but it will all make sense. Some muthafuckas just don't pay enough attention.

Most rappers I talk to come from broken families and their brothers and sisters are all in jail or dead or something. What's going on with us? It's like slavery never ended. People call this civilization and progress? When is this madness going to end?
It probably won't end. They have a plan for us. It's not a friendly plan, you know. It's a plan to incarcerate all Black males from the age of 18 to 30 most of us have been to jail. They wanna make sure that by 2112 damn near every Black man in the United States has been to jail. And it's getting outa hand. Muthafuckas are goin to jail for goddamn nothing. What it's doin is giving you a prior. Every time you go to jail for something stupid you have a prior. You go to jail for drinking or you go to jail cause you had a little weed on you, some stupid shit. Then later if you go to jail cause you had a gun on you or you're sellin some dope, then all those little stupid priors from before are gonna make you get like 19 years. Over some really dumb shit, though! I was reading it takes $60,000 to keep a muthafucka in jail for a year. That's bullshit—just give us the 60 thousand and we don't have to fuckin steal no more, we don't have to deal no more. Put the 60 thousand in my hand.

It's ridiculous. Once you go to jail, when come out you're on parole and the laws are so strict, you can hardly move—you're back in jail.
Prison is the best business to invest your money in right now. If you invest in a prison you're guaranteed to make the money. That's what money muthafuckas are doing, they're investing their money in prisons. That's tragic. They've got all these prisons and they gotta fill them up, and they target the poor people. Poor people are the most likely to commit a crime, cause they don't have any options. They gotta do something in the street to make their money, or they use drugs to cope with their everyday situation. They're filling all the jails up with poor people. Ain't too many rich muthafuckas in jail. Mostly poor and mostly Black. Fuck it, that's life and that's what we have to deal with.

The people who are creating these situations for us, they're suffering for it. They're not happy people. They might have money, cars, houses, but I've never met any of those people who are happy; they are all miserable people. To me they are the ones who are really living in hell.

What Zodiac sign are you?
I'm a Leo. Born on August 12.

What Happened To The World
When you a kid you don't understand. You're looking at everything on TV and you see stuff going on at school, and you don't understand life. But you have dreams and ambitions and it's all good shit. It all feels good and you can't wait to accomplish the things that you wanna do. It all looks good and sounds good. But then when you get older all of that disappears. You realize that you have to work for the system or you ain't gonna survive. You have to do something you really don't want to do. Man, what happened to the dream? What happened to the things that I wanted to do for real. Then you start paying attention to the news and politics and you get sharper and sharper, and you realize: What happened to this place? This ain't what I thought. Some muthafuckas stay in the dream though, they never come out of their kid way of thinking, because they haven't been exposed to nothing real. But when you in the streets you're constantly be exposed to something real. You just wanna figure out what the fuck is goin on, what can I do to make sure I don't get caught up in this bullshit.

Black kids grow up fast because you're exposed to so many things at an early age.
We're growin up with some fuckin ghouls and goblins, man! A little kid gets scared at night and his parents come to comfort him, show him there's nothing hiding under the bed. For us, at that time you're getting tucked in, muthafuckas are outside of your window for real. It's kinda scary. Muthafuckas is fighting, cussing and shit, gunshots. If you a girl muthafuckas is takin advantage of you. It might be a family member, it might be whoever. They could be on drugs and they're not even in their right mind. Black girls are getting taken advantage of by the time they're 9, 10. They don't even have a muthafucka think twice before touching them. They've already been tested so many times, "What the fuck, I know how to have sex, I'll just start fuckin some niggaz." By 13, 14 you got a baby. You've already been exposed to sex by family members or muthafuckas your family leave you with, shit like that. You automatically know about it.

Another thing that's killing our people is the bad food they eat and unhealthy lifestyle they live. So many people I know have diabetes or heart disease or cancer.
I know. I went to the doctor the other day and he said my blood pressure is a little high. He said, "You better slow down on all that shit you be doing—drinking sodas, partying, going hard every night." You gotta be cool.

Our Heroes
That's the song featuring Dub 20 and J-Stalin. MG made that beat too. That's about our heroes in the streets. I'm not talkin about me personally, but the majority of the youth, our heroes are drug dealers and killers and muthafuckas who show pure brute force. It's not to glamorize it or nothing. It hardens us. It makes us soldiers, it prepares us. We know for a fact we gonna go to jail, you just dread that day. All my life I knew that one day I'd end up goin to jail for something. I had that thought in the back of my mind and I always hated that. That song right there is for all the dudes who really stood for something and had a positive message, even though they was hustlin and doin something illegal. They still gave us inspiration and hope. That's what that song is. That song's for the people who're locked up or didn't make it. You still gonna be our hero. I know what I know now, and I'm Muslim. But you did know something that I didn't know at the time and you inspired me.

The Movement
That's me and Planet Asia. Roblo made that beat. Planet Asia is hella tight, and I want my people to know he tight. People don't know that them kinda dudes is what made me want to rap. On that I really had to go in because of how dope he is. I didn't wanna be the fuckin one slackin on there, so I went all in on that song.

What's the project you're working on right now?
I'm workin on another album called "Murder Weapon". The reason why I'm callin it that is because I was the "Secret Weapon" and now I'm the "Murder Weapon". I'm killin 'em as far as this music go. I'm the one you can use for inspiration. I'm the one you can take back to college with you, the one you can take on the road with you. That's what the "Murder Weapon" album is. So far it's unbelievable! I don't got no features or nothing on it neither. The critics always say I have too many features on my shit. I'm not even tryin to have features. If I have somebody featured on my album I'm really gonna have two verses. You gonna get a lotta Jack. You gonna hear a whole lotta Jack.

That would be my only complaint about "Tear Gas". I wanted to hear you a little more. I just want to get into that Jacka mode and chill out.
That's what "Murder Weapon" is. Practically every song is a solo song from me. That's probably why I normally try to give them a lotta songs on an album, cause I have some solo songs. "Tear Gas" had like 4 solo songs. I had more solo songs I was gonna put on the album, but I couldn't clear the samples. Otherwise I woulda had 3 or 4 more solo songs on there. They were all sampled beats and I didn't have time to clear them. People will still get those songs though, I'll put 'em out.

You probably had a lot more songs that didn't make the album?
I had like 45 songs to pick 19 out of. I'll put 'em out. I got Demolition Men mixtapes comin out and I got another street album comin out. I'll put 'em out. That was 45 songs for "Tear Gas". For "Murder Weapon" I've got like 20 beats to pick from and I already got 13-14 songs done. "Tear Gas" had so many songs, I'm mad they didn't make the album. I had a song that Erk The Jerk made—I'm really disappointed that song didn't make it. I'm gonna have to put it out on a mixtape or something.

The Greatest Alive
Man, that song! Roblo made the beats. Everyone that hear that beat like it, that's one of them songs. If somebody got E-40 and Mitchy Slick on a song they want to make it a single. But I didn't wanna do that, I wanted to make a song that E-40 wanna do. He want me to come with this Mobb shit, so that's why I came with that one.

There's a lot of new artists coming out making music that's based in Hip Hop, but they're taking the music in different and creative directions. You have artists like M.I.A., you have Rye Rye, Blaqstarr and the whole Baltimore Club sound, DJ Diplo in Philadelphia and Santigold, K'Naan, Kid Cudi. I feel like your music is similar to that, it could be accepted by a different audience.
Yeah, K'Naan. That's the shit I listen to. I just went and bought K'Naan's album. The first song, soon as I heard it I said, this dude kinda reminds me of me.

I'd love to hear some of your music remixed by a DJ like Diplo or DJ Sega. It would be really mind blowing.

They Don't Know Me
Roblo made that beat. Freeway had come out here, we was in San Francisco, just going to the studio to do a song. I had a CD full of beats, but that was the first one on the CD. Soon as he heard it, he was like this is the one. So he dropped a rap. You know Freeway don't write. He's like Jay-Z, he don't use a pen, he don't use his phone. He just sits there and zones out and comes up with a 16. He just started bobbin his head to the beat and mumblin and moving is mouth a little bit. He did that for about 15 minutes and he had a rap ready. It sounded good! It was dope. Just bein in the studio with another artist like that, seeing how he works. When he came out here I hooked him up with a couple of other dudes to do music with too. He did the same shit—didn't write nothing, bobbed his head to the beat, and came with the music.

How did you select the artists to feature on "Tear Gas"?
It just happened. I didn't ask for Freeway. I didn't ask for Paul Wall. I didn't ask for nobody. They just called. We already friends and we was gonna do music anyway, so this was just the perfect opportunity for us to work together. I'm workin on an album, let's do it! When they come to town we just go to the studio and knock it out. Like Devin The Dude, he came to town, and the dude MG who made that beat, we just went to the studio and he did one for me. He did a verse and a hook for me, picked the beat, came up with the concept and everything. He was just a real dude! It was just meant to me I guess.

Dream
That was another beat that I knew, they ain't never heard me on a beat like that. I just wanted to do it so I knocked it down. That's one of my favorite songs on the album, "Dream". I thought about Ampachino because this is his dream, rappin is his dream. I knew he was gonna murder that, and he murdered it. Then I thought about Zion I, and he murdered it too. He really came with some shit with some thought. Some food. Let you know, this is how you do dope shit. You don't have to do what the next nigga's doin. You do your own shit. A lot of people go somewhere and they hear something and they do it like that. That's OK, it's good to have certain sounds on a project that people can relate to, just soften them up to the album. You gotta have shit that's gonna make 'em wanna listen to the album. Once you get them in the door and they get a chance to hear the other shit, then they really appreciate it. They fuckin love it, man, and they wanna put everybody else up on the shit.

When I first put your album on I wasn't hearing anything I was familiar with, so I knew it was going to be a classic, something original. Some music you hear it and it catches you right away because it's similar to something you've already heard. But for me, the albums that I love the most are usually ones that it takes me several listens to get into. After hearing your CD "Tear Gas" a few times it started to open up, and it just kept getting better.
I'm glad you felt that way about "Tear Gas". I think that when people first listen to it, it actually goes over there head. It's like, wait a minute, I didn't catch this, lemme listen to it again. People always call me back later. I left the album in Seattle with one of my brothers and he called me a week later, he was like, "I finally got a chance to really realize what was goin on with that album and I really love it." He made me feel great. I know it's not easy to penetrate right away. It's easy to listen to, but it's a lot that's being done and being said. It takes some time to get.

It's intricate, but not in a mental way. It's more on the emotional level, like it just came together magically.

Won't Be Right
This song is about everything that's goin on in the streets. We know how to make the money, whether it's hustlin, sellin CD's, whatever it is we'll do it. But in the process people die, people go to jail. It's the life, but it ain't gonna be right till the dudes who sacrifice with me is outa jail and they're free. That's what the

> "WE'RE GROWIN UP WITH SOME FUCKIN GHOULS AND GOBLINS, MAN! A LITTLE KID GETS SCARED AT NIGHT AND HIS PARENTS COME TO COMFORT HIM, SHOW HIM THERE'S NOTHING HIDING UNDER THE BED. FOR US, AT THAT TIME YOU'RE GETTING TUCKED IN, MUTHAFUCKAS ARE OUTSIDE OF YOUR WINDOW FOR REAL."

song is about, and Cellski made the beat. He's just a big time beat tweaker! When you hear that beat, if you know Cellski then you automatically know that it's a Cellski track. A lotta people like that song, because when you first listen to the album that's one song that will hit you quick. All that other stuff is for like when you're on your way to LA or something and you're just listening.

I like the way the singing vocals on some of the songs, they're like way in the background, like a radio playing far away in the song, like a movie. Are those samples or did people sing those parts?
We have people come in and do background vocals. See, once I get the beat I gotta really work on it and add what I wanna have in there too. Sometimes we have to sample a woman's voice or we gotta have somebody come sing background, like way in the background so you gotta rack your brain trying to hear it.

It reminds me of how a late sixties girl group would have three or four girls harmonizing in the background and then you had the lead vocalist. You have layers like that. I hear that a lot in "Tear Gas".

Keep Calling
That's the track with Devin. We recorded it here. He picked out the beat, he came up with the chorus, he came up with pretty much everything. I was just cool, go in there and rock. He went in there and laid some shit, and then I went in and laid mine. Then on the last verse to that song I switched it up a little bit, took it a little deeper, some more food for thought. Even in a song like that you can throw something positive in there.

You worked with all different types of artists on this album, from straight up Gangsta rappers to Hip Hop rappers like Zion I.
I wasn't really trippin offa who was hot at the time. Or just because they're on the radio right now, let's get with them. Naw. I really wanted to do some shit with people that I'm really friends with, and they really want to do it. I wanted to get with people that just want to get down on a track with me. I didn't have to pay 'em. I didn't have to do no ass-kissin. We all had the same vision, we just wanted to do it. That brought a good vibe to this album.

That's the way a true creative union happens. It's not just some job you do for a few thousand dollars and move on.
We really spent time together. If I didn't know you already, I got to know you then. After that we all kept contact with each other. We're great friends now.

How long did you work on this album?
Probably close to a year. It was really hard trying to find production for this album. That's what took me the longest, getting the production. Once I got the beats it was pretty much done, in my eyes. Just rock wit 'em. It came together beautifully. I hope every project I do comes together this smooth and easy. The things I been doin in the studio lately—this is to much. I don't know what's happening right now, this is too good to be true. To the point that I'm nervous.

What do you mean?
Ever since we did the "Tear Gas" album I've been workin. The songs that we're doing now, I can't even explain them. I need everybody else to listen to them so I can hear what they think and understand what they are. It's just some crazy shit. And it's really good. When I'm in the studio makin a song it's always at least about 10 people there. These are some real serious critics, no yes men. Ain't no fuckin groupies or none of that shit. Real straight up brute honest opinions in there. It's just crazy the shit I've made since "Tear Gas". I've really stepped the bar up higher.

When you're recording an album you feel comfortable having a lot of people around you?
Yeah. At first I didn't used to want PK and them, cause I felt like PK didn't understand the music. I didn't wanna hear his opinion. But now I want them all in there. I want them to hear it cause I'm excited about it. I won't even start makin a song if I'm not excited about it. I want everybody to be in on it, get that energy in the room.

Where did you record the album?
I did some songs in Seattle. I did some in Alaska…I actually started off doing "Summer" in Alaska. In Seattle me and MG did "What Happened To The World". But most of the songs we recorded in 17 Hertz here in the Bay. "Girls" was recorded at PK's house.

Girls
I'm not a person that would like that song, but I love that song. How did you pull that off?
I was a big fan of the Beastie Boys. I always felt like that song was slept on. I used to love that song. So when I heard that beat, I instantly liked it. At first I didn't think it would fit in with the other shit on the album. It does though. The response I keep getting off it is that people the same way I felt about that song. That's the main reason that I did it.

Scared Money
That's the one with Krondon and AP.9. That's like a real Southern California sounding beat. Like a gang-banger's beat. I knew that was a real West Coast sound. I'm like, that's that Gangsta shit right here! I gotta get Krondon on this cause he's got that sound. I wanted to have Krondon do the chorus cause I know he really understands that music. That's just one of them Gangsta sounds.

> "I REALLY WOULD LIKE TO HERE MORE PEOPLE TRY. JUST GO AHEAD AND TRY TO DO SOMETHING DIFFERENT. BUT MAKE IT TIGHT! MAKE IT GOOD TO WHERE EVEN IF YOU IS A THUG OR A HOOD OR WHATEVER YOU ARE, YOUR PEOPLE GONNA LIKE IT BECAUSE THEY FEEL YOU."

How did you hear about Krondon?
I heard him on a mixtape one time, and that boy gassed the shit out of it! He's real lyrical but he's got that Southern California accent and you could tell he's from LA. The way he rap and the kinda shit that he come up with, the boy is ridiculous. I became a fan of his shit instantly.

You seem to be very excited about all of the artists you featured on the album. You're a big fan of these artists.
Yeah, because they're real people. They go through real life shit and they real humble. Not all Hollywood. They'll fuck you up if you cross 'em, but they cool muthafuckas.

Summer
My boy MG produced that track. When he gave me the beat I started listening to it and—man, it's a great beat! I came up with a style to it first, just something to ride the drum pattern. I did my verse and I wrote the chorus. It was just a dope chorus, remind me of something Frank Sinatra would've said. I got my boy Rydah J. Klyde on there talkin about a guy

who ended up in jail and he used to love the summertime. He'd go to all the events and he could drive his car around and get all dressed up and look fly. But now he's in prison for the summer. I was just talkin about life in general: Summer don't love us.

To me that song gets the overall feeling of the album. Why did you choose to put that as the first song?
I felt like that song would be a great opening for the album because it jumps right to the point. I wanted them to hear something that I really loved. I love every song on the album and I put every song on there for a reason. "Summer" was the song I wanted them to hear first.

What I love about the whole "Tear Gas" album is that you thought a lot about how you put it together. It's not just 19 separate tracks, it's a complete work, a classic. To me this really is an introduction to The Jacka.
I've had a chance to really live life and now I know how to put an album together. Every time I come with a project it ain't easy.
I gotta go through things, I gotta feel certain emotions, just live life and put it into a song. As time turns things change. We gotta talk about what's goin on right now. I just want to put the life into the music.

Just A Celebrity
I always loved this beat. I think The Inkredibles made that beat. When I was in the studio my boy Sky Baller ended up being there. He hopped right on it. We did it all in a day, and as soon as I heard it I was like, "Man this is something they need to hear." We doin this music, but we still active with the people. Everybody else is just wanna be celebrities. They wanna be like someone on TV and have the same things they got on TV, instead of being a real person. That's what we do, we just keepin it real.

This record has a different feeling from other Rap out there. It's got a psychedelic feel to it. It has a strange and beautiful mood.
Yeah it is, man! It's psychedelic. I'm glad you like that song.

I like all the songs. Even a people that don't listen to Rap could feel this album. People who like Pop music will like this album and people who like ghetto street Rap like this album. You're walking that fine line.
I appreciate that. I just want to bring everything to everybody. That's why I did certain songs. On this album you gonna get a chance to feel things that everybody feel. I didn't just make it for one audience, I made it for everybody.

On the same note, you didn't cater to specific markets the way some rappers are doing. A lot of artists make a song for the girls, a song for the thugs, one for the grandmas—but they're moving with the intention to sell and make money. That's not what you're doing, that business approach. You're coming from the heart so you music speaks to all people.
I didn't do a song for the kids or the women or nothing. I didn't just have it all planned out. I just went with what sounds good and I wanted people to hear.

Glamorous Lifestyle
It's just about a guy and the girls like him because he's a bad guy. They're attracted to him because he seems like he's handling his business and he's takin care of himself. The beat—I love the drums in that beat! That's what really moved me, the drums, the congas was playin. Traxamillion made that track. It's an up-tempo beat, and the up-tempo master is Andre Nickatina, so I had to get him on there. I knew he was gonna murder this. I didn't think it would be a single, but I knew it would be a good song, something muthafuckas can really have a good time to. They ended up liking it and it ended up being the single.

When you listen to a classic album like a Curtis Mayfield or Stevie Wonder record, the whole album has a consistent feeling. That's the way "Tear Gas" flows. It almost feels like the same person made all the tracks.
Right. Because a lot of the producers I work with know me so well. They're like, I wanna see how you sound on this. Lemme see how you sound on this beat. They like my voice and my style and they want to put me with this beat. A lotta rappers might not rap to certain beats because it's not going with the way that they flow. You gotta come up with a flow, make something up to go with the beat. It could be slow, fast, whatever, you come up with something for it. That's how you get better, by trying to come up with something. Try to make something dope, cause that's what we here for.

You always take a lot of risks. The beats you use don't fit in with the Mobb sound or the Hyphy sound or Crunk or LA Gangsta sound. They're not typical in any way—I hear a lot of tribal beats and sounds from Africa or Asia.
I really would like to here more people try. Just go ahead and try to do something different. But make it tight! Make it good to where even if you is a thug or a hood or whatever you are, your people gonna like it because they feel you. They gotta feel what you're sayin. I feel shit that ain't even Rap because I hear what they be saying. What he sayin—I don't give a shit what kinda music it is—if I like what he's sayin I'm gonna listen. I'll play all kindsa shit because I like listening to different people. It gets me goin. Music is like movies—you can get as creative as you want. I'll do just about anything, but I don't wanna make nothing wack at all. I'm gonna make sure that everything we do is dope. And it's gotta be something fresh and something new.

I think you could take just about any track and make it into a great song. You have music in you.
I like when I go to a producer and he has something already set up; he's not lettin me be in my comfort zone. He's bringing certain beats cause he's tryin to bring the best outa me. Them the kinda producers that I like to work with. I just do whatever they tell me to do, see their vision. If I'm able to do that, that's dope. I got some music from a dude named Child from Project Groundation, he's a Reggae DJ. This dude's got some crazy production over at his house. I go over there and do songs that people could never imagine. To me it's a new sound.

Did he do any production for this album?
No, we just started workin after the album was done. We got our own album we're workin on. He's doin all the beats and I'm gonna be rappin. •

INTERVIEW WITH TOO SHORT

BY KEITA JONES • PHOTOS BY BLACK DOG BONE

How have you seen the Oakland Rap scene change in the past 15 years?
There's not enough hope. People had that sparkle in their eye when "Tell me When to Go" came out and Keak Da Sneak was all over BET, but it faded away when the Hyphy thing didn't become Crunk. Instead of rollin with what you got, everybody was disappointed. If you got Anchorage, Alaska, Vancouver, Seattle, Portland, Denver, San Diego, Salt Lake, Phoenix, Vegas, the Bay, LA and all these cities checkin for what you doin, how could you not be pacified? Why look at it as a failure? In all the cities I just named if you put on some Keak Da Sneak, Mistah FAB or Messy Marv, they all start going stupid. They look just like the Bay, they talk just like the Bay. They go hella stupid. They love the Bay music. They reason I know is because I done shows up there with all Bay artists. Everybody's tryna convince me that the Bay is a failure because the Bay ain't platinum. Fuck that! How many fuckin cities and areas do you know where Hip-Hop artists who are not on a national level can eat without having a day job? They have money and drive Benzes and own the richest property. The Bay Area Hip-Hop scene feeds a lot of people. I'm the one person you're not gonna convince that that Hyphy was a failure. I have conversations with people from the Bay who are like "Atlanta is the shit!" Atlanta got labels setting up shop and giving artists 10-15% and muthafuckas in the Bay is getting 100%. You call that a failure? "Oh, we not on BET or MTV, we not performing at the awards shows." I'm like man, if you was doin that shit, you'd be getting raped. You'd be getting 10% of your money and still be fuckin complaining.

What made you decide to form your label Up All Night?
I was always an independent man doing something. I had Dangerous Music and I had $hort Records, this is just another venture for me. I have a lot of music that I wanted to put out. I wanted to come a new with a fresh start. I wanted a name that reflected my work habits.

This is your third label. Why have you changed the name over the years?
There's always a logical business reason why. There's paperwork. This time around it was a vibe. I wanted to do something new. We always had something going on in the recording studio called the Up All Night Crew. Because we liked to hang out all night and party and shit I flipped it to Up All Night Crew. I didn't want a label called Too $hort records. Dangerous Music was a partnership that dissolved in the late 90's.

Who are the artists that you currently have signed to Up All Night?
Right now it's just The Pack, but I have a lot of other groups that I'm working closely with now like Hoodstarz and the Murder Mob out of Atlanta. I'm in the Bay looking to expand to more Bay Area music. I'm moving the studios so we should be completely relocated within the next 30 to 60 days. Me, Mistah FAB and Keak Da Sneak are meeting with Thizz Ent. I'm about to merge my company with Thizz as a sister company all in honor of Mac Dre and the Bay. Bay artists need a home and something they can say is ours. Public Relations wise Thizz is not the most popular label out the Bay but of all the independent labels, Thizz has the biggest brand of the Bay and that's what I respect. Mac Dre was a friend of mine so in the name of Mac Dre we gonna throw up the T, let people know Thizz is what it iz. We not gonna separate, we gonna join forces.

What prompted the move from Atlanta back to the Bay?
I feel there's a need for guidance in the Bay within the music industry. Not to say I'm coming back to tell Keak Da Sneak, Mistah FAB or Messy Marv what to do. I want to have a hand on the next guys entering the game after them. When I looked around, all the teenagers and people in high school, people you meet and know they been bangin on the drum machine, got the rhymes, the swagger and image, don't really know the proper procedure to get out there and launch their careers. I would prefer for my label to be Bay Area based than Atlanta based. In Atlanta they are all about grooming an artist, go to an A & R, getting a few hundred thousand, shoot your video. They all about getting deals on major labels and I'm not all about that.

What are the plans for Up All Night in 2008?
We have a lot of music in the can slated to be mixed and mastered to be released. We were never in the mixtape game but now we recorded so much music we gonna release mixtapes and get them on the street. People think of mixtapes featuring rappers rapping over someone else's beats but our music is all original. We wanna get the music out and heard and get the Up All Night name heard. The Pack is signed to Jive so they have nationwide exposure going on.

What was the idea behind your last Jive album, "Get Off the Stage"?
I was playing with words. People might look at me like: look at this old muthafucka, get yo ass off the stage! It's about those 60 guys on the stage who stands up behind the rapper while he does his show and make the rapper look bad. You got five dudes hugging on you, five dudes with mics and one rapper and everybody singing all the words. It's just a bunch of dudes looking like they humpin on each other's butts and stuff. It's like: man, why don't you get off the fuckin stage and let ya boy rap? Everybody wants to stand on stage with a rapper, that's the fuckin wackest shit I ever seen in the history of Hip-Hop. The album is a ten song album I put out to fulfill the obligation to end my contract with Jive. I tried to put it on a Bay Area vibe, but it's more or less something to bump in your car.

Now that you're off Jive, can we expect "The History Channel" to come out?
I don't know what the new album's gonna be called, but me and E-40 just sat up in the studio the other day and made a couple of songs. We always make songs. When we made "The History Channel" back then, we recorded about 8 or 9 songs. We still have those songs and four of them still feel good now. There's no telling right now. 40's one of my best friends in the Rap game so there's definitely more 40 and Too $hort comin at you.

Jive did you all shady with that one.
They didn't want us getting together. It's not even a matter of them thinking the album wasn't gonna be good, they just didn't want us working together. Jive always had a policy of not wanting Jive artists to work together. All these years R. Kelly was working with everybody and their momma except Jive artists. It was like that even before Jive went Pop. They got Tribe Called Quest, Too $hort, Spice-1, Mystikal, UGK. You'd think they be

> "I WAS ALWAYS AN INDEPENDENT MAN DOING SOMETHING. I HAD DANGEROUS MUSIC AND I HAD $HORT RECORDS, THIS IS JUST ANOTHER VENTURE FOR ME. I HAVE A LOT OF MUSIC THAT I WANTED TO PUT OUT. I WANTED TO COME A NEW WITH A FRESH START. I WANTED A NAME THAT REFLECTED MY WORK HABITS."

like "Hey we got all these guys let's go on tour." Def Jam did it. Jive didn't want us to be friends. I was in they ear a while back about it. We had a showcase with everybody I just named and I was like, "Yo this is a tour right here." But Jive didn't want no part of it. And the new guy in the label at the time was Keith Murray, gold right out the box and I'm like, "This is the perfect shit, let's go, we got the South, we got the West, the East."

You were recording an album with UGK. What's going to come of it now?
We did about seven songs. I mentioned this to Scarface and David Banner. I didn't say anything to Bun yet, he's still down, but we should get all the songs Pimp had with everybody and add some stuff to it and give all the profit to him so his kids can have the option to do whatever they need to do. It doesn't take a lot to send his baby's momma money every month, but it does do a lot more if you put a fund away for his kids. I know he was dude where if it was me he would be like, "We gotta do something for $hort."

What was your relationship with Pimp C?
That was like my little brother. He was one the best friends I ever had. I didn't talk to him much when he was in jail, but I would talk to his mother periodically. I would see Bun B in Atlanta and wrote him letters. As soon as he got out I was one of the first people he looked up and was like, "what we doin? Let's kick it. Meet me in the studio." I spent a lot of time with them on the road, in the studio in Atlanta. They used to come to my house, I would go to their house. We was tight, we used to always hang out.

How did the relationship come about?
Just being labelmates and having the same following and crowd. We did a lot of shows together. Tour. When you go on tour with another group that's a bonding where you find those friendships with people you around everyday.

How would you like Pimp C to be remembered?
The people who know the story know the truth, but the people who don't know are missing that fact that Pimp C was very influential to the South sound. The South is hot now, but he was one of the people who pioneered that popular South sound. The songs that make you wanna bounce, the slow songs, the way he did the hooks with that twang in the rhymes. It was a joke in the early pioneering days of Southern rappers. I always commended Bun B on putting the name out and he did it with "UGK For Life", "Free Pimp C". Putting it on every verse, putting it on shirts. It was a "Free Pimp C" campaign. Pimp C's name was bigger than UGK off the campaign.

"The Corrupter Soundtrack" is one of my favorite soundtracks. Jive had all these mainstream artists but kept them in the underground.
They never knew how popular Too $hort and UGK was. They kind of measured the numbers of what you sell and they assume things, but living in New York it never sunk in. They could never realize what UGK meant to so many fans or what Too $hort meant. The way people would fall out if they saw me, Pimp C or Bun B wouldn't happen in New York, so it never registered to them that they had a roster of mega stars. They still don't know it. Not to mention Clipse or E-40. They had cult rappers with millions of fans buying records with no videos or singles. If they had a Def Jam approach they could have easily went to the Pop era and kept Hip-Hop alive, but they traded one for the other.

What do you think caused the demise of Dangerous Crew?
We were onto something good when I had the studio in West Oakland, but it was the move to Atlanta. Everybody came with me. I was in the comfort zone, my mom retired we was throwin parties at the house. In the case of Ant Banks, Atlanta was far away, he wanted to be close to his family and at home. The same with Pee Wee my keyboard player. Shorty B who played the guitar stayed. We did a lot of work over the years but without Ant Banks, we had to make different moves. Ant Banks was the backbone, he oversaw everything, he did the mixing and mastering.

Is there chance of a reunion album?
Probably a greatest hits album volume one and two. We gonna start getting the music on iTunes. Fatha Dom still got the swag. My man Goldy jumped off in the real estate, got the money, doing his thang. Just like Ant Banks who dipped off the real estate. You start making money other ways and suddenly rappin ain't as fly no more. I haven't seen Ant Diddley Dog, I don't know where he at, but he and Rappin Ron had some serious flows.

The Infamous Luniz battle. People still talk about that to this day
That started off as us just having fun in the studio and it turned out to be a historical event. The skill level was so high between Yuk and Num and Rappin Ron and Ant Diddley Dog, it turned out to be real battle.

I heard you're doing some stuff with Youth Uprising in East Oakland?
I teach a class, a music industry class. I donated a Pro Tools studio and help them put together some independent projects and have the kids do all the engineering, do all the beats all the songs. My job is to teach them how to put the music out. I do it for the love. You got to be 13-24, go up there, it's totally free. You can be from anywhere in the Bay. They even have van services where you can get picked up and dropped off.

What is your response to the people who say you're not an appropriate role model for these kids?
I'm not over there saying, "this is how you be a man" or doing counseling or something I'm not qualified to do. I over there teaching the kids to put out music. I'm not over there playing with a kid's mind talking about pimping, or this is how you get girls, it's strictly music. If the kids try to get me to say all that stuff, I shrug it off. I treat the kids like a 25 year old adult. I'm not gonna sit there and handle somebody's kid the wrong way, I stay in my place. At the same time, who do you have who is gonna go in there and help these kids chase their dreams? I'm from East Oakland. The people I know who can potentially help these kids are scared to go over there, they don't want to be a part of it, they say it's ghetto or it's dangerous or worthless. When I go in that building I see so many talented kids that just need a chance to shine. They not askin for handouts they just want a chance. •

C MURDER INTERVIEW

BY BLACK DOG BONE • PHOTOS BY MARCUS HANSCHEN

TRU first came out hard on a street level, now you've broken into the mainstream. How do you manage to keep a balance trying to keep your old fans happy and your mainstream audience?
We just keep on makin the music how we want, we basically make street music. Then we take a few songs that we feel can be put on that worldwide level, clean 'em up a little bit. But mainly me, I just make street music. Then P and Silkk, they can do both sides. Then we just work with whatever beats we got and do it. We gonna always have the streets, no matter what, cause that's all we be talkin about. It's the same things we been talkin about.

People say that TRU are real commercial now. Do you think you're more commercial now?
Naw, I think we just grew in the game so much that we can make both kinds of music, we can play both sides of the game. Me personally, all I can make is street music.

Do you feel a pressure at this time to maintain this level and please a wider and wider audience?
Me personally, I don't feel like that. I still make the kinda music I make. I just get nasty and say what I wanna say. I don't feel pressure to have to please nobody. I'm makin what I wanna make, and I know I'm makin straight street music. I ain't even trippin on that. It's the same with P and Silkk, they do what they wanna do. P on a level to where he know exactly what the market needs, and he's gonna give it to 'em. That's why we where we at, and I'm gonna let him make all the decisions cause I know he knows what he's doin.

Are you happy with where you are right now? You feel like you're in a good place?
Yeah. I feel like we're in a good position right now. We're workin our album, doin our thing, makin all the right moves. We're gonna start the next tour, I think that's the main thing. People want us right now and we need to get out there for them to see our faces, so that's what we're doin right now. We're makin moves to get out there and do some shows and tour.

You're doing a tour to promote this TRU album?
We been doin shows in and out, but we're gonna start tourin in August. It's gonna be a big ol' tour, it's called The No Limit Only Tour. The whole month of August.
Rap comes from the streets, and TRU is no exception, but when you get big things change. Things that you hated when you were at the bottom, now you've become that. I ain't trippin on all that shit. People gonna say what they want. They know better than to come around me talkin all that kinda shit. I don't even be listening to all the bullshit in the street right now. At the point I am right now, there's too much muthafuckin talkin out there. That's why we in the situation we at, we done made a decision and we run up on a muthafucka yappin and talkin they mouth. Gonna stomp 'em. That's how we is right now. Muthafucka can't never tell me I ain't no street nigga and I ain't makin no street music.

I'm glad to hear it from you. You know how people talk--they love you when you're down and hate you when you blow up.
That's what I can't understand. But they ain't got the guts to come to a niggaz face and say it direct. That will make you a man, you dig?

Nobody's going to say it to you...

> "I STILL MAKE THE KINDA MUSIC I MAKE. I JUST GET NASTY AND SAY WHAT I WANNA SAY. I DON'T FEEL PRESSURE TO HAVE TO PLEASE NOBODY. I'M MAKIN WHAT I WANNA MAKE, AND I KNOW I'M MAKIN STRAIGHT STREET MUSIC."

But it's cool. When I walk up on them they don't have to tell me nothing. I'm gonna have it myself. Too much niggaz runnin they mouth out there in the streets right now. Tryna put a stop to that. So it's on, you dig?

No Limit has never toured out here in California. People are waiting.
We know that. We know there's a big space right now where people need to see us. That's the main thing right now. We about to come out there and handle our business and give our fans the chance to see us again.

When you compare this new TRU album to the last one which one do you like better?
Me, I like this one. This one is worldwide, it's a universal album. I feel it.

It seems like No Limit has done just about everything possible--from films to shoes--what type of plans do you have next?
Mainly right now we're focusing on the music business more and our clothing line, that's where we at right now. We're gettin back into the music real serious with it, and the clothing line. That's where we really puttin our attention now. I'm startin to work on my next album already, so I can put together the best C-Murder album ever. That album gonna be straight street. I'm gonna handle that, work on my shit, you dig?

Are you signing new artists on No Limit?
Yeah, we just signed four or five new artists. We got DIG, we got Tataye, some dudes from New Orleans, and we just signed some more people to The Pound, some production.

Do you think there's a lot of good things happening with Rap right now?
I think the mainly the thing about the industry right now is the radio. The radio makin and breakin people right now. That's where the industry at right now, it's all about radio and video play. So that's what we lookin at. If the radio is what's makin and breakin artists, then we gonna put out a lotta radio songs. Whoever get on the radio gonna sell, that's where it is right now. That's just a part of the game.

When No Limit started you never got any radio play, but you somehow broke through.
At that point in time it was all about a street buzz and doin what you're doin, makin quality music. It ain't like that right now. Right now whatever's hittin on the radio, they're pickin it up. Right now if you're not on the radio you ain't happening.

You really think so?
I know so. I'm just sittin back analyzing the game, that's what I do, I'm analyzing the game.

For a long time street Rap could never get any radio play, but still people like E-40 and Master P who were selling major units.
We don't just wanna sell major units, we wanna sell our units to the street and catch the radio buzz. That's just part of being a good business man. Throw a few songs on the radio and let them hear that so you can grow markets, that's all a nigga doin. Why not when you could?

But the people who like the street stuff are very different from the radio crowd, and when they hear you on the radio they feel like you sold out.
That's they muthafuckin business to me. I ain't never gonna be trippin on another nigga. That's their opinion, I ain't trippin on that. People gonna have an opinion about everything. That shit don't even bother me. I don't think twice about that shit.

But your fans are important to you, right?
Yeah, dog, but I ain't gonna be trippin on no nigga if a nigga tellin me I sold out. Ain't no muthafuckin fan to me.

Do you think it's good thing to keep putting out so much material? Sometimes it's better to keep the public wanting more than they can get.
I don't know. You gotta just go with it, see what happens. If it don't work you change it up.

You had a couple singles out on this album, how'd they do?
We had "Hoody Hooo" and "TRU Homies", they did real good. We're about to drop another single called "Bounce That Thing". That's more of a street song. We only had one crossover single, that was "Hoody Hooo". But it was so rowdy that it was like underground also.

You don't come out here to the Bay anymore?
No, I don't get out there. I just stay home. Wherever my home is, that's where I stay. When I lived in the Bay, I stayed in the Bay.

Question about TRU?
TRU ain't never gonna die. We're gonna always be on time and we'll always be together cause we're family. Muthafuckas ain't never infiltrated on what we did. Lotta muthafuckas out there right now--I don't know what's goin on with 'em--but the business, it's just like the dope game, the business got so big that it's bad right now. It's fucked up right now, industry's fucked up right now.

Why do you feel that way?
I don't know, I just feel like that, something ain't right. I don't know, I'll find out.

We saw the East Coast happen, then the West Coast was happening and the South, where do you think it's gonna move next? What do you see happening in the industry?
The industry change every couple years. The East holdin it down right now.

You don't see much happening in the West?
Not except for Snoop, and I consider him as one of us.

You remember how it was in the Bay when you were here, it was hot.
you think you're commercial re and do some shows and tour. •

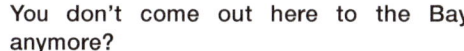

INTERVIEW WITH BUN B

BY MATT SONZALA • PHOTOS BY DERON NEBLETT

UGK came up in Port Arthur, TX, a small town along the coast of the Gulf of Mexico, and y'all always really seemed rooted in the Gulf Coast musical tradition. You came with that real Southern funk that kind of set the standard for Southern hip-hop. What were you and Pimp listening to when you first came together?

When UGK first came together it wasn't like it was just me and Pimp. Pimp was in a group and I was in a group, so we were all part of this larger clique type situation. The group that Pimp and I ended up forming came more out of circumstance. It was originally a four man group and the other two dudes basically quit. But coming up we as a group listened to all Hip-Hop. We were big fans of people like EPMD, the Juice Crew, I think the biggest direct influence on us nationally would have been the Geto Boys, OG Style, the first Royal Flush album, the Def IV, all of this stuff is prior to us releasing music. We were also big fans of Philly hip-hop, Cool C, Steady B, that whole movement. Definitely KRS ONE, Public Enemy. Back then I assume everybody listened to all the same stuff because there really wasn't room to differentiate. We were all…everything was new, you know?

When I hear your sound, the production of Pimp C, even the cadence in your voice, I hear a lot of similarities to other music coming from your region, all along the Gulf Coast. I know you've worked with members of The Meters, was that the kind of music you guys came up on before Rap?

Well yeah, if you wanna talk before Rap, in my house, with my parents being Cajun, there was a lot of Blues and a lot of Creole music. In my house you had a lot of Bobby Blue Bland, Z.Z. Hill, but you also had Solomon Burke and like Step Rideau. As far as Cajun music is concerned I remember more song titles than artists, cause none of that shit was playing on the radio. "Sittin' at the La La Waitin' For My Ya Ya." The La La in Cajun talk is the dance, that's what they call the big dance, and your Ya Ya is your woman. And the "Joe Pete" is a song and Joe Pete is an infamous ladies man, messin' with all these women, and his main woman found out what he was up to and got at him. But a lot of that shit, when you deal with Blues music, Cajun music, Creole music, roots music, any type of world music, African drum or Indian type stuff, a lot of that stuff deals with real life situations. You talk about "my woman left me," that's real. Most of those dudes don't write those songs while they got a woman. Heartbreak was something that people used to be more honest about. On a lot of those Blues records you hear that stuff. I hear a lot of that influence in your music.

Absolutely, and Pimp even more. As a producer, he had a much stronger musical ear. He had a lot of Blues influence, he had a real strong R&B influence from a lot of the great group's from the 60's and 70's. From Maze to the Isley Brothers, the Bar-Kay's, The Ohio Players, that whole real Funk era where the bass was the dominant sound. The Parliament-Funkadelic stuff.

Back when I used to travel and do a lot of stories for Murder Dog, I would go to cities all over the U.S. and interview all the underground artists, and when I would ask people who their influences were, UGK came up all the time. And I think one of the things they admired was the fact that when you came out, you really represented where you were from.

With us, even with the first EP with Big Tyme Recordz, we took our lead as far as gaining different markets from the Geto Boys. The Geto Boys were the only ones we knew that had made real noise outside of the region. You had RP Cola, DJ's back in the day like Wiz and Lonnie Mack, and shit like that, Houston was goin' hard. You had Steve Fournier. Steve Fournier's record pool was one of the biggest record pools in Hip-Hop period. And that happened right out the gate.

He also did the Houston column in The Source back when it started before anybody did that.

Man, that was in the Source and the Rap Pages days, the Rap Sheet, Beat Down. We took our direct influence from people who basically their mission statement was "Rep Houston, Rep Texas, Rep the South". We just took that, we just tried to follow the path that the Geto Boys had already made.

A lot of people credit you doing "Big Pimpin'" with Jay-Z for taking UGK mainstream, but I don't think people realize how big UGK were in the streets and how much of a market UGK had totally under the radar. It was kind of a world unto its own back then.

UGK's success is based on very practical stuff. Chad and I are from a small town called Port Arthur, TX, population, 50,000. So for us, we'd get calls from like, Lafayette, New Iberia, Appaloosas, Tyler, Shreveport. These aren't even media markets, so it was more a matter of, let's give these people something. A lot of these clubs only held 400-500 people. There really wasn't a lot of money involved in it. We remember when the Geto Boys came to the Connections Skating Rink in Beaumont in 1991. Scarface actually came into the bathroom and battled with K-Rino and them. And I'm in the bathroom freestyling too. It's me, DA from the Blac Moncs, he was called Big Six back then when we were in high school. We were in the bathroom freestyling like real MC's. And Scarface—this was back in the suit days, he had his suit on—he came in the bathroom and probably said one rhyme and that was a wrap for everybody. That kind of shit inspired me. I've tried to make myself that kind of an accessible MC, like Scarface made himself accessible to me. Even if I can't just hang out with everybody all night. I'm definitely gonna come and acknowledge the cipher.

Did Pimp battle back then?

Yeah, Pimp battled, but he was more into beats back then. Pimp was an MC, but Pimp gave up a lot of concentration as far as rapping was concerned to produce and to

> "PIMP WAS AN MC, BUT PIMP GAVE UP A LOT OF CONCENTRATION AS FAR AS RAPPING WAS CONCERNED TO PRODUCE AND TO GIVE ME MORE OF AN OUTLET, TO GIVE ME MORE OF AN OPPORTUNITY."

give me more of an outlet, to give me more of an opportunity. Pimp really started freestyling again probably back when we were doing "Ridin' Dirty" and "Super Tight" and 3-2 was in the mix with UGK a lot. That's pretty much all me and 3-2 did was sit around and freestyle all day. Like literally all day. And Pimp was like, fuck that shit. Every now and then he would be making the beat, and we'd be sitting around freestyling and shit while he'd be making the beat. Because Pimp would always start his songs with his drums. And we'd always have that to rap to while he built shit around it. And Pimp got tired of that shit and started jumping in that shit. Pimp started letting other producers come in and we started getting tracks from like N.O. Joe and it took a little bit off of him and it gave him room to do more of what he wanted to do, which was really get back into being an MC. A lot of what Pimp was doin' in his last couple years, especially after his release from prison, a lot of what he was doin' was freestyling.

When UGK first really started hitting, I have to tell you, it got to the point where I was sick of hearing "Tell Me Something Good". That had to be one of the biggest Rap songs on the radio in Houston ever.

As raw as y'all were back then, how did you end up breaking into the radio?
What happened in Houston was, we entered this contest called "Houston Home Jams", DJ Reggie Reg and Greg Street. Reggie Reg used to come to the record store at the King's Flea Market where we used to work, that's the guy that put UGK out first. Reg was one of the first people to hear any of the first studio recorded stuff that we did as UGK. And he was like "Yo, you need to enter that 'Tell Me Something Good' in the Home Jams." And this was recorded for an album to come out and Home Jams was for the up and coming artists. He was like, "You ain't got no album out, so you qualify." We talked about it and we joined Home Jams on the last night of a two week thing and won. The winner was supposed to be pressed up by BPM Studios, you was supposed to get your single pressed up. When they found out that we were already signed to a record label, they disqualified us. But people called so much that they eventually had to add it. For probably a month we had a hot record on the radio in rotation with no product to sell. It was a big issue because it was basically against policy to promote a record that wasn't available for retail, but the demand was so high they had to play it. They were risking losing listeners because at the time they weren't the only game.

There were three stations in Houston at that time, at least three. Majic 102, The Box and 1590 Raps.

The record came out on February 21st, 1992. Between then and May 1st when we signed to Jive we had sold upwards of 50,000 independent albums basically without really knowing what we were doing. The only reason we halfway knew what we were doing was because Russell at Big Tyme Recordz who put out our record had a record store, so he understood the concept of warehouses, and all of this. We were one of the first people to be independently distributed by Southwest Wholesale. We weren't the first, but we were one of the first Rap groups to be distributed by them independently. But like us, Street Military with Beat Box back in the day, ESG with Perrion and people like that, we were some of the key people that helped Southwest Wholesale grow into a major recording industry in the mid to late 90's.

Those were some very different times for Houston.
Absolutely. We were kind of taking our cue from what the Oakland music community was doing. Oakland was basically making music for Oakland, marketing and distributing it straight to Oakland people, and Oakland people were supporting it. Instead of just trying to make Rap like we were from New York, why don't we just make Texas music for Texas motherfuckers, just like the Geto Boys was doing and maybe one of these motherfuckers would pop just like "Mand Playin' Tricks".
And it did.
It actually did.

You were one of the first groups out of Houston to sign to a major deal like that.
Yeah, back then it was us, Johnny Quest had his deal with Tommy Boy, Street Military were getting ready to get with Wild Pitch, you had the College Boys, they really went toward more narrative shit. People think that the boom a few years ago was the beginning for Houston but no, we had major label situations before that. The tide of Houston just really kind of changed I think.

Houston had a few different waves. When Southwest Wholesale really started to grow, that really set a whole new lane for Houston. That was right around the time when y'all did "Big Pimpin'". That was 1999, right?
We recorded "Big Pimpin'" in 1999. It came out in late 1999 and we shot the video right around this time of year in 2000 at Carnival in Trinidad. It was nine years ago, which is insane.

How much of a change did you see after that? How big of a turning point was that for UGK?
There's no way to downplay it at all. It really was. For the markets that we already had, this was a victory for people who had been down with UGK for years. Tellin' everybody that UGK's the shit, all of that shit, and people would be like, "Naw, fuck that shit, it's all about this dude or that dude." At the time it was all about Jay Z. And Jay Z said, "I want to work with UGK." Jay Z could work with anybody if he wanted to. It was all good. We understood that if New York didn't get a chance to embrace UGK, it had nothing to do with the consumers in New York not liking us, we had never been presented to them. I can recall many times going up to New York and telling people, "I made 'Front, Back, Side to Side,' I made, 'Pocket Full Of Stones,' I made, 'One Day'." People'd be like, "Yo I never knew the same people made all those records!" Cause there was no visuals attached to none of that shit.

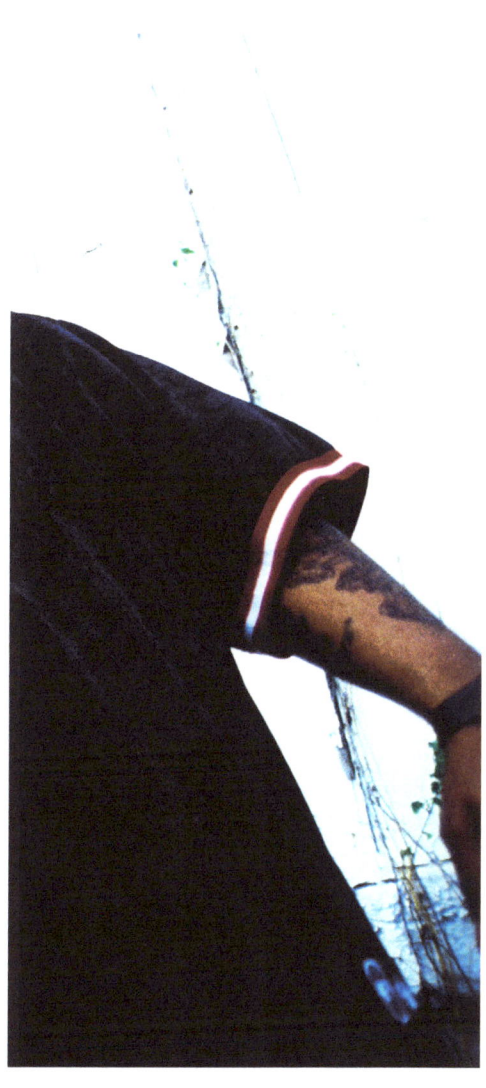

After that, you and Pimp got on every song. It became some shit to really collect every song y'all were on at the time. Y'all seemed to be featured in some capacity on everybody's stuff.
We always worked with people like Three-6-Mafia. You can tell people who had maybe just jumped on the bandwagon and people who we had just really wanted to record with us. At the same time that we had one of the biggest Pop records of the year, we also had what is arguably the biggest street record of the year, which is "Sippin' on Sizzurp" with Three-6-Mafia. It was really a one-two punch. You have to give Paul and Juicy credit. The summer of 2000 was a UGK summer, but it wasn't soley because of UGK. We just got presented with two incredible opportunities to make two incredible records that to this day still pop. Like it's not even a problem. These records are nine years old right now. "Big Pimpin'" was recorded in the Fall of 1999, "Sippin' on Sizzurp" was recorded on Super Bowl Sunday 2000 in Atlanta.

On this new UGK album, are you personally piecing the album together? What was the process like putting this album together without Pimp C?
We were in the process of making this album already. A lot of the concepts and themes that you hear on this album were originally conceived during the Underground Kings double-album session. A couple of these songs are songs that grew out of those sessions. At the same time, a lot of the production that Pimp was doing was not solo production. A lot of the production on the last album were co-produced by some of his protégés. DJ B-Do, Steve Below, Averexx. With the structure being there and a lot of the production themes already set up, I was able to go into the studio with the people who had been in the studio with Pimp, creating this music. With the exception of Akon and Manny Fresh, the other producers on the album are up and coming, and as close to the original Pimp C sound as you're gonna get. These are people that Pimp C personally was grooming. You got DJ B-Do, who's a member of the Underdogs from Port Arthur, Averexx that's also from Port Arthur, and Cory Mo from Houston and Steve Below from Dallas. Everybody that we tried to get on this album, I wanted to make sure the features made sense to UGK fans and that they made sense to people that knew him personally. We had both known Lil Wayne since he was a kid and Lil Wayne really wanted to be part of the album. We didn't want it to seem advantageous, you know? We got Big Gipp from the Goodie Mob, E-40, B-Legit, 8Ball & MJG, people who definitely make sense recording with UGK and people that if you been following UGK you know that we fuck with.

I think that's important because we've all heard some albums that have come out after artists' deaths with crazy features and way off-base shit that doesn't seem right. I don't know if people understand the history between UGK and Goodie Mob and The Click and 8Ball & MJG
Something that people probably don't even know is that UGK recorded a "Dirty South" remix with Goodie Mob, but they never used it. This

> **"WE RECORDED "BIG PIMPIN'" IN 1999. IT CAME OUT IN LATE 1999 AND WE SHOT THE VIDEO RIGHT AROUND THIS TIME OF YEAR IN 2000 AT CARNIVAL IN TRINIDAD. IT WAS NINE YEARS AGO, WHICH IS INSANE."**

album is mixed and mastered by Mike Dean, which is probably the best hands you can get touching music right now. That's history there. The video is gonna be more of a retrospective. Like, I'm not in the video as far as like set up shots in cars and silly shit like that. I'm really trying to take UGK from what some people would call legendary status to what I would like to see as iconic status. Not necessarily for me but for Pimp, because of his contributions as a writer, as a producer and just as a spearhead to the movement. People are just starting to see now, in retrospect, how much of a contribution he really made. Not just to the Southern Hip-Hop movement, but to Hip-Hop in general. And man I want to thank a magazine like Murder Dog for even fucking existing. Out of all the people who we ever wanted to call and get ads placed and get the records rated, I think Murder Dog probably was the first glossy covered magazine to call UGK and ask, "Can we do a story?" They were the first magazine to call and offer us covers. All that type of shit. A lot of UGK's firsts as far as print media is concerned coincides with Murder Dog. Looking back, on Hip-Hop, I'm not sure if a lot of us would have touched as many people, or covered as much ground as we were able to cover without the support of a magazine like Murder Dog. So for me, I want to thank the magazine and all the people over the years, especially Black Dog who was always a real big pusher for people like us. And yourself Matt for actually trying to impress upon people the truth behind the music we were trying to create. And to see through all the bullshit of people trying to cloud us with and really see what Chad and I were really trying to do with music. And we were really able to accomplish during the course of our career just making real honest music from where we were from. On behalf of the UGK family I want to thank journalists like you who go out to the Port Arthurs, who go out to the Louisville's and go out to the Greenville's and go out to the Jacksonville's, and find this music that's viable. Find this music that's relatable, that's real and true and giving motherfuckers an outlet. Much Love to Murder Dog, for real. •

REMEMBERING DJ SCREW

(July 20, 1971 – November 16, 2000)
CONDUCTED BY BLACK DOG BONE • PHOTO BY BLACK DOG BONE

Robert Earl Davis, Jr, known to the world as DJ Screw, passed away on 11/16/00. He suffered an apparent heart attack, fueling speculation that the rumors of his drug use are true. Police suspect he may have overdosed on codeine, but tests to prove that take weeks for a conclusive answer. In one of his last interviews, he claimed he had given up lean and fry, saying that it was not a good role model for the children. His family states that he had a history of heart problems, having had between 4-6 heart attacks previous to this last fatal attack. He was buried in Smithville, TX, where his family is from. It's a small town outside of Austin.

D-Wreck
people at the radio station, they wondering why ain't nobody else around here is making that much noise in the music game that been up there to the radio station trying to get their records played, trying to get interviewed, trying to get to that next level. Screw never went over there cause that's just how he is. The distributor, Southwest Wholesale, a lot of major record labels have come at this man to try to get him to enter into deals with them because they know the influence he has but…The lack of greed that he had, I can't even explain it. A lot of people got that confused with saying that this man is not ambitious. This man is very ambitious. The fact of him being ambitious is why he didn't have to go and run around here and jump on the first distribution deal that was presented to him cause he was making so much money through his Screw shop, just doing what he loved to do and what he wanted to do. He never had to walk outside of those parameters to do what other people wanted him to do to get his money. He was making his money. He wasn't wanting for nothing. And the amount of peace that he had by being that type of person, you just don't see that too often. That's rare and that's what amazed me about him. You could say somebody's not ambitious or they dumb or this or that. I can't call a genius dumb. I can't call a perfectionist unambitious. Cause to him it was art.

Hawk
He gave us our chance at doing what we're doing to try to go nationwide. We just regular locals and he blew us up without us even knowing. It's a major blow. It's like Tupac to the West Coast. Biggie to the East. Screw to the South. I still sit back and trip. I just can't believe it. I can't believe it.

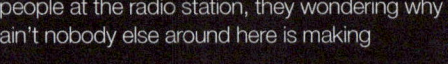

I mean, he was so humble as far as giving us the opportunity to be somebody and didn't expect anything for doing it. and I consider that to be real love because what he was doin', his thrill was seein' us strive to achieve because he know we started in his house on grey tapes, these tapes built us up to making our own tapes, you know and just him giving all he had to see the Click **make it and expected nothing from it, you know. A thank you was** enough for him. That's why I thanked him when I saw him because he made me what I am today. For real.

Man, that was a good dude. I promise man, I love Screw to death. I love him. I mean this is one person who will be sorely missed.

Ronnie Spencer
I gave him his first disc jockey job at Almeda Skating Rink. From then on he took it further in the game. He started slowing music down. I taught him how to blend. He took that and flipped it. What this man did is created a sound in the South that everybody love around the world and it'll never be another Screw. So I want the world to know it'll never be another Screw, he's dead, may he rest in peace and Houston, mainly we got to appreciate the good things he did. He sent my niece to see the president because she was an honor roll student. He helped me as an individual, he helped Swisha House, he helped Jam Down. All these labels that's coming out now that got a Screwed-Up Click artist, Southside Playaz, AL D, Fat Pat, he's dead, Mafioso, he's dead, even me Ronnie Spencer, and that's me speaking. I wouldna never made 'One day you're here, the next day you're gone' if it wasn't for Screw. And I want the world to feel what I'm feeling.

He felt his death. He knew what was happening and if you listen to a Screw tape you can see Screw feeling in his music. Screw's idols was Tupac and Nate Dogg. Now he got a special song that he always play is called "I Don't Wanna Hurt No More", by Nate Dogg. We're gonna play that song at his funeral and at his wake and his celebration. Now I've done a lot the past four days for him because like I say I lost a son. And this man laying to rest is a part of me. Cause I taught him a lot in this world. So I wanna say Screw, rest in peace, I love you.

INTERVIEW WITH EC ILLA

BY BLACK DOG BONE • PHOTO BY MATT SONZALA

You've got a new album coming out called "Natural Born Illa." When is that record dropping?
May 29th. The album's completed. It should be available nationally via a number of independent distributors. It's beautiful, a beautiful album – my best work to date. I'm very comfortable with the record. I think it's a good representation of me and the little style that I've created.

Could you describe your rap style for fans who haven't heard it before?
Yeah. I would say that it is, if you could imagine Gangsta Rap with very minimal keyboard in the production. So I mean, most Gangsta Rap today is made almost exclusively on keyboard, you know. Really, what I do is a little bit old-school flavor where it's a hundred percent samples – even the bass tones and the bass lines that I make are me fuckin' with the pitch on the bass lines and shit on a sampler. I use MPC-3000 exclusively. No keyboards. So it kind of tweaks the sound a little bit. Imagine if you were to get Three 6 Mafia or one of the harder Gangsta acts and told them 'Make an album with no keyboards.' The beats might sound like something that I do.

"Natural Born Illa" will be your first full-length album since 1997. What's the first single going to be?
The first single is the cut called 'Don't Get Me Started,' and the b-side is 'Too Raw' featuring Father Tyme, whose album I'm actually producing and putting out later this year on the same label.

I picture you as being to Chicago what Esham is to Detroit as far as being on top of your respective games. Would you agree?
Well, in terms of the hip-hop side of things I've taken it a few steps further than the next man. The Gangsta shit in Chicago, there's a

number of groups that, five years ago, got scooped up when Chicago was blowin' up with the whole situation between Do or Die, Psychodrama, Snypaz, Twista. There was a point when Chicago was kind of hot and labels came and scooped a lot of acts. This was the same period that I got the major distribution with Universal. But I've been doing independent music since '91-'92. So even though these cats have been around also for a long time as well in the circles, they weren't putting out music. So I've been around a minute and got some good knowledge of the independent game. I know how to get records in the stores; I know how to make people know about the records. And that's the type of shit that happens by the time you get past the decade of being in the game. I take that as an absolute compliment to even be compared to what Esham is doing. I mean, when I just started rapping I would see his shit in the stores and wonder how was it getting there. 'Cause it was way different from everything else that you would see in the stores, and I hoped that people would feel the same way about what I was doing. People become intrigued because 'It sounds as good as some major label shit, but how did it get here?' The average consumer doesn't realize the pain and strife it takes just to get them to even acknowledge its existence.

the music game is not here. New York and L.A. for the most part, and now Atlanta's got a little somethin' and other places are sproutin' up. But for some reason, the Midwest in general and Chicago in particular have been neglected. So there hasn't been a whole lot to like. And the fact that I'm independent after 10 years in the game, still, even after respectable sales history, is proof. It's difficult to show your face around these parts. There's absolutely no radio support – I mean zero. Not a little; nothing. So they don't fuck with no independents or no local artists on the radio. Now that The Box is gone – can't even get a video on TV on some independent shit – it's difficult. So it's an uphill battle. It's like a barren tundra here in terms of the rap game. But I defy anybody to deny that Chicago has definitely got some of the most talent of any spot in this world, between the Twistas and these different cats. People be comin' with some all the way original shit against the odds. The fact that I get some props when I think back and realize the struggle, I pat myself on the back 'cause this shit is an uphill battle to say the least.

Do you feel like there would be an easy way out, perhaps even selling out, and maybe you just choose not to for some reason?

No. I would say the handful of acts that have managed to establish themselves have been lucky. But, for the most part, there's maybe a half dozen to 10 groups that people know and respect. And they're able to survive in the game and put out shit independently, like that CWAL Ballaz I sent you. That was pretty much an exclusively local release that went on to sell 15,000 to 20,000 Soundscan. Twista does real good with his Legit Ballin' shit. So it can be done and there is a certain level of respect, but I think Chicago has been trained to be consumers of other music this whole time. We've been stifled so hard. I don't been to sound like I'm whining and complaining, but if you live here you know this as a fact. We've been stifled and people have been trained to like everybody's music. They buy the Atlanta shit, they buy the New York shit, they buy the California shit. The Chicago shit, they don't even know what it's about because they haven't been presented in the correct fashion. So there's a lot left to be exploited in the market. Hopefully someday we'll get what we deserve.

Where can fans get copies of all of your older CDs that are still available?
Wicked Entertainment is still pressing and selling the 'Illa LP.' They have a Web site, wickedentertainment.com. I'm pretty sure it's

> "IMAGINE IF YOU WERE TO GET THREE 6 MAFIA OR ONE OF THE HARDER GANGSTA ACTS AND TOLD THEM 'MAKE AN ALBUM WITH NO KEYBOARDS.' THE BEATS MIGHT SOUND LIKE SOMETHING THAT I DO."

What did you release before your first nationally available album, "Illa LP," dropped in 1995?
Prior to that I had 'Live From The Ill E.P.' and I had a double album in '93. Independents weren't doing double albums in '93 really. That's even pre-Master P shit. That was called 'Ill State Of Mind.' And I had little 12-inches when vinyl was a little more prevalent in '92. I had my first album, which was called 'Invisible Man,' in '91. So this is the 10th year of me putting out product. Even prior to that I was running around trying to show my face in the streets of Chi.

How long have you lived in Chicago and what do you like most about the rap scene there?
I've lived in Chicago all my life. I mean, I don't know if there's too much I can say that I like about the scene in Chicago. It's really been neglected and given the cold shoulder from the music business. Really, it's obvious that we should be at least the third powerhouse in the game. I mean, we've got way more urban area than even New York and L.A. in terms of actual miles and actual space of ghetto. There's lots of streets and there's lots of people buying music, but unfortunately

I don't think there is an easy way out. The rap game now is super-saturated. I think, maybe, in '95 we in Chicago had opportunity. I'm not gonna say that we missed, but when Crucial Conflict had a gold record, Do or Die had a gold record and they came a-knockin' – and there wasn't two million rap records out at that time – that probably would have been the time to exploit it a little more. But (a) we were younger and (b) we were just doin' what we like to do the way we like to do it. I believe all of us felt that that was gonna make the million dollars anyway. Psychodrama ended up gettin' scooped by Suave House. They got this thing off Eightball's album with Master P and Mystikal and everybody at the peak of P's popularity. So you would see Psychodrama on TV with Master P. In that period, that was a big deal. Do or Die getting scooped up by Rap-A-Lot, you know, number one record in the country, Billboard. Twista's getting this so-called lucrative deal with Atlantic at that time, and I'm getting distribution from Universal. It seemed like we were on point, and I think we all felt that we were doing the right thing. Look what was happening. But the fact that we were independent and lacked experience in the game ended up maybe bitin' us in the hand. How is your support in Chicago? Do they come out and support all the acts in the city?

available on there. The Universal shit, if you can find it, would be most likely found at a big site like amazon.com or some place that keeps a lot of major label back stock. But I have a store and I can't get that shit. So that shit is odd. Obviously, it might be my optimism but I think it's cool in the whole story. There's this album you can't find that should really be the easiest album to find. I mean, I'm not trippin' off it. I'm just cool, you know? If you can track it down, track it down. You'll love it.

I haven't heard of too many rappers that own record shops like the one you run on North Ridge in Chicago. What's it like being an artist and CD shop owner at the same time?
I kind of felt like I spent all this time in the rap game, I run my own record label and I was doing publicity for myself. I learned the whole ins and outs of the independent distribution. So I was producing the music, I was writing the music, I was recording the music, I was pressing the music, I was distributing the music, I was publicizing the music and I really had a certain degree of experience in most facets of the game. I felt like that was a little bit the final frontier. In addition, my way of thinking was, 'Look. I'm in between these records. I'm producing these acts. And this is a way for me to get a royalty off

of everybody's fuckin' album.' Every record I sell in here, I get a piece of that shit. Why am I gonna sit around and every couple years drop an album and struggle to stay afloat in the game when I can benefit from millions of dollars they're spending on Nelly's album… and, at the same time, promote these independent groups and put people up on this other music. I'm getting a cut of everything. It's my own little world where I'm the CEO of the biggest record label in the world. It's The Tip CDs & Tapes. I sell everybody's shit and I get a cut off of everybody's shit.

Are most of the Chicago rap acts you've mentioned your peers, or did you grow up listening to some of them?
I would say we kind of built this scene together and it's really developed over the last 10 years. There were obviously those before me, but they're not really active anymore. There's a few groups I can remember listening to – there was O.C.U. and Ten Tray – that were putting out in the late-'80s and having some decent distribution. But none of those cats are actively putting out music anymore, or at least to my knowledge. The Legendary Traxters and the Twistas and the Do or Dies and everybody – we all were trying to do this at the same time. We're all still caught in this motherfucker.

Aside from your work on the "CWAL Ballaz," "Killa Beats" and "Wicked Streets of Chi" compilations, fans have had to wait patiently since '97 for your follow-up to "Power Moves." What can they expect from the "Natural Born Illa" album?
Everything's new. The whole sound is new and it's really what E.C. was to '95 is what E.C. is to 2001 – it's a new flavor. It's my same shit, but if you haven't heard it in four years, it comes back and the production is tighter than ever. I've got the sweet guest appearances. I'm real, real confident in this shit, not in just that I felt I made a good album. I felt like I made a groundbreaking album. This shit don't sound like nobody's album; this is my own thing. And that's where the potential for great success is. It's not just that I do good music – a lot of cats out here do music and everybody's puttin' out their CD. But my good music doesn't sound like nobody's good music. So I separate myself that way. I think I look different, I act different, my beats are different and my raps are different. And it's all good. So with that in mind, anybody that checks it out I'm sure is gonna love it. The next goal is to make sure everybody checks it out. •

How long have you been working on this new album?
Ride Wit Us Or Collide Wit Us. We been workin on it about 3 months. 20 songs on there. Bangin.
It's gonna be a classic. Best album to come out this year. And we're not just sayin that cause it's out album. When you hear it you'll know what we mean.
It's original. We got the bangin beats, we got the bomb rhymes. We hot. That's point blank.

I heard that you started your own label?
Outlaw Records. We also got Outlaw Clothing coming and Outlaw Films comin. We the CEO's. Us four.

This is the first time you'll be coming out without 2Pac.
Absolutely. I'm real excited about it. We've grown a lot. We had to step it up, and I don't think we'll disappoint 'em at all. I think we might be better than people even think we are. We recorded like 5 albums that y'all didn't even hear. Over the years buildin up.

What happened to all those recordings?
We have about 4 albums right now about to come out. We got a whole 'nother album done right now. We got the Jersey M.O.B. compilation, Napoleon presents The Bonapartes and The Blood Brothers.

When did you record those albums?
We keep workin. We stay in the studio. That's what we love to do. We got something to prove. Outlaw Records, tryin to shut the game down.

You stay in LA now or are you still in the East Coast?
LA. We recorded all our shit in LA.

How did the Outlawz come together and how did you meet 2Pac?
We all linked to each other from childhood. It was something that had to happen. We all were linked in someway or another from childhood. E.D.I. and Kastro grew up together. Pac is Kastro's cousin. And I grew up with Kadafi (rest in peace). Kadafi is Pac's brother. He brought me, Napolean and Fatal to the group. Fatal's locked down right now too, he's doin a solo thing too. That's how it happened basically. It was a family thing.

What was the age difference?
Pac was three years older than E.D.I. and six years older than me. Pac created The Outlawz. He was the first Outlaw, he was the general.

You were in 2Pac's shadow for a long time. How do you think the world is going to take you now?
We like to let our music speak for itself. We have a lotta fans. From bein on all that Pac stuff we got our own fanbase now. They lovin us for all our past work, but we never put an album out. We way better than we used to be. So when they hear it they gonna love it. Go get the album and you will see. Ain't nobody fuckin with us. We got a lotta fans. We're just tryin to be independent and blow Outlaw Records up. We're tryin to go platinum independent.

How did you end up working with Bayside for distribution?
Spice 1 hooked that up, as a matter of fact. Spice 1 doin something with Bayside. Then he gave 'em a call lettin 'em know we was tryin to do it independent, and they jumped on it. They're excited just like us. They didn't even have to hear the music. They signed us cause they have faith in us, they seen where our heart is at.

When you first met 2Pac did you ever think he would be this big?
Two members of the group knew him all their life, so they always thought he was gonna be this big. We always knew 2Pac was gonna be this big. 2Pac was born a star. You just know when somebody got it.

You think that people are born stars?
For sure. Some people got it, some people don't.

I don't believe that people are born with it, I think people learn.
Some people can learn it. But if you knew a person like Pac all your life you would say that he was born a star. All people--not just us--all people knew that about him. You knew he was gonna do something special.
The ones who didn't know, they know now.
Do you think The Outlawz are stars?
Absolutely. Pac wouldn'ta fucked with us if he didn't see that light in us also. Do you think we're stars?

I like what you're doing, but you were always were working with 2Pac....
You mean we have to prove ourselves now.

People are wondering if the Outlawz can stand on their own.
That's what we want them to say. Pac ain't been here for like three years now. We're still here, we're still bringin the raw. Muthafuckas is gonna see. We wanna prove ourselves.

> "RIDE WIT US OR COLLIDE WIT US. WE BEEN WORKIN ON IT ABOUT 3 MONTHS. 20 SONGS ON THERE. BANGIN. IT'S GONNA BE A CLASSIC. BEST ALBUM TO COME OUT THIS YEAR. AND WE'RE NOT JUST SAYIN THAT CAUSE IT'S OUT ALBUM. WHEN YOU HEAR IT YOU'LL KNOW WHAT WE MEAN."

> "I'M REAL EXCITED ABOUT IT. WE'VE GROWN A LOT. WE HAD TO STEP IT UP, AND I DON'T THINK WE'LL DISAPPOINT 'EM AT ALL. I THINK WE MIGHT BE BETTER THAN PEOPLE EVEN THINK WE ARE. WE RECORDED LIKE 5 ALBUMS THAT Y'ALL DIDN'T EVEN HEAR OVER THE YEARS BUILDIN UP."

I really appreciate rappers who don't give a fuck about anything and just keep doing it.
Keeping it gutter, somebody gotta do it for the streets, everybody can't do this pretty shit. All this glamorous ass shit, not everybody living that life. You gotta tell 'em what your really living. You selling drugs, you rap about that. You really doing this to feed the streets. It might be ugly, but you're just painting a pretty picture with some ugly ass paint, that's how I look at it.

Do you get a lot of negative feedback from the media for what you rap about?
Yeah, they complain about it. But it is what it is, other people talk about it. They just don't do it in the way that I do. But I don't do this shit for no critics, I don't give a fuck.

What inspires you to make music?
I just love it, I just like rap. I just put my stamp on it. Doing the music is better than other stuff, it won't put me in jail. The music is a good opportunity for a black person in America to do this shit and make a living off of it. I don't take it for granted. There's a lot of black people in jail without a lot of opportunity to feed their family and I'm getting that through the music. Whatever magnitude it might be, however rich I might or might not get, just eve having the opportunity as a black man in America to make money off of this is a good feeling.

Ever since seeing your videos and listening to your music, I feel like you have that star quality.
That why despite no radio play, I'm still here. I still maintain a presence without going over the top. I built a core fan base and these rappers they listen me, they look at what I do and the moves I make and the things I say. I just continue to pour into it 100 percent while trying to survive. That's what keeps me going.

A lot of rapper talk about being hardcore but when I listen to your music it feels like you are coming from a real place.
I'm really from the gutter man. I'm from the no food in the house, no electricity, no water, that type of shit. I came from that. A lot of times when rappers talk about being hardcore it sounds forced. It just comes natural to me. And still have a lot to learn but I try to give to the youngsters a different side, not just the party, party, fuck bitches and get high. I try to give them something deeper than that on all my projects.
When you were growing up in the ghetto did you understand about freedom or the black panthers or Malcolm X?
I read a lot of books, understood about that aspect, I was aware of the Black Panthers, Malcolm X. I just read a book on George L. Jackson. Soledad Brother, it's one of my favorite books. I'm definitely into that aspect. I'm all about that, black power. I hope Obama do something for black people before he get out of office. When I make the music, it's definitely street and gangstsa, you gotta grab the audience. Once they are listening, once I got 'em then I go really deep. I wanna give them my struggle first, then also what I learn and my audience can grow with me. I can't force it and give them what I'm not though. I'm still thugging in the street and getting high, I'm in the street everyday doing my thing. I got to tell them that. But I know that that's not everything and there's more to it.

It's a funny thing but this 20th Anniversary issue, we are dedicating it to George Jackson. The beginning of Murder Dog comes from that. After reading books like George Jackson and Malcolm X , that's where it all started, Murder Dog. The thing about George Jackson is that he's hardcore and revolutionary, but he still has that emotional quality. I feel like a lot of people try to be hardcore but don't have that emotional quality.
Yeah, they don't show any vulnerability,

they don't show that they're human beings. You don't know where you are going and you don't know where you come from and people like George Jackson, they're part of our history.

When you got the Interscope deal you moved to LA, what was that like, coming from Gary?

It was defiantly a change up and then when I got dropped from Interscope, I had to start over. I was broke, I didn't have no money left. I had to hustle like I did in Gary. I had to hustle in the streets of LA. I had to start fucking with the Bloods, the Crips. I know a lot of niggas in the streets, I'm a street nigga from Gary Indiana so when I go to LA or any city I go and intermingle with the street niggas. I was just out here doing my thing, went to jail out here couple of times, got caught with a couple pounds of weed, I already had a gun charge in Gary. Then I got another gun charge here in LA, I had to go to LA county. And once I got out of there I had that on my record and it was just harder to rap.

How did you start rapping again after that?

I just got back in the studio. I didn't have a fan base yet so it didn't matter, I was fresh. I was fresh to the game. If I had put out a record while I was on Interscope, and then shit got fucked up, it would've been bad. I wouldn't have been able to do what I had to do. I'm kind of glad I didn't drop an album while I was on Interscope because they wouldn't have pushed me anyways. When I came back out and was doing more underground shit it was more fresh. It wasn't easy, I'm not saying it was easy. It was an uphill battle. It was like going halfway up the hill and then falling down and then you have to fucking go all the way back up. And I'm still climbing up, I have still room to grow.

In LA who did you start working with for production?

I was working with my homeboy Josh and my homeboy Sid and I was getting beats from him. And then after that people started doing tracks for me and sending me beats, cause I was putting mixed tapes out on the internet and people started hearing my shit.

Did you work with Finger roll after you moved to LA?

Well, he moved to Atlanta and I was out here. He was doing his thing and I was doing mine. We was both trying to get established in the Game.

What got you started doing rap when you were in Gary?

I don't know, I was just bored, there wasn't nothing else to do. I was bored and I saw the other muthafuckas doing it and I was like "fuck it". I was just selling dope and getting fired from every job. Not doing what I was supposed to do so it was good that I gave it a try.

Did you grow up in a big family?

I grew up with my mom and my dad, I was the oldest of three. I have a brother and a sister. I got a whole lot of uncles that lived in the house with my grandma. So yeah I got a big family.

What did you grow up listening to?

All my uncles, while I was growing up, they was listenin to Geto Boys. So I listened to a lot of the Geto Boys.

You probably related a lot to them because they were talking about what you were living.

Yeah, it was like having a relative on CD. Or on a tape, cause it wasn't CDs then, it was tape.

Are there any artists on the underground scene that you think are good right now?

I'm it, I'm the best. Ain't nobody out there, no competition. Other than people doing there shit commercially as far as underground, ain't nobody doing it like me.

So you are based in LA mainly?

Yeah, I got my studio at my house, and I just grind it out and make music. I got a whole lot of people I work with out here. I've been working with Mike Dean as of late. I'm working Suppaville, a lot of young up and coming guys.

Your videos have a really dark grimy feel, who directs them?

I direct the videos. I got a guy who comes in a helps me direct but basically all my video concepts come from me. I come and either write it out or tell the director how I want it. I write the songs so I gotta kinda see how they are coming out. 90 percent of the time the come out kinda dope.

You have a big fan base online as well.

Yeah, all the little white kids from the burbs find out about me on the internet. The videos play a big part of that. And they be like "this guy really be doing what he rapping about". It was like when Iceberg Slim was writing books and he was really pimping, I'm on the streets doing what I rap about. I'm making music that's really thug. So it's like this cult following.

They can reach out and touch it they can really see it.

> "I JUST GOT BACK IN THE STUDIO. I DIDN'T HAVE A FAN BASE YET SO IT DIDN'T MATTER, I WAS FRESH. I WAS FRESH TO THE GAME. IF I HAD PUT OUT A RECORD WHILE I WAS ON INTERSCOPE, AND THEN SHIT GOT FUCKED UP..."

When you are in the studio, what sort of sound are you going for?

It depends on the mood. I think I'm one of the most versatile rappers in the game right now. I don't like limit myself to nothing. I just did a whole album with Madlib that I'm about to put out, and a lot of people don't even know who Madlib is. And that's just in addition to the hardcore shit I do.

How did the project with Madlib come about? He's more of a backpacker, lyrical type of rapper.

We've got mutual friends. And he got weird ass sample beats but it was dope. He wanted somebody to put some gangsta shit over it. We just finished the album.

What are some of your favorite songs that you've done?

Probably the last song I did, it's called 'Shit, can't tell me shit', and then there's a song I did called 'Whole Thang' with Young Chop. I just did a song with young Chop. Those are the songs I'm excited about now.

Have you seen you seen yourself change as a rapper?

Definitely, you see yourself evolve and grow and you get better, as a rapper and a song writer and every thing. I sound way different than I sounded when I first started rapping with Finger Roll. I kinda grew up behind the mike, my manhood started behind the mike. You can definitely see the growth, I wanted go farther than I seen anybody go. I think I accomplished that but I still got a long way to go.

So what are you working on at the moment?

I'm going to put out my new project, 'Straight

Killa Part 2'. So that's what I'm working on right now. It'll be out around Christmas, I just put out my street album ESPN, then my album with Madlib, that'll be out in January.

And what label are you on right now?
I got my own label, ESPN, it's independent.

I haven't talked to you in a while!
Man, we go back like 10 years. You remember when I was first doing stuff. Murder Dog came to Gary and did the Murder Dog article! I got in the magazine!

Murder Dog was were probably the first magazine to do anything on you.
Yeah. I wanna get on the cover. What I gotta do to get on the front cover?

For sure. Let's do a cover sometime. Maybe for the 20th Anniversary issue.
I wanna be on the cover. What do I gotta do to be on the cover? I live in California; I'll do a photo shot, whatever. I'll come wherever you're at. It's big! Big for me, big for the magazine.

In your video, the fuck the world video you're running from the police and you get caught. I was wondering why you get caught? Why don't you just escape? Does it represent your life?
I think that it's just reality. But I feel like am free, just a force in the game. I've been doing my shit since I was 21, 22 and now I'm at the point where I've come to another level. I've got the underground on lock. I'm probably the king of that. As far as commercial success, it comes, it goes. I'm not really worried about that, I just want to put out good music. My fans really just love me, everyone else is just bandwagon.

I wanted to talk about the Gary sound, it's very dark and grimy. Where do you think that's coming from?
Well it's the environment, it's the poverty. The world we grow up in. That's what fuels the music. The place has been in an economic crisis for the last thirty years. Growing up in Gary as a youth it was a lot of crazy, a lot of drugs, a lot of murder. There was drug addicts and there was pimps in my household, cops in my household, hoes in my household. It was a big mix of shit. Growing up around that I didn't let it take me under and I used rap as an outlet. I started out with Finger roll, just chilling out in his studio, listening to him making music and smoking weed. When I could get on the mike I took full advantage, I took advantage more than most people do, that why I shined, I think.

How old where you when you started working with Finger roll? What's he up to right now?
I was around 21. Finger roll started me up. If it wasn't for Finger roll I wouldn't be rapping right now. He's in Atlanta still producing, that's my homie, we still talk.

What was the rap scene like in Gary when you where growing up?
It was like, Grind Family, CPA, Finger Roll, Mutt Dogg and Jeff, Thugged out, it was Rick Jilla. It was all these guys and I was like the little man on the totem pole at that point. I had to show that I could rap the best, I had to put myself in the best position. That took a bit of time but then a year and a half, two years back, I got a deal with Interscope. I got a deal real quick. But I got dropped from Interscope a year later though. There was a lot of rappers at that point. There are still a lot of rappers but back then it was more of a thing, there was more respect. Now anybody can put a mike in their bedroom and start rapping. But then everybody was rapping in Gary and when everyone started fading out I just stepped up and took control of the scene. I turned the rap scene in Gary into me. I made myself the voice of the whole city.

About your new album, it was going to come out later but it came out earlier, why was that?
It got leaked, so I just dropped it. I just gave the people what they wanted. It's pretty much 18 tracks, everything post the whole Young Jeezy thing. I just had a lot of shit to get done so I just put that out. I just did it old school with having people fuck with it in the industry, it's a real street album. That what I was aiming for.

How would you compare it to your previous albums?
It's pretty consistent from the last project. From the BFK to the Cold day in hell, when I was with Jeezy and then not with him, my shit stayed pretty consistent. You can go back to my first tapes, everything I put out is solid. It ain't never been a dull moment with me. My tours too, now I do all the big festivals, a lot of show. From my standpoint I'm doing a lot. I just the best in the game but I'm the most underrated. But I ain't worried about that, that'll come.

You were one the first artists in Gary to get picked up by a major label.
From Gary, yeah. My current manager, he was an intern there and he pitched my music. But when they changed management he got fired from the label and I got fired from the label. We just kept working, with all the music and all the knowledge that we got. We used it to our advantage, we used it to propel me to where I'm at now. I'm way bigger now than when I was on Interscope. When I was on Interscope nobody knew who I was cause I wasn't promoted or anything of that nature. It was a good learning experience for me though, I took everything I learn while I was there to move forward in my career. I might've not put an album out but the knowledge that I gained was priceless. •

> "I KINDA GREW UP BEHIND THE MIKE, MY MANHOOD STARTED BEHIND THE MIKE. YOU CAN DEFINITELY SEE THE GROWTH, I WANTED GO FARTHER THAN I SEEN ANYBODY GO."

SANTIGOLD INTERVIEW

BY BLACK DOG BONE • PHOTO BY CRAIG WETHERBY

A lot of times you are compared to M.I.A. You are very different from each other, but both are female artists that are doing something different. Both are doing music that's related to Hip Hop, and you're not coming across as sex objects like a lot of female artists out there.
There are not enough female artists, especially women of color, that are pushing boundaries and trying to do something new and musical and artistic and creative. So there's a camaraderie among those of us who are.

It's exciting to see this new movement of women artists. You have a unique sound and incorporate many different styles. I love the CD you did with Diplo "Top Rankin Dub".
And Bad Brains, Punk Rock…I grew up listening to all that music. I grew up listening to Rock and Hip Hop and Reggae and all kinds of stuff. My Dad was a real music collector and he listened to mostly Jazz and Reggae and Soul, or like Fela and World music. So I listened to that. He took me to see James Brown and Fela Kuti when I was really little. I grew up in a house where music was really appreciated. Then my older sister listened to a lot of Rock. She was into Bad Brains and Punk Rock, and she listened to classic Rock like Jimi Hendrix and the Doors or Led Zeppelin and Joni Mitchell. And at school, I went to a mostly White school, a private school. People were listening to The Cure and Slits and Talking Heads and stuff like that. So I knew all that music. And then I knew Hip Hop cause everybody in my neighborhood was into Hip Hop. I was listening to Salt-N-Pepa and LL Cool J and all that stuff. As a child I had the opportunity to get exposed to a lot of different music; I grew up really appreciating different kinds of music.

That's what I like about your music. It's so broad. I was surprised when I first heard you used to be in a Punk band called Stiffed and worked closely with Bad Brains.
Yeah. They were like my heroes, so it was amazing for me too.

When did you start doing Punk music?
I didn't even start singing my own stuff until later. As a kid I didn't really want to be a singer or an artist. I wanted to be an artist, but not in that way. I wanted to make music. I bought some production equipment when I was 15. But it was a hobby. Then I wanted to have my own record label, so when I went to college I started working at Sony at Epic Records. I tried to do that, like I wanted to be a music executive, but then I realized I didn't like the business side. Then I started songwriting for other artists. I did that for a while, and then finally I started my band Stiffed. That wasn't until like 8 years ago.

As a songwriter did you play instruments or write lyrics?
I can do a little bit of both. I play a little guitar and bass and keyboards, just enough to write. I'm not good at it, but I can write songs on instrument—I write lyrics and I write melody, I write everything. So I was writing for other artists. I wrote a record for a girl named Res that came out on MCA in 2001. That was the first professional songwriting I did. Since then I've written for Lily Allen, Ashlee Simpson and some other artists. That lead me to say actually I want to write songs for myself.

I'm glad you did. I was talking to Diplo earlier and he was talking about you. Are you working with him on the project he and Switch are doing with the Dancehall Reggae artists?
The "Major Lazer" record? I did a song on there with Lexus, it's called "Hold the Line". I think it's going to have two titles, "I'll Make Ya" and "Hold the Line". It's so sick, it's one my favorite songs that I've done recently. I love it, it's really good. Originally when they started working on that project I went down to Kingston with them. I was in the studio with a bunch of Dancehall artists. As they were putting it together I went there and it was really cool to be able to get on one of the songs.

Do you think you'll work with M.I.A. or Rye Rye in the future?
I'm sure. We all come out of the same crew. We're all very supportive of each other and involved with each other. Maya and I actually did a song together about a year and a half ago called "Get It Up"; that's also on the mixtape that I did with Diplo, the "Top Rankin" mixtape.

How did you start working with Diplo? Was it a Philadelphia connection?
No, we have a lot of mutual friends. I met him through my friend Spank Rock. He's a really good friend of mine, and he introduced me to Diplo. Also my friend Amanda Blank. It's just a family of progressive artists who are interested in pioneering some new territory and breaking doing boundaries. Diplo, me, Spank Rock, Amanda Blank, Trouble Andrew, M.I.A., a whole bunch of people.

Where is most of the music going on in Philadelphia?
It's weird, cause I live in Brooklyn but I'm from Philadelphia. Philadelphia is cheaper to live in than New York so more artists can live there and actually sustain themselves while they're trying to figure out what it is they want to do. You're more free to just create and not be all stressed out about how you're gonna pay your bills in the meantime.
Artists are broke most of the time, so it's good to have a city that's easier on you. I moved back to Philly when I started my band Stiffed. I lived there while I was trying to figure some stuff out. I had the space and there's a lot of musicians, there's a lot of great musicians in Philadelphia. I do find that Philadelphia's a bit conservative though. You can come up with cool stuff while you're there, but then once you have something cool you have to leave Philadelphia because there's no music industry there. Also people are more open in New York. Even though we're all from Philly

> **"THERE ARE NOT ENOUGH FEMALE ARTISTS, ESPECIALLY WOMEN OF COLOR, THAT ARE PUSHING BOUNDARIES AND TRYING TO DO SOMETHING NEW AND MUSICAL AND ARTISTIC AND CREATIVE."**

I didn't meet Diplo or anybody until I came to New York. New York is where everybody has to come to make something jump off. Then once you blow up in New York, then people in Philly start paying attention. It's an interesting phenomena. Philly is a great place to cultivate new ideas, but if you want to make something with that you've got to leave.

What is the difference between the Baltimore sound and what you're doing?
What I'm doing is very different from the Baltimore sound. There's not much Baltimore sound in my music at all. Spank Rock is from Baltimore, so he's got more of that influence. Him and Alex, that's XXXchange the one he did the first record with. They're from Baltimore, so there's more of that Baltimore sound in their music. I like the Baltimore sound, and that's in my music. As far as Bass music and Club music, there is some of that in my music. Baltimore music is way more specific, my music is more broad. My

music actually blends so many different styles together that I don't think it fits into any specific category. It's got some Dub and it's got some Electronic, some Punk Rock, some Reggae. I can't really see it even being called Club music at all.

It would be cool if you did a whole album of cover songs, like of Post-Punk artists like The Slits, Fall, Gang of Four, Joy Division. And with Diplo producing it.
What's interesting about Diplo is he comes more from a DJ background. So when he works with me it's fun because he's never actually worked with a real songwriter before. I write Pop songs, and I write with instruments. I wrote most of my record with a guy named John Hill. John and I both come from more of a Rock background. As far as how I approach the songwriting, it's more Pop song structures. So with someone like Diplo, that was his first time working with artists that make songs like that. Diplo's the type of producer that's more track based, which is not what I do. He actually didn't work on that much of my record, he worked on "Unstoppable" and he worked with John and I on a couple of other tracks. What I'm sayin is, I'd rather bring Diplo in once I've already written a song. Maybe I'd start with him, but I don't know about doing a whole Rock record with him cause he comes from a whole different sensibility. That's what's cool about him and about working with him or somebody like Switch, which comes from a House music background. He is all about crazy sounds, like comin up with sounds that you've never heard before. Or choppin up vocals and makin the vocals become sort of like instruments. What's cool about those two workin together is that everybody's got different strengths. The same thing when they came to work on my project with John and I—they brought some of that sensibility to what we were doing. It's all of working together to step outside of our comfort zones that creates the new fresh sound. I don't think that any of us inherently would come up with that same sound by ourselves.

I understand. You come from that Rock/Punk background where you use a guitar or bass to write a song, with chord structures. Then when Diplo or Switch come in they cut it up and make Techno/Tribal club records. What are you working on now?
I'm about to go on another US tour, then another Europe tour, and then I'm done touring for a while. Then I'm gonna start workin on my next record.

When you perform what type of audience do you get? Is it more of a Rap audience or a Rock audience?
It's a really mixed audience because it's a little bit of everything for all different people. I really have a diverse audience, which I like. A lot of people come from the Indie background. And then with these collaborations I've been doing like the song with Jay Z ("Brooklyn We Go Hard"), that opened up a whole new audience. Then the mix with Lil Wayne, and Three 6 Mafia did a mix of one of my songs—that really brought me into the Hip Hop world more. I'm doin a song with Ferrell and Julian Casablanca for the Converse thing. And I did the song with N.E.R.D. and that's more Pop. I feel like over the course of the year my audience has been becoming more and more broad.

I feel like we need more people like you and M.I.A. in the Hip Hop world. As a woman and as an artist in general, you are an inspiration. You show that you don't have to just sell sex to be a successful in music. It's all about the music. We don't have enough people who have a passion for music—it's not just business for you.
Right. It's interesting to watch what's going on with Hip Hop right now. People like T.I. and Jay Z and Lil Wayne, people that are respected, are taking a risk in working with artists like us, people that are doing something different. That's doing good things for the state of Hip Hop, cause now people are more willing to take risks. Hip Hop for a long time has been dying because nobody takes risks, everybody does the same thing, wears the same clothes, says the same thing, uses the same producers. It's just dead. It doesn't help music grow at all. Finally now some of these artists that are in the forefront are pushing forward and saying, "This shit is cool," and reaching out and trying to introduce new things into their music. I think that's gonna help the music overall. •

> "THAT'S WHAT'S COOL ABOUT HIM AND ABOUT WORKING WITH HIM OR SOMEBODY LIKE SWITCH, WHICH COMES FROM A HOUSE MUSIC BACKGROUND. HE IS ALL ABOUT CRAZY SOUNDS, LIKE COMIN UP WITH SOUNDS THAT YOU'VE NEVER HEARD BEFORE."

RBL POSSE

INTERVIEW & PHOTO BY BLACK DOG BONE

The Bay is coming into a good period right now.
I feel the same way, cause everybody in the Bay is startin to network a little more now. We're bringin that vibe back to where it was in the early '90's when E-40, Spice 1 and all of us used to perform our shows and it was like love. But then everybody started goin their separate ways. Major labels started comin through, picked up people like Mac Mall, me, JT. That kinda separated everybody, broke up that Bay unity that used to be there. Now everybody's goin back to that independence. That's puttin us all back in the game, everybody's startin to control and own our own shit. We learned from our past mistakes as far as signin with the majors real quick just to get a deal. We all had it goin independent from the gate. We shoulda just stuck with it.

When you're independent you make ten times more money...
That's what I'm on right now. Even with Atlantic, they put out my last album. It sold over 150,000 copies. That was a disappointment to them, but to me on an independent level I woulda been real happy with it. We sold like 30,000 copies of "How We Comin". If that was me bein independent that's ghetto platinum. It's a big difference.

It's good to see the Bay back on the independent track.
Right. The Bay is used to pushin 50-100,000 units max and be satisfied, go on to the next, keep it consistent. The majors, once you get with them and you ain't satisfied 'em with 150-200, they put you on the shelf for one or two years and you fightin 'em up outta that. That's what I went through with Atlantic. They tried to shelf me and they kinda tried to shelf Twista too. Twista started getting more feedback from bein on Puffy's tape and stuff like that. He blew himself back up and they got interested in him again. I had to wriggle myself outta that situation. Now I'm back independent. I'm ready to keep it consistent, at least every 9 months to a year I'm tryin to drop an album.

What's the album you're putting out now?
RBL Hostile Takeover. Bootleg was something we just put out there to hold us over. I had my album ready, but I didn't know who was gonna distribute it. I wanted to take it to City Hall, but they didn't have the budget to do the marketing and promotions. So I took it over to Brandon at Bayside. He showed me some love and plus he knew the history on RBL, cause he grew up in Hunters Point. Right now it's swell, we're releasing May 8th. Hostile Takeover is a whole new beginning. After that Hitman's tape is droppin. We got like seven groups on the Right Way roster--Alias, Collide, Military Minded, Prime Minister and Young Thugs.

> "WE'RE BRINGIN THAT VIBE BACK TO WHERE IT WAS IN THE EARLY '90'S WHEN E-40, SPICE 1 AND ALL OF US USED TO PERFORM OUR SHOWS AND IT WAS LIKE LOVE. BUT THEN EVERYBODY STARTED GOIN THEIR SEPARATE WAYS. MAJOR LABELS STARTED COMIN THROUGH, PICKED UP PEOPLE LIKE MAC MALL, ME, JT. THAT KINDA SEPARATED EVERYBODY, BROKE UP THAT BAY UNITY THAT USED TO BE THERE. NOW EVERYBODY'S GOIN BACK TO THAT INDEPENDENCE. THAT'S PUTTIN US ALL BACK IN THE GAME, EVERYBODY'S STARTIN TO CONTROL AND OWN OUR OWN SHIT."

Are all your artists from the Bay?
All from either San Francisco or Oakland originally. And Prime Minister's from Sacramento.

Are you making beats for these new projects?
I'm doin like 70% of the work. And I got a coupla new dudes who are underground. I like underground people who are doin shit. I like to put them on the map, cause they're easier to work with. I got Nick Nasty outta Oakland and another dude outta Mississippi called C-Dog. We're doin all the production. We're called R Rated & Dangerous Music, us three.

With RBL albums you were doing all the beats. The first two were classic albums.
Exactly. And those albums was mainly just us. We didn't have too many features, just underground people like Cellski. I went back to the roots on this one--I did all the production and I got all underground cats who are hungry, who still got the love of music. The love kinda left me after all this business and music industry bullshit got into me. When you listen to my first album you can tell that we was havin fun on that album. Just clownin around on up tempo tracks. We started getting more business oriented when Ruthless By Law came up. By the time Atlantic got us it was strictly business. I kinda took the fun and the love out of it.

Things are better for you now?
I'm happy. I got more control of what's goin on. Right now I'm tryin to find the right home for us, and hopefully Bayside's that right home. It's kinda hard to figure out the right place to be, the right people who ready to get behind you and put that money behind you and really believe in you instead of treatin you like just another number or another check. We're tryin to get that all situated and get my whole catalog back. Hopefully I'ma take that over to Bayside or somewhere that's good and put the whole catalog out.

INSANE CLOWN POSSE

BY BLACK DOG BONE • PHOTO BY JOHNNY BUZZERIO

When you first started wearing clown faces and al that, how did people react to you?
They hated it. I remember we opened up for Esham and the entire crowd--they didn't boo us off, but they didn't move. I've never seen anything like that to this day. They just stood there and looked at us. We said Throw your hands in the air, and nobody would move. It was unbelievable. In all my years of doing shows, all throughout Europe too, I've played new markets in Spain, Germany, but I've never seen anything like that.

What kind of reaction do you get now?
We're on our own headlining tours now. If you look in Pollstar Magazine, we have the number 25 top grossing tour in the United States. Out of all the tours, including Grunge music, Rap music, Rock music, every tour out there including Walt Disney On Ice and all that kinda shit, we have the number 25 top grossing tour. Right now we average 3,000 people a night every night, no matter where we play in the United States.

Doesn't all that touring burn you out?
Big time. I landed myself into a mental institution twice because I was on the road so long that my brain just stops working. I had kind of a breakdown twice.

When you're on tour do you drink or do drugs?
To be totally honest with you, no. That's really unusual, because you won't find a lot of bands--Rock or Rap--that don't do that. Shaggy, he drinks every now and then and Twiztid, they smoke a lot of weed. But I don't do anything. I think I'm more addicted to sleeping pills than anything else. But there's not a whole lotta drinkin and drugs goin on in our bus.

When I listen to your music I thought you might be dropping a lot of acid.
I seems like we would be, but no. The last tour we did, which ended about 3 months ago, our opening act was Krayzie Bone of Bone Thugs. I'll tell you why he was our opening act, cause even though Krayzie Bone might sell more records than us, he doesn't draw to a concert what we draw. So a lotta times we have big name rappers opening for us. Krayzie Bone did a whole tour with us. We also did a lotta shows with Snoop Dogg opening for us. We get a long with rappers a lot better than we get along with Rock & Roll bands.

What kind of audience do you draw? It's a Rock audience?
Naw, I wouldn't say that. In that way it's mixed. It's half a Rap audience. It depends on the situation. It's weird cause when you're not on the radio and you're not on MTV or BET, you never know what your audience will be till you get to that city. It's whatever part of town caught onto you first. Like for example when we played Denver we have a big Latino audience. It's whatever part of town started bumpin your shit first.

It also is influenced by the way you've been marketed by Def Jam. I'm sure a lot of people would love your shit if they were exposed to you.
I think you're right. I hope that if other people wake up like Murder Dog--you're always the first to cover anything interesting. In fact I don't buy any other magazines except Murder Dog. Dead serious. My boss doesn't buy any other magazine but Murder Dog either cause it's all shit. Murder Dog's the only real shit out there. The whole thing about ICP and Twiztid is that people don't know how to categorize us. Rap, Rock or whatever, we kinda float around.

After that first show when everybody just stood there, how did your fanbase build?
When we first did that first show when everybody just stared at us, that was before we had sold any records. Then we sold a lotta records before we did our second concert. When everybody came to that one, they were to see us that time. First time we were opening for Esham, second time we just played ourselves. Everybody in the house was there to see us.

How much later was that from your first show?
About 9 months. Ever since that second show every show we've played in Detroit has sold out.

Now the audience is wearing clown make-up to. Is that just in Detroit?
No, that's everywhere. More outside of Detroit than in Detroit.

Where are you the biggest?
According to our concert merchandise figures and Soundscan record sales, Detroit is our fifteenth biggest market. There are fourteen other places where we're bigger. Phoenix. Austin. St. Louis. Chicago. Pittsburgh. Boston. Cincinnati. Seattle. Denver. Those are all bigger than Detroit for us.

And they all show up wearing clown makeup?
Yeah. Even when we play a city where we're not all that popular, the few people that might show up, they have clown makeup on. Everybody does.

In the beginning you went by a different name, Inner City Posse. What made you change your name?
Inner City Posse was a street gang. When we first started off rappin, that's what we went by. Pretty soon all the other gangs started kickin

> "IT FITS WITH OUR VOICES. TO ME CARNIVAL MUSIC IS BEAUTIFUL. I LOVE ORGANS AND I LOVE CARNIVAL MUSIC. AND THE THING IS, IT'S A LOT EASIER TO BE A CLOWN. EVERY RAPPER FROM THE WEST TO THE SOUTH TO THE EAST, EVERY RAPPER TALKS ABOUT HOW COOL THEY ARE, HOW HARD THEY ARE, HOW MUCH MONEY THEY GOT, HOW TOUGH THEY ARE, WHAT A PLAYER, WHAT A BALLER THEY ARE. BUT ICP, WE'RE CLOWNS, WE'RE FOOLS. WE TALK ABOUT HOW STUPID WE ARE, HOW UGLY WE ARE. THAT'S WHY PEOPLE CAN RELATE TO US, BECAUSE EVERYBODY, EVEN THOSE RAPPERS, EVERYBODY'S A FOOL. BUT EVERYBODY TRIES TO BE COOL. WITH ICP IT'S OK JUST TO BE A GOOF, JUST TO BE A FOOL."

our ass really bad. We started gettin popular, because of the records not because of the gang bein tough. Then everybody quit and it was just down to like 5 of us left in our whole crew. So we switched our name and became Insane Clown Posse.

When you started you had a bigger group?
It was just a bigger crew. It was four rappers, but a whole buncha muthafuckas.

When you first started did you have a different sound?
Yeah, it was Gangsta Rap. Like old NWA.

You weren't wearing the clown faces?
We weren't wearin clown makeup. We were just Gangsta rappin, thuggin.

The whole concept with the clowns, how did that come about?
In 1994 when the gang was over with. We switched and joined The Dark Carnival, which is kinda like our religion. It's who we are, it's what we are. It was meant to be. That's why Inner City Posse never worked. It's the wicked shit. It'll never go away.

Did the change come gradually or suddenly?
It was kinda like catchin the holy ghost. It all happened over night. Very suddenly. The ghost of the Dark Carnival approached us and from then on we were Insane Clown Posse.

You two are the original members? Did you grow up together?
We grew up in the suburbs until about 7th grade. Then we moved to the city and we dropped outta school. We were kinda wannabe gang bangers. But in short we got our asses kicked all the time. We didn't really understand that these gangs in Southwest Detroit had been there for generations and generations. We kinda moved into the neighborhood and said, Hey let's start our own gang. We didn't know anything about it. We got our asses kicked real bad. My mom's house got shot up, I got shot in the shoulder. We totally didn't belong in what we were doin cause we were really from the suburbs. We had no idea what we were doing.

What suburb did you come from?
Oakpark.

How long have you been doing this?
We've been rappin since 1989. Our first release was in 1992.

Who else has been doing production for Insane Clown Posse?
There's a guy outta Detroit named Mike E. Clark. He has been with us since day one. To this day only Mike Clark and Esham have done our shit. Esham did a couple songs for us, but everything else has been Mike E. Clark. Mike E. Clark also does George Clinton, he's done a lotta Kid Rock, he even did some stuff for Esham.

Did you do a lot of shows with Esham?
Back then we used to always try to put together the ultimate show with ICP, Esham and Kid Rock all at one show. ICP, we said we'll open the show. But Kid Rock and Esham could never get along and decide who would go on last. Everybody wanted to play last. Esham didn't wanna go on before Kid Rock and Kid Rock didn't wanna go on before Esham. So it never happened. Back then ICP was a bigger draw than in Detroit than both of them, but we agreed to open up. But today Kid Rock is way bigger than ICP. Kid Rock now plays The Palace in Detroit, it holds 18,000 people.

He crossed over to a whole different market.
There you go. And his market is very fragile. They'll disappear as quick as they came. When you build your following from the underground they'll be your fans for life. ICP fans just love ICP. Same with Esham.

You're right. Those fans will never go away. I wonder if you'll ever do a tour with all the Detroit wicked shit together.
We did a movie that comes out in January. When we were making the movie last year we flew Esham out to New York and we talked about doin a tour together and about possibly doin a record together. They weren't into the idea. I'm gonna be totally honest with you. I don't think they'll ever be a tour with us and Esham because of the fact that Esham wouldn't wanna go on before Twiztid. And Twiztid sells more records than he does across the country, because we've been pushing them nationally. The only way Esham would ever tour with ICP is if Esham went on right before us and that would make Twiztid look bad. It's a big thing with egos. And it really does matter cause fans take notice to that stuff. Fans wonder why they are goin on before them. It's a hard situation. So I don't think it'll ever happen.

So ICP is always touring?
Non stop.

Who is Alex?
Alex is our manager. He's the owner of Psychopathic Records. We been with Alex since we started in 1990. We started it all out together--me, Shaggy and Alex.

Who were you listening to when you first started?
When I first started my influences were Geto Boys, NWA and Esham.

What are you listening to now?
Right now I'm listening to Bone Thugs, Krayzie Bone. I'm really excited that NWA reunited. I'm praying they'll do an album together, absolutely praying. I was in LA 2 weeks ago and I went to an Ice T concert. Everybody was there--Cypress Hill was there, The Alcoholics, King T--we were hangin out with all those guys. And even though we're not on the radio, they're all big fans of us. We were really excited about that. We did a song with Ice T before, but I didn't know that any of those people would have any idea who we were.

So you were listening to a lot of West Coast Rap?
It's really odd cause to this day I'm a huge West Coast Rap fan. Shaggy, the other half of the group, is a big East Coast Rap fan. He doesn't like too much West Coast Rap and I don't like too much East Coast Rap.

You have conflicts?
In the bus, yeah. On the CD player.

How do you get along after working together for so long?
We're best friends. And we'll always be together.

When I listen to all the Insane Clown Posse records I can see you have changed and developed a lot. I feel like you had a master plan.
That's all the Dark Carnival. It's the six joker cards.

Can you explain a little about the joker cards, how each one represents one album. How did that concept come about?
Like I said earlier, it's sorta like catchin the holy ghost. It was dawned to us by the spirits of the Dark Carnival.

It just came into your mind?
Like a dream. Nothing made sense until that happened. Now it all makes sense. Every album, there are a lotta messages underneath our music. Those messages are to be told to the people that need to hear them. We talk a lot about anti racism. We don't like racism at all. And if you look at it, all our records seem to sell in the suburbs, and that's the people that are most racist. Those are the people that need to hear it. It all works out.

Where do all the names come from for your albums?
They come to me. It's like somebody injects a thought into my mind. Even if I don't like it I have to roll with it, cause it's the Dark Carnival. It's the way it has to be. We're like prophets

of the Dark Carnival. Very underground and very hidden. Yet in our own world everything makes perfect sense to us. But on the outside looking in, it seems like it makes no sense. But to be a follower of Insane Clown Posse, a Jugalo, it makes perfect sense. We have five jokers cards, and I don't know what the sixth jokers card, the last jokers card is gonna be called. I haven't been told yet. It'll come to me, but I don't know when that is. It might be tomorrow, it might be next year. But I can't even start workin on that album until it comes to me.

Then you will get your whole concept around the card?
Right. That started in '91 when we released the first jokers card, Carnival Of Carnage. All of our album covers are just a jokes card--a black cover with a clown face.

Who does all the artwork for the jokers cards?
Shaggy. He doesn't draw anything except for those. He's not an artist like that, he doesn't draw anything but when it's time to come up with the image for the jokers card it comes to him.

After the last joker card comes what's the future for Insane Clown Posse?
There's a lot more to ICP than the jokers cards. Well, we're gonna do solo records, but we're still gonna be with each other. I'm gonna do a Violent J album and he's gonna do a Shaggy album. He'll be all over my album and I'll be all over his album.

The solo albums will be coming out next year?
Yeah. And then we have a group album with Twiztid called Dark Lotus. That's all four of us together. Then we have the next jokers card. And after the jokers card we'll have to see what happens. I've got so much ahead of me right now with Dark Lotus and with my solo record. But our solo record isn't really a solo record. It's still ICP, but it's gonna be me on all the songs. We'll never make music without each other or without Mike E. Clark.

Will the record be called ICP or Violent J?
It'll be called Violent J, but Shaggy'll be on a buncha songs. You know the Geto Boys? The Geto Boys do solo albums, and they don't even talk about the Geto Boys on their solo albums. Scarface will release a solo album and there's no sign of Willie D. We're not like that. Our solo records might as well be ICP.

You'll be working with the same producer, when did Mike Clark start doing your production?
I'd say Riddlebox. The third jokers card is when we started messin with guitars and stuff like that.

You use a lot of Gypsy carnival type sounds in your music. Where did that come from?
It fits with our voices. To me carnival music is beautiful. I love organs and I love carnival music. And the thing is, it's a lot easier to be a clown. Every rapper from the West to the South to the East, every rapper talks about how cool they are, how hard they are, how much money they got, how tough they are, what a player, what a baller they are. But ICP, we're clowns, we're fools. We talk about how stupid we are, how ugly we are. That's why people can relate to us, because everybody, even those rappers, everybody's a fool. But everybody tries to be cool. With ICP it's OK just to be a goof, just to be a fool.

Like when you talk about gang banging and how you got your ass kicked. Most people, even if they do get their ass kicked, they'll never say it.
Yeah, we get our asses kicked. It's a lot easier to be yourself and to be a clown. If you've ever seen one of our concerts, I might slip and fall on my back in the middle of the show, but it doesn't matter because I'm a clown. I can come out and wear shoes that only cost five dollars. I can be a goof. I can drop the microphone in the middle of the song. Nothing really matters, it's OK at our concerts. That's why we put the carnival music too, because there's no rapper out there that puts carnival music in their music. We wanted to have that feeling that it's OK to be crazy and to do your own thing. We have no rules. If you listen to our last album, The Amazing Jeckel Bros., the first song and the last song on the album sound completely different. The last song is really slow and has piano. We can be really subtle and soft. Or we can be savage serial killers. ICP will go anywhere. Anywhere we wanna go in music. I'm gonna make a dance song. I'm gonna make a Gangsta Rap song. I'm gonna make a Booty track. I'll make anything I want, because I'm a clown and I can do whatever I want.

Most people seem to want to be like everybody else, but you just went off and did your own thing. What made you want to break off and do something different? Were you always like that?
When we were kids, me and Shaggy, we were always kinda picked on and made fun of. On our first record ever, Dog Beats, it was only on cassette, we were kinda Gangsta/hard. And we knew that wasn't us. And our gang ICP, Inner City Posse, had this reputation that it was tough--that really wasn't us. There was no hiding what we really were. Then the Dark Carnival reached us and said, You guys are perfect for what I'm tryin to say, you can be the spokespeople for us. Whatever the Dark Carnival is. Ever since then we just came out with our product, who we are, not what other people would think is cool or what other people would think would work. Listen, in the beginning when we first started out, everybody used to tell me, "Hey you guys are really great, but you shouldn't wear the clown makeup, that's stupid." Everybody said that. Now you know what they say? They say, "You guys suck, but the fact that you wear clown makeup is the only reason you're popular." People are always trying to find a way to put you down. You know what I mean? Before the reason why we were not popular was because we wore clown makeup. And now the only reason we are popular is because we wear clown makeup. To really block yourself outta that is to only communicate with you and your fans. That's exactly what we do.

Even though you're clowns your music is not a joke. It's deep. Do you write your lyrics together or separately?
We both write the lyrics. But back what we used to listen to before we made records--like if you listen to Ice Cube's first album, that's pretty much what ICP was like at first. He had one song that told a story--once upon a time in the projects. Then he had another song that was just Gangsta. He had another song about a girl. Back then Rap, every song sounded so different from the next. That's our influences. In our music every song has to be different. Every song has to be sayin something. Every song has to have a story or a deed to it. Just like our tours. When we come to town we're not just ICP live in concert. Like the tour we're on now is the Wicked Clowns From Outer Space Tour. We have Martians that come out on stage. It's keeping your record entertaining. I always tell people that never have heard us, Even if hate Rap music you'll find something entertaining about our record. You'll find something that you'll life.

Sometimes your music reminds me of early Ice Cube and the Lench Mob. It's a crime that you've been marketed as a Rock group. Most Rap buyers have never heard your shit.
Every album that we put out sells a million copies. I think we have a million fans and it never grows. It just maintains a million fans. The people that know us love us, and the other people they just don't know us.

I know there are some other acts signed to Psychopathic Records like Twiztid. Does Insane Clown Posse own Psychopathic Records?
When we started out in 1991 or '92 we started Psychopathic Records. We were the only group on our label. We did a tour. A lotta

the other rappers in Detroit stay in Detroit, but Insane Clown Posse doesn't. We tour, we go nationwide, we play everywhere. One day we did a tour and the House of Krazees were the opening act for us. After about 10 shows the House of Krazees' manager pulled them off the tour. Two of the three members of House of Krazees didn't understand why and they hated the whole fuckin idea that their dumb-ass manager pulled them off the tour when they were doin so good out there. The group House of Krazees wasn't gettin along anyway so they broke up and they left the House of Krazees. Two of them joined us at Psychopathic Records and we took them in and started Twiztid.

Twiztid formed when they came to Psychopathic?
Right. They were breakin up though, they were having trouble for years. Walt doesn't know the first fuckin thing about the music business.

House of Krazees was an amazing group.....
They were musically because Twiztid was doin the music. But House of Krazees couldn't exist without the guys from Twiztid cause they were 2/3's of the group.
The other member of House of Krazees, Soul, he has a new group called Half Breed.

I haven't heard about that.
I'll tell you one thing, a lot of rappers from Detroit--I'm not gonna mention names--they tell you how many records they've sold and they tell you how big they are and how large their fanbase is and on and on and on. The only thing I have to say about that is check the Soundscan, check the billboard charts. Twiztid alone sells more records than any of them. We do, sure, but even Twiztid outsells every other group from Detroit. I'm not sayin that as a matter of opinion, I'm tellin you as a matter of fact. Check the Soundscan. And I'll tell you why it sells, because what we're doin here at Psychopathic Records is takin the wicked shit that Detroit is famous for and we're spreadin it across the nation. We're goin on tour, even if we only play for 50 people or if we play for 5,000 people, we're goin on tour and we're workin our asses off. That's the reason that we're sellin so many records. What we do, the wicked shit, the horror rap or whatever you wanna call it, which Esham basically created in Detroit, what we do doesn't only work in Detroit, it can sell records everywhere. You just gotta get off your ass and go out there. That's what we're doin.

I love what you're doing and I want to support Detroit Rap 100%.
You definitely are. Every time I pick up Murder Dog I see a story about Esham or Natas or even groups from other states that haven't exploded yet but are heavy on the underground. It's unbelievable. You're the first magazine to be on top of all that shit, you're gonna cover this stuff before it's on the cover of Rolling Stone.

The reason we never did anything on Insane Clown Posse is because your label never approached us or sent your product.
I'll tell you why you never got our product. Our label Psychopathic Records is a Hip Hop label, but Island/Def Jam does our distribution and Island/Def Jam, when they work our records, when they do our promotions, they consider us Alternative Rock. Instead of goin to the Rap magazines like Murder Dog they go to the Rock magazines. Even though we don't play any instruments and we do strictly Rap, that's what we do, the record company only promotes us to a Rock audience.

That's fucked up. A lot of people who listen to Rap would love what you're doing.
Tell me about it. I know that and you know that, but unfortunately my stupid-ass record company, Island/Def Jam, doesn't have the first fuckin clue of what's goin on.

Don't you get mad when you see your records in the Rock section at a record store. You don't sound anything like Rock.
I used to get mad, but now I'm so tired and I just say Fuck it. We tour, we entertain our fans. I love our fans and our fans keep buying our albums no matter what we put out. And I really don't care any more about fighting with my record company. Like the people at Def Jam, they'll never understand ICP. Even though we're on Def Jam, they'll never understand us. I'm through trying, and if I did explain my situation to them and they were on point and they were marketing us correctly and everything was fine, then they would all the sudden fire their president and hire someone new and then I'd have to start all over again. The only label that I'm concerned about is Psychopathic Records. That's ICP and Twiztid and Dark Lotus.

Are you planning to sign new acts to the label?
It's just us for now, but we're always looking for somebody new. I hate to say this, and a lot of rappers will disagree with this, but this is the truth. If there's no gimmick, if there's no theatrics, or there's no story behind the

> "ONCE EVERYONE'S TIRED OF THEM AND WANTS TO KILL THE GUYS, THEY GET SOMETHING NEW. LIKE MASTER P. MASTER P'S BEEN ON THE UNDERGROUND FOREVER. BUT ONCE RADIO GOT AHOLD OF HIM AND MTV GOT AHOLD OF HIM HE WAS ONLY POPULAR FOR ONE YEAR. NOW HE'S GONE. I BET HE WISHES NOW THAT HE NEVER WENT MAINSTREAM. HE'S BEEN AROUND FOR YEARS. BUT WHEN HE WENT MAINSTREAM HE ONLY LASTED A YEAR. THAT'S WHY I'LL NEVER GO ON RADIO. FUCK RADIO! I'LL NEVER LET THAT HAPPEN TO PSYCHOPATHIC EVER."

rappers, then we don't wanna have nothing to do with 'em. I want exciting acts. I want stage presence. I want something you could make a comic book off of. I want gimmicks and theatrics.

When you tour in different places have you found other artists that have been influenced by ICP and do it like you?
Yeah. All the time. Sometimes they play shows with us. Sometimes they just come out on different labels. There's a lotta things, mostly in the Rock world though. There's a lotta Rock bands out there that rip us off. The rappers all rip Esham off. All the rappers rip off Esham and all the Rock & Rollers rip us off. There seemed to be a lot going on in Detroit--with Esham, Insane Clown Posse, Kid Rock, Twiztid, House of Crazies--but the media didn't recognize it for a long time.

With the exception of Murder Dog covering this stuff, nothing's changed. It's still so much goin on in Detroit and the world hasn't caught on to it. Murder Dog is the first.

How did this whole clown concept come about?
When our gang broke up, the Inner City Posse that was gettin our asses kicked, it dawned on us. We weren't goin anywhere no matter what happened, we were gonna keep doin it. It's like, we're from Detroit, let's do the wicked shit, let's quit tryin to be LA, let's quit tryin to be New York, let's do what we really feel-- Detroit streets. The streets in Detroit, you can just feel the wicked shit everywhere in Detroit. It's just the way the whole community is. It's like New Orleans and Cajun cooking. If you're a rapper from Detroit and you're not doin the wicked shit, I don't know where the fuck you're from. It's all over Detroit, it is Detroit.

was a big fan of Esham back then. I'm not such a big fan of his newer records. He's more for the radio, you can tell he's tryin to get on the radio. I'm out here with two platinum albums and two gold albums certified, and

> **"I WAS FUCKIN WITH THE GUY. COME ON DOWN TO THE SHOW, IT'S GONNA BE A LOTTA FUN, WE'RE GONNA DO SOME OF OUR RADIO HITS.... BUT WHAT I REALLY WANNA SAY WHILE WE'RE HERE ON THE RADIO-- HE'S LIKE, WHAT'S THAT?! I'M LIKE, FUCK RADIO! UNDERGROUND FOREVER! FUCK RADIO! FUCK THIS STATION! THE GUY WAS STUNNED. THE DJ DIDN'T KNOW WHAT TO DO. THERE WAS A GUY FROM MY RECORD LABEL, A GUY FROM DEF JAM, HE WAS JUST LOOKIN AT ME, HIS MOUTH DROPPED OPEN. THAT WAS EXCELLENT. I WISH I HAD A CASSETTE OF THAT."**

Detroit has such an exciting Rap scene, very different from what's going on in the South or the West or any place.
You're absolutely right. Insane Clown Posse was one of the first to start that off with Esham. We used to work together a lot back in the day.

Some of your early material was produced by Esham?
Yeah, our older stuff was. And if you look back before NWA in Compton there was no Gangsta Rap. After NWA was born all the Gangsta Rap started comin up outta LA, it started blowin up. That's what Detroit's like. It's something brand new. It hasn't really caught on yet, but it's going to and it is happening right now.

I think Esham influenced a lot of Detroit Rap, with the dark wicked lyrics...
Yes. Esham influenced us. He was the first to do this wicked shit. So did the old Geto Boys. That's why on our latest album we covered the Geto Boys song "Assassin".

Esham was using Heavy Metal rifts on his early albums. Were you doing that too?
We didn't really get into the guitar stuff in the beginning until we started touring. Once we started playing live shows we started to see what the crowd really liked. They liked the guitars and stuff like that, so we started adding it into our music. Any songs with guitar in it, the crowds would go like 10 times more crazy.

When you perform do you have a full band or do you use samples?
It's just us and samples. But in the studio we have a whole band.

When you first started out in Detroit Esham was doing shit. Who else was there?
When we started out there were two names on top of the Detroit music scene. There was Esham and Kid Rock.

But Kid Rock wasn't doing what he's doing now, he was more Hip Hop....
Right. He was doin Hip Hop, but he was not doin the wicked shit. He was doin Hip Hop, but it wasn't anything like Esham or what people call horror Rap, what Detroit's famous for. Kid Rock never did any of that. Which is cool cause Kid Rock's not really from Detroit. He's from a town like 50 miles outside of Detroit called Mt. Clemens. I think maybe what was going on in Detroit wasn't really influencing him out there.

It seems like Esham had a big influence on the whole Detroit scene.
Without a doubt.

Are you a little younger than Esham?
No, we're about the same age. But Esham came out first and he hit so hard in Detroit. He was so popular in Detroit that he influenced us, he influenced House of Krazees, he influenced everybody. He was so Detroit. Back then Esham was so much representing Detroit, it was excellent and it was great. I

I'm like: Fuck the radio! I'm still like: Fuck the radio. But Esham's old stuff was so great that you can't help but be influenced, you wanna be just like that. It was so good.

Didn't he appear on your albums and do some production for Insane Clown Posse?
Yeah, he was on our first and second records.

How many records do you have out?
We have five albums and four EP's.

Are they all Insane Clown Posse, or did Inner City Posse have any records out?
There's one ep called Inner City Posse. It's very hard to find. Very much a collector's item. They sell 'em on the Internet for about $200 a cassette.

What was the first Insane Clown Posse album?
The first one was Carnival of Carnage. It came out in '92.

That one sold gold?
No that one isn't gold or platinum. It's at about 300,000 copies. Then the second album, The Ringmaster, and that also is at about 300,000 records. The third album is The Riddlebox, that's gold. The fourth album is The Great Millenko and that's platinum. '97 that came out. The fifth album is The Amazing Jeckel Brothers, that's our new album and that's platinum. Also we have a record out called Forgotten Freshness, which is a double CD of hard to find, rare released songs. That's gold.

I know you were influenced by Esham. But you went on a whole different road with it. I don't think there's anybody out there doing anything like you.

Not really. Not in the Rap world or the Rock world. That's good music. Anything different and original is good music. Last time I spoke to you I hadn't heard the new Natas record. But now I have and I like it a lot. I think that's the best record Natas has ever done. It's very different. It's really really different. I like it a lot.

I saw so many articles about Eminem, but he never talked about what's going on in Detroit.
He never does.

I'm sure he knows about it, he was probably influenced by it.
He was, without a doubt. Back for all of the 90's Esham, Kid Rock, Twiztid, House of Krazees, and Insane Clown Posse--all of us kinda grew up together. We grew up doin shows together or hating each other. We were at the same places and we knew the same people. But Eminem, he kinda came outta nowhere. I think he started rapping one day and about a month later he got a record deal. It kinda exploded. He didn't come up with us. We never did shows with him and he never put out his own records on the streets. He just kinda appeared one day and got signed by Dr. Dre. He wasn't part of a family almost.

When I found out about the sound coming from Detroit it was exciting.
Eminem, he's not part of that sound. That sound was born by Esham, Insane Clown Posse, Natas. These are the forefathers of that sound.

Twiztid's album is tight.
They're sellin 3,000 copies a week and it's not getting any radio play or anything. Check the Soundscan on it, it sold like 150,000 copies. And that's fact. A lotta people say they sold 5 million copies, but on the Soundscan they only did like 40,000. But I give you the straight facts. They're selling really really good.

Do you ever tour our here in California?
Yeah, we just did San Francisco, San Diego, LA, Ventura, Palo Alto, all over California. We'll be back though in like two months.

What the definition of a Jugalo?
It's people who don't always wanna be cool. Someone who isn't always concerned about looking cool and being tough. People that follow the jokers card, they follow all of our albums. We have Jugalo parties and all the Jugalo show up. It's people who enjoy our music and think the same way we do. People that live, breath and die just like us. Jugalos, that's just another word the followers of Insane Clown Posse.

Where do you have Jugalo parties?
All over the country. When we tour. Let's say we have a show in Chicago at the Roseland Theater. We'll rent out the House Of Blues the next day and we'll tell all our fans at the concert, we'll say Show up at the House Of Blues tomorrow. When they show up at the House Of Blues there'll be free drinks and we'll get on stage and perform, and let them get up and rap, things like that.

Do you and Shaggy always wear the clown makeup?
Yeah. Anytime we're out in public. But when we're out alone on our own, naw, we won't wear it. Like if we're goin into a supermarket at midnight or something. But anytime that we're anywhere in public we wear it.

If you go into a club where other rappers are do they look at you like you're crazy or what?
No, because most of the Rap world, they know who we are, and they respect us. Because we sell so many records. Like we did a song with Snoop Dogg, and I thought Snoop wouldn't wanna do it. But he dug it. He's like, These guys are doin something original. I think some of the younger rappers, the up and coming rappers, they feel they have something to prove, so they'll diss us. After they've been in the business for a while they start to respect it. Cause ICP, we ain't fuckin with nobody, we're just doin our thing. I think other rappers respect that. You'd think that a lotta people would just say, Fuck them. But they really aren't like that. Like we're really good friends with Krayzie Bone, we're really tight with him. He kinda broke it down for me when he said, Anybody that's out there makin the money, doin it anyway they can, we respect that.

I heard that Krayzie Bone is working on a Heavy Metal/Rock album.
Yeah, he's doin something really weird. People are gonna be really shocked by what he's got comin up.
I think a fusion between Rock and Hip Hop was inevitable, but Esham and Insane Clown Posse were the first to do it. To be totally honest with you, I think the first one to do anything to do with horror Rap or the wicked shit was the Geto Boys. They did it in 1986. It was on the song "Assassins" on the very first Geto Boys album called Makin Trouble.

Scarface has been influenced by groups like Black Sabbath, and Bushwick Bill too.
100%. They were the first ones to do whatever it is that we do. If you go all the way back to 1986, they were doin it. I believe that they influenced Esham and Esham took it to another level and influenced everybody else. On that Geto Boys first album they only had like two songs about the wicked shit, the rest were regular Rap. But Esham took his influence from those two songs and made whole albums about it.

Do you ever listen to Rock or Heavy Metal like Led Zeppelin or Guns N Roses?
We did a song with Flash from Guns N Roses. He played guitar on a song for us. And I'm a big fan of Pearl Jam. We don't really get along too well with Korn or Limp Bizkit.

Why's that?
Mostly because of shit talkin. They'll say things and we'll say things and it get back to each other. It's like Korn and Limp Bizkit are a crew, they hang out together. And ICP and Twiztid are a crew. It's kind of a battle goin on between us and them. We almost beat Korn's ass at Woodstock. That was our first time meeting them face to face, at Woodstock. Their body guards were lookin at our body guards, and they were all lookin at each other. It was really weird, but nothing happened, we got along. We were supposed to do the Family Values Tour with 'em this summer, and they threw us off it because our crowd and our music is so violent. After Woodstock Limp Bizkit got in trouble cause they said that they were inciting riots. Limp Bizkit was headlining the Family Values Tour and they had to clean up the image. So they threw us off the tour.

Being so different you've probably been through some hard times in this music business. Did you ever just want to give up?
We've always done things on our own, so we've never really faced the problems. We don't really do other tours. All the touring we do is on our own. We don't go to Rap conventions. We don't go to Rock conventions. We do everything on our own. So even though it was tough in the beginning we didn't know it could be better. We've always done things on our own.

But now you're gettin paid.
Yeah. Now things are excellent. But I can honestly say I've never once thought about giving up. Bad as it was back in the day, I never thought about giving up. I always knew it would work. I knew it would take years. It took forever. But every record we released sold more than the last. And all the old stuff keeps sellin more. Everybody wants all six jokers cards. They don't just want the fourth or fifth, they want 'em all.

What's behind Dogbeats? Is that about your producer?
Dogbeats was before any carnival-ness. That was just us Gangsta rappin. We weren't touched by the Dark Carnival. We were just rappin about Southwest Detroit. That's just Gangsta Rap.

Does Mike Clark come up with all the music on his own or do you work together?
We very very very much work together on everything.

What are you using to get those sounds?
You have al lot of carnival and gypsy music. All kinda keyboards and organs. He's got tons and tons of stuff. Sound byte samples, whatever we can find. I like using sound effects in our music like screams and howls, and stuff from scary Halloween records. I collect Halloween music. Every year at Halloween I buy CD's of all the Halloween music I can find. And I use it in my music all year around.

What music do you really like?
You wouldn't believe it because there's no influence. Our favorite Rap is NWA and Ice Cube. MC Ren. I'd say MC Ren is probably my all time favorite. I love his voice, I love his delivery, everything about MC Ren. I like all of his solo records. It's like he hasn't changed in ten years. But he's allowed to sound like that because he originated that. Like the whole Gangsta Gangsta shoot-em-up--he does the same kinda raps. But it's OK cause he was the first to do that. I really enjoy his music. We tried to get him on our album and he agreed to rap on our album. And then he said, I don't know anything about the group, send me some CD's and some videos. I sent him some stuff, and that was the last we ever heard of him. He didn't wanna do it anymore. I even asked Snoop Dogg to call MC Ren and tell him to be on our record, but he wouldn't do it. When he saw the video he was like, Fuck that! But I love him still. I also heard that Ice Cube hates us. We were doing some shows with WC and I heard that Ice Cube told WC to not show up. And WC didn't show up. Then WC called us and this is exactly what he said: I'm not showing up because Ice Cube told me not to. I was like, Couldn't you think of something better to tell us? You had to tell us the truth?

I wonder what Ice Cube has against ICP?
Ice Cube's friends with the band Korn. Korn is our bitter enemies.

Why is that?
It's not business stuff. Our touring agents office is in Korn's managers office. We had a billboard up in LA, a big ICP billboard. And the guys from Korn were making fun of the billboard in front of our touring agent. We were like, Fuck them! And they were like, Tell them to fuck off! When Ice Cube was touring with Korn on the Family Values Tour. And Dub C was gonna tour with us. Ice Cube said, Fuck them. I wonder if Ice Cube knows that I'm his biggest fan. I don't care about the personal stuff, I love the music.

Can you name your ten favorite albums?
Both NWA albums: Niggaz 4 Life and Straight Outta Compton. Michael Jackson's last two albums: History and Dangerous. MC Ren: Ruthless For Life and The Villain In Black. I like Pearl Jam's first two albums: Ten and Verses.

What is it you like about Pearl Jam?
The vocals. The lead singer, his name is Eddy Vetter, he's gifted from god. His singing completely mesmerizes me. I love Eddy Vetter's singing. Then I like Prince: Sign Of The Times. And The Geto Boys Grip It! On That Other Level. Those would be my favorite albums.

I'm not surprised that you like Ice Cube. Some of your beats remind me of Lench Mob's beats.
Without a doubt what made ICP ICP was that kinda music. I even love Ice Cube's new shit. I love it.

Do you spend a lot of money buying CD's?
Yeah, I have a humongous CD collection.

Do you buy Rap or other music?
No, I hate Rap? I don't like any NY Rap at all, except Wu Tang. I hate Nas. Hate JAY-Z. Hate that shit. At the same time Shaggy loves that shit. He loves that shit, I hate it. They're boring and they all sound exactly the same and they're so boring. I can't stand it. I like West Coast Rap. But I buy a lotta different music. Anything from classic Rock to R & B to old Rap, some new Rap. I like Ol' Dirty Bastard's new record.

Do you buy old carnival and gypsy music?
Oh yeah. Anything I can find. I sleep to that at night. I have a really slow carousal CD, and I sleep to it.

What's the story with that Faygo soda and ICP?
It's a soda that's made in Detroit. It's really inexpensive and cheap--it's only 80 cents for a 2-liter--and mostly poor people drink it. I grew up drinking Faygo. We always put it in our raps, "I'm sippin on a Faygo, bla bla bla..." It's kinda like a Detroit thing. One day we threw it on a crowd and everybody cheered. Now we go through maybe 300 2-liters a show. Non stop Faygo!

It's all over everybody, all sticky and everything. Doesn't your clown makeup come off?
No, we have grease paint so it stays on. We can ever sweat through the makeup and it won't come off.

Do you put your own makeup on or does someone else do it?
We do it ourselves.

Every time you perform you throw Faygo at the crowd. When you tour do you take Faygo with you?
Listen to this. We have a whole semi truck full of it following us. And it has to go back to Detroit and reload three times every time for the tour. We throw an enormous amount of Faygo off the stage. Absolutely unlike anything you've ever seen.

What do the people in charge of the venue say?
They won't book us unless they know what we're about. They come in the night before our show and put plastic all over the speakers, all over the venue. They totally tape it up. Then they have like a hundred guys mopping up after our concert. They're ready for it. Hell yeah. Everybody knows what ICP's about when we they do a concert. The reason we do it is because--because it doesn't make any sense. And it's better not to make sense! Have fun!

Everything doesn't have to make sense. People always want a reason for everything.
Yeah, what's the point? There is no point. The point is to have fun. Like why do you like music? I don't know why I like music. It's magic.

> "OUR FAVORITE RAP IS NWA AND ICE CUBE. MC REN. I'D SAY MC REN IS PROBABLY MY ALL TIME FAVORITE. I LOVE HIS VOICE, I LOVE HIS DELIVERY, EVERYTHING ABOUT MC REN. I LIKE ALL OF HIS SOLO RECORDS. IT'S LIKE HE HASN'T CHANGED IN TEN YEARS."

When did you really break through selling major units and getting such a big turn out at your shows?
That's the most incredible part of our story. Cause there is no time that it happened. Little by little by little. There was no big record. There was not big event. There was nothing. Little by little by little. More and more and more. That's why it doesn't seem like we ever hit. There wasn't like one summer when Boom! everything hit. It just built up slowly. And now we can put 3,000 people anywhere in the country. Last year we could put 2,500 anywhere, and the year before that it was 2,000. It's slowly but surely caught on in the underground.

And you never catered to the radio or TV.
Fuck radio. I hate radio. I hate MTV, BET, VH1, fuck all of them.

I truly believe that radio basically kills music.
Yeah. It gives it a time limit. It makes it only popular for a couple months. And then it's on to a new thing. Once everyone's tired of them and wants to kill the guys, they get something new. Like Master P. Master P's been on the underground forever. But once radio got ahold of him and MTV got ahold of him he was only popular for one year. Now he's gone. I bet he wishes now that he never went mainstream. He's been around for years. But when he went mainstream he only lasted a year. That's why I'll never go on radio. Fuck radio! I'll never let that happen to Psychopathic ever. We did an interview in Dallas on a radio station about 3 weeks ago. I waited till we were live on the radio and I said, Fuck radio! And they took us off the air real quick and shoved us outta the building. But I had waited till we were on the air, and at first I was talkin like everything was cool. The DJ really didn't have any idea about ICP or what was goin on. He just knew that we were popular so he had us on there. I was like, Come on down to the show. The show was really sold out, but I was fuckin with the guy. Come on down to the show, it's gonna be a lotta fun, we're gonna do some of our radio hits....But what I really wanna say while we're here on the radio--he's like, What's that?! I'm like, Fuck radio! Underground forever! Fuck radio! Fuck this station! The guy was stunned. The DJ didn't know what to do. There was a guy from my record label, a guy from Def Jam, he was just lookin at me, his mouth dropped open. That was excellent. I wish I had a cassette of that.

Most people don't have the guts to do it.
I don't give a fuck. I hate radio. Another reason I did that in Dallas, Dallas has always been one of our big cities. One time we threw a dart on a map board and it landed on Dallas. So we drove to Dallas and made our record really popular there. We promoted it and handed out CD samplers. We really made Dallas work for us. This was in '94. We were signed to Jive Records. They didn't believe ICP could be popular outside of Detroit. So we threw a dart on a map and it landed on Dallas Texas. We went there and stayed for 2 months, and we worked our asses off. Next thing you know we were popular in Dallas. We wanted to prove to the record company that ICP can work outside of Detroit. Ever since then Dallas has been a big market for us. Then when I showed up at that concert 3 weeks ago there was this guy there that worked for Def Jam and he goes, I'm gonna take you guys to do this radio interview. I said, How long you worked for Def Jam? He said about three weeks. He didn't have any idea what ICP was about. Everybody at Def Jam knows we don't fuck with radio. On the way down to the radio station I said, You know we've been around in Dallas for years, we sell a lotta records here. I said, What are we gonna do this stupid radio interview for? He's like, Ah man this is really gonna put you over, if they start playin your record you're gonna be huge in Dallas. So I had to make sure that don't happen.

You've been always working with East Coast labels. How do you do in the East Coast?
We do better in New York than we do in LA. We do good in New York City. Just like everywhere else, it's kids comin from the suburb I think. I don't really know who comes to our shows in New York. I just do it the same no matter where it is.

What about the Bay Area?
We're not very popular in the Bay Area yet. Although we've played down there, just recently. There was about a thousand people there each night, which is OK. We're good for 3,000 everywhere else. And the Bay Area, a lotta people live there. I think we could be a lot bigger than we are right now. Murder Dog is gonna really help us out on that I know.

Why did you decide to use six cards? You could have had twelve cards or--
It totally came to me. Just like that it came to me and said, There will be six faces of the Dark Carnival. After all six have risen the end will consume us all. That might be the end of ICP. It might be the end of the world! I don't know. I have no fuckin clue. I'm havin fun doin it though. •

You just put out a movie on video. How did that come together?
Me and Mac Mall been talkin about this movie since '94 when Snoop came out with that movie, Murder Was The Case. We both had seen it and it was real cool, but we thought it coulda been longer and they shoulda really pursued it by puttin out videos and stuff like people are doin now. We didn't have the position or the know-how, we just had the vision for it. When P did I'm Bout It I got to participate in that, and it inspired me to get off my ass and make the vision reality. Soon as I came up with the idea to start it, in '98 about this same time last year, I called Mall and said let's do this movie. So we started puttin together some plots and started shootin it one scene at a time. We wrote the screenplay at Mall's house on the 13th floor, the penthouse section. We got the pictures took for the front cover and wrote the movie all in the same night. We wrote the whole script, put down what we visualized and took notes basically. The next morning we were shootin.

How did you get the budget to do the film?
Doin this movie, we was payin for it day by day. We started shootin the movie April of last year. We didn't complete shootin it until October. We would shoot every other weekend, sometimes we'd shoot every other month cause money was tight. We was doin songs, sellin 'em at a blow-out rate. Normally I'd charge like 2,000 a song, Mall charge about 45-5,000. Instead of chargin 2 I might charge 500 or 700. Mac might come down to 15 or a G. We basically did that to generate these funds quickly and formulate the plan. I didn't see no mountains, I didn't see no obstacles. I'm sayin I'm goin for broke, man. I put my head down and I'm runnin through all the opponents and obstacles If there's a brick wall there, then there's gonna be a hole in it. Everybody that was involved in the project was a first timer, wasn't nobody already got some stripes or something. All beginners with a vision. Everybody brought something to the table to make it reality. The casting was done the day we started shooting. When it was time to shoot, I grabbed people off the street, "Play this part." Some people didn't believe it could be done, some people was laughin, cause we didn't have a big crew—we basically had three people.

What's the name of the film?
The title of the movie is Beware Of Those. The title for the movie was originally different, and I was talkin with a friend of mine and he said the title should be something saucier. I remembered a song I done with E-40 and Celly Cel in '95 called "Beware Of Those". So we took that title right there and applied it to this movie. It made a lotta sense to call it Beware Of Those because it's a lot of different aspects in the movie that related to the name.

Beware Of Those **sounds like a warning to watch out for playa hatas...**
It's more than just playa hatas. You gotta beware of your family, your brother, you gotta beware of your girl. Some of the people who you think are tellin you right are really tellin you wrong and they don't love you. It's bigger than just individuals.

You did the whole thing from scratch.
Everything, from buying the film to editing, to processing, to transferring—how much film to buy, how many feet to get. It was 16 mm, camera, DAT machine and lights. And it's a lotta hidden costs that you not gonna know about. Your camera crew is one cost, the equipment is another cost, buyin your film is another cost, transferring is another

> "IT'S MORE THAN JUST PLAYA HATAS. YOU GOTTA BEWARE OF YOUR FAMILY, YOUR BROTHER, YOU GOTTA BEWARE OF YOUR GIRL ... THEY DON'T LOVE YOU. IT'S BIGGER THAN JUST INDIVIDUALS."

cost, editing your film is another cost, gettin your pictures done for your cover is another cost, manufacturing your videos is another cost. Some people got budgets, we didn't have none—we paid for it as we went along. Some days we spent everything. There was no such thing as a bank account, it still ain't no such thing as that, and we got 3-4 more projects on the table as we speak. What separates us from everybody else in this industry is that those who got money are scared to spend it and scared to go for broke. I come from bein broke, it's an art to bein broke. You just can't be broke and not have skills. When you broke you'll do something drastic when everything ain't happening fast enough for you. When you broke you gotta have that faith and know that you're gonna make your dreams come to reality.

You're determined to succeed. What keeps you going?
I'm out here doin nothing illegal, and I'm lookin at everybody else who doin stuff illegal prospering in the music business. I'm like damn, why god hold me back? The thing is god will only help you if you help yourself. If you ain't willin to stay up till three, four in the morning, be up at six or seven, be willin to take the humiliation and the low budget end. People like to criticize everything low budget. If you come out with an album low budget, nobody's feelin you. If your cover ain't in color they ain't feelin you. We was willin to put everything on the table and come up under that microscope. We under that microscope right now. Right now there's about 3,000 movies circulating and half the movies I gave out for free.
It's hard to break into a new market, especially if you're independent. People won't check out a CD or a movie that's low budget even if it's good. When something comes from a major company with major money and the major push, the public automatically expects it to be good.

Right now you got a movie out called Penitentiary Chances on Dogday Films, from some Latino brothers.
I bought their movie. The movie is about 30 minutes long, it's a real simple movie, the quality might not be that good, but they get an A for effort because they done it. I give 'em credit and I bought their tape and I watched that tape—when other people come I show 'em, these boys did it. And they got another movie just came out called Veteranos. I got an lotta inspiration from them. They was the first people to do a movie in the Bay Area, with the exception of Consequences that was done back in '89. And we followed right behind them. They was the first and they get credit and props from JT and Mac Mall.

After being signed to Priority, how does it feel to be independent again?
Where I'm at right now in this game, I feel like got a degree on one level in this independent game. If I never sign a contract ever in my life, I know how to make a tape, I know how to put it out. If I gotta press a hundred copies, I'm gonna make my profit, I'm gonna make some bread off of it. Just to know how to do it is a gift. If a person work a job, they might work it for 5 years, they depend on this job for their well being. Their family depend on this job for their well begin. What happens when the people cut you off? Can you go out and get it on your

own? That's the difference from the people who sign to major labels. They got big money, they got Benzes and all that shit—I ain't never had a Benz. But then when they wanna go do a compilation they gotta ask permission. Or you gotta ask them for the budget and you got 3-400,000—you a fool, you a dumb-ass house nigga. Feel me? You sittin there arguing with the label, when you can just say fuck y'all, I'm gonna do it with you or without you. See, I'm not abiding by the rules that they set, I'm not goin by the industry standards. If I feel that I'm not bein treated fair in a contract I just flip the script and let 'em know that they can't stop me.

You played an important role in shaping the Bay Area independent Rap scene.
What you got here in the Bay is the uniquest game in the country. We was known first for puttin out tapes independent, starting with Too Short and E-40. They was the pioneers of this independent shit. Now we carry the torch and the legacy on. Me, I came into the game with no distribution deal. I had to print the tapes and put it out at 16-17 years old, as the executive producer. It's my company, my shit, we gonna do it how I wanna do it.

You tell us don't put out an album, we put out three or four. You tell us don't do this, we put out a movie. You can't never stop us cause we puttin it down. Nobody can stop you when you're doin something positive.

You've been working on the film for the last two years?
For the last one year. My studio got robbed in February of 1998, so that set me back in terms of my recording. I used that time to get my film done. It was like a blessing in disguise, cause I got a new studio and my movie got done.

What happened with your studio?
If you leave your house unguarded that's what happens. I was movin around a lot, so at this particular spot where I had my studio there was a lotta individuals in and outta the building.

They took everything?
Everything except my DAT tapes. I took those DAT tapes and put out GLP, The Package and I put out Fillmoe To Hunters Point.

How did you feel when you got robbed?
I feel like: Beware Of Those. Beware of those around me. That's why I named my movie that, because a lotta scannless things happened to me. But it only made me stronger.

Do you know who took it?
No, it's the ghetto. The ghetto took it. It's gone, but I charge it to the game because that comes with the territory. When you take losses you set yourself up for bigger successes, bigger goals. Like DMX say, whenever you go through suffering, look for the good within that suffering so you can benefit off of it. If you go through suffering and don't find no good in it then you wasted your time. It was wasted pain. I had to suck it in and blow it out. I was slippin, that was it.

I feel like you've been through a lot of hard times in these last couple years, but it didn't bring you down, it made you stronger.
That pain and that loss fueled my desire to be successful even more. It made me drive harder toward doin something that no one has done. Mac Mall gave me his full support, we're like brothers. We been doin this for a long time and in these last years we got closer and closer. In the movie people can see that we work good together.

Who else is in the film?
Killa Tay, Mob Figaz, Guce, Tha Gamblaz, Ray Luv, a friend of mine named Laron Mayfield (he also is an associate producer in this movie). There's some females in the movie too, but they ain't no rappers.

Is it a serious film or a comedy?
It's a mixture of the seriousness of livin the ghetto life, the funny things that go on in the community, the different things that happen. It's a combination of comedy, a drama and a message. The core of the movie is a message. It's different stories that's going on in the movie, but they're all based on makin the right decision and not fallin up under peer pressure. Beware of those, make your own decisions, be on the path that you wanna go down.

What role do you play in the film?
Since this was my first movie I wanted to put out the image out there. I was the one that played the sucker in the story—you didn't kill nobody, you didn't do this or do that—I played the role of how I really was in my life. I wasn't killin hella people out there. I wasn't no big dope dealer. I was a strugglin man tryin to get a job. Fallin out with my girl, always tryin to get $20-$30 from her. I'm tryin to make it in the music, I'm havin conflict, it's not cool. That's what this whole movie is about—strugglin and doin it the right way. Tryin it the wrong way, gettin in trouble and bumpin your head and then comin back the doin it the right way finally, and then bubble. When you get blessed to bubble like that, it ain't no end to it cause you went through the pain and the sacrifice and the struggle.

I think it's good that you went through all that struggle. Otherwise you wouldn't be doing what you're doing.
I wouldn't. I might be satisfied or comfortable right now. Now I'm dangerous. I'm very dangerous at this point in time. If the wrong amount of money get in my hands it's gonna be stupid around here. If they never put it in my hands, I'm just gonna get it right here myself.

You had no previous experience with film?
Never had no background, never been to school to learn about it. I only took notes from watchin other movies. I took notes from watchin other students. I took notes from people who were studying. I watched them and sucked up the information and tried to benefit.

So many people go to film school for years and they never come out with anything good. You did it with no money or experience, just your determination.
The Black man been held back for so long. Our generation is gonna be the generation to break the chains. We're not gonna wait for the big companies and the corporations. They only fuck with you when they see you bubblin, they only fuck with you when they see they can make money out of you. They don't give a fuck about you or the music you're doing.

A couple years ago Master P couldn't get a review in Source. Now he's gettin every cover. Every cover is a No Limit artist. He got tired of asking them to put him on, so he made himself so valuable that they had to put him on if they wanna sell magazines.

> "NO, IT'S THE GHETTO. THE GHETTO TOOK IT. IT'S GONE, BUT I CHARGE IT TO THE GAME BECAUSE THAT COMES WITH THE TERRITORY. WHEN YOU TAKE LOSSES YOU SET YOURSELF UP FOR BIGGER SUCCESSES, BIGGER GOALS."

Like me, if I wait for someone to fund my projects right now I won't be worth nothing, because I'll be right in there with those other million Black men who might not have the vision of gettin beyond this ditch that we in. Everybody wanna make it, but are you willin to sacrifice? Are you willin to go through the pain? That's the difference between us and a lotta other people. There are other people like us, everybody get their time to shine, everybody get their chance to do some pioneer type stuff. We got blessed to do this one, based upon our desire.

You didn't give up.
It turned me into some thing vicious! That movie, when you look at it, you're gonna see. When you look at my interview at the end of the movie too. That was on our last day of editing the movie, my face hella ashy. I ain't goin home, I ain't takin no bath, I ain't doin nothing—I'm stayin right here, I'm not movin up out this muthafucka till this shit's finished. I knew that once I got one complete copy of this beta, I'm makin my own copies. My first copies of the movie had a black and white print-out with tape around it. Then me and Mall, we're puttin the stickers on the tapes. We're doin manufacturing and distribution. Promotin, sellin 'em, whatever we gotta do to make sure the people get the movie. The people gonna get the movie, man, fuck the rest. I feel like I got something to prove to everybody who was down with me and who did leave. I can't be mad at 'em, but they left me at a critical time when I needed them the most, when I took a loss at the studio, when I was goin through it with Priority and I was tryin to stand my ground. Since we wasn't gettin the money like P and them was gettin, they wasn't havin faith no more in me.

Do you feel bitter about all that?
I couldn't be mad cause they got to eat, they got children to feed. Man, go get your money. No hard feelins, man. But I'm JT and I'm Get Low and I'm GLP. I'm gonna do my thang with y'all or without y'all. If everybody leaves, I still got me. I'll make my own beats, negotiate my own deals, I'll promote my own shit. I'm the rapper, I'm the director, I'm a writer. I didn't really prosper on the level of nationwide and a lotta financial success, havin big money. But all my trials and tribulations and struggles turned me into a cold cold cold individual. I don't see no mountains right now man. I don't. I'm gonna bubble regardless of anybody's help. •

MOBFIGAZ
INTERVIEW & PHOTO BY BLACK DOG BONE

The Mob Figaz are: Husalah, Rydah J. Klyde, The Jacka, Fed-X and AP.9
We gonna bring it back to the essence. We're gonna let 'em know what the Bay Area really represent. Like niggaz gettin 455 high performance engines, young niggaz gettin away from police, niggaz gotta have that shit. The real shit, nigga. D boys, the real mainy thugs nigga. None of that LA or Bay Area bullshit. The Bay, they lost it, but now everything is evolving back to the Bay, cause they be lookin for it. And that's why we here, Mob Figaz, that's why we're kings of the West, holdin it down. We're all from different parts of the Bay Area, but we reside in Pittsburgh. We all performed in the record store in Pittsburg called The Music Depot one day. We was all separate rappers, we wasn't a group yet. We was all at the tape store rappin and Bobby G (AWOL Records) was up there. We was rippin it and they was lovin it. He's like, C-Bo's startin his own label and he's lookin for some groups. We shot him the tape, he heard it, he liked it. He had just got outta jail, next couple days he swooped us. We went to the lab that very day. C-Bo was workin on his Till My Casket Drops album, he gave us a spot on there. That's how we hooked up with C-Bo right there, plain and simple. •

LIL WAYNE INTERVIEW

BY BLACK DOG BONE • PHOTO BY MARCUS HANSCHEN

> "I THINK THE HIGHLIGHT WAS JUST BEIN ON STAGE EVERY DAY. IF I COULD WAKE UP EVERY DAY AND BE ON STAGE, THAT'S ALL I WANT."

This last year you spent a lot of time on the road. How was it for you?
It was nice. We had been a whole buncha tours before that one.

It didn't stress you out, the travelling, bad food, hectic schedule…
It ain't stress me out. Life's stressful, it wasn't just the tour. It was a good tour. Money. I gotta eat, so I ain't give a fuck.

You got paid a lot of money on the tour?
Yeah, you get paid a lotta money.

What were the highlights of the tour?
I think the highlight was just bein on stage every day. If I could wake up every day and be on stage, that's all I want.

You really like performing.
I love to be on stage and perform.

You're about to release another album. What are we going to get on this new album?
It's a whole different Lil Wayne. I ain't little no more. On my last album everybody was expectin for it to be childish and talkin about school and shit, but I'm a nigga off the block. Now on this one I'm just gonna be upgrade, I'm gonna be 30 steps higher or something.

I heard you turned 18. You never used to cuss on record before….
I'm cursin on this one, yeah. The first one I did that just to make a name for myself. They be like, That's Lil' Wayne, young nigga, he don't curse and shit. Right now I already made the name, so I be like Fuck it. I got a lotta shit I wanna say and I can't say it without cursin.

Which Cash Money album do you like the best?
Ain't none of 'em, cause everything just gets better. I like my new shit. I like BG's new shit. I like Juvey's new shit. I ain't got no favorite.

You like the new albums better than any of the previous releases?
I like all the new albums better because it's like we graduatin every time we make a new album.

All of you are always together, do you influence each other?
Yeah, we get influenced by each other. We'll go to the studio and we're all gonna be on a song, if I hear Juvey spit his verse, then I'll go write my verse. When me and BG spit our verse, we'll be like fuck. It's like we be in competition amongst each other.

You all got along on the tour, bein on the bus every day?
Yeah, but we got different buses though. We all got different buses. Me and Slim ride on one bus. Baby and Juvey and BG ride on one bus. Mannie got his own bus. It was all good. The tour was regular. Niggaz was just out there getting their money.

You probably saw the whole country. Did you get a chance to check out some of the towns?
I saw the whole fuckin US. I go to the mall in a lotta cities. Like if we get to a city early I'd go to the mall at like 10 in the mornin. Cause if we're doin a show in a city that night then everybody gonna be in the mall getting their shit. If they see the muthafucka who they're goin to see, muthafuckas would be goin crazy. So I go early in the mornin and get everything I need to get. But fuck, all them cities ain't shit. I like home better. I'd rather be at home.

Did your fans ever see you when you were in the mall?
Yeah, they'd go crazy. You got different kindsa fans. One might run up to you and want an autograph. Another one wants a picture another one wants dick.

You go out on your own or with the whole camp?
Sometimes I got with the clique, sometimes I got with my own squad, the niggaz I fuck with. However I go, I don't take security. My niggaz are my niggaz. My security be on my waist.

It sounds like you had a lot of fun on the tour.
It was fun. We about to go out again on November 10. That's gonna be a Cash Money tour. I think we bout to go with Ludicris, Lil' Kim, Trick Daddy. But it's our tour. Holler.

What do you think of the Baller Blockin movie?
It's funny, man, cause niggaz tryna act. It's like they cut a camera on us and say action, and we did what we do every day. When they say cut, we stop.

Did someone come and try to train you how to act?
Naw, we ain't doin no actin classes, none of that shit. Niggaz ain't tryin to be no actors out here. That was extra money to put in our pocket. Fuck it, we got up on the world makin a movie and we don't know shit about acting. Let's do it.

Were you nervous to be on camera?
Nervous? Come on now! I got a super star face, nigga. We just did it.

You're happy about your new album?
I'm not happy about it, I'm sure about it. I'm sure about my new album. It's gonna be real big. Big. My shit uncut. You know how hard it is to get a whole brick uncut these days with no cut on it? It's hard. I'm puttin it out with no cut.

What are you doing right now?
I'm in the studio. I'm just chillin. They're mixin my new album. I ain't doin nothin though.

When do you find time to write?
I think of a rap every day, and I just write it down when I have time. I ain't got no drug habits, so I keep raps in my mind. I ain't got no drug habits to wipe it out. I'm coming up with amazing stuff every day.

Last time we talked you were upset with your personal life. How's your personal life?
My daughter's doin fine. She's about to be two November 29th. I don't see her enough. Shit, she's about to be two years old! As far as my personal life, everything is Rap. Everything is money, everything is Rap.

What were you listening to last year?
Jay-Z, that's all I listened to. Jay-Z, that's it. I be listenin to Inner Circle too. •

> "IT'S A WHOLE DIFFERENT LIL WAYNE. I AIN'T LITTLE NO MORE. ON MY LAST ALBUM EVERYBODY WAS EXPECTIN FOR IT TO BE CHILDISH AND TALKIN ABOUT SCHOOL AND SHIT, BUT I'M A NIGGA OFF THE BLOCK. NOW ON THIS ONE I'M JUST GONNA BE UPGRADE, I'M GONNA BE 30 STEPS HIGHER OR SOMETHING."

INTERVIEW WITH BAD AZZ

BY BLACK DOG BONE • PHOTO COURTESY DEF JAM

How did you first connect with Priority?
I was doin some work with Snoop and Tha Dogg Pound on Doggy Style Records/Death Row. Things got kinda shaky in the business, you know how things were not right over there. Upon leavin I came to Priority with a demo that I had done with three songs on it. Priority already had a deal on the table with the Eastsidaz Crew, which is Snoop's group now. I was gonna be a part of that group, I was one of the three members. Instead of taking the deal as the Eastsidaz group, I took the deal as Bad Azz the solo artist.

The Eastsidaz formed a while back?
Yeah. We were gonna change the name from the LBC Crew to the Eastsidaz. LBC Crew was the name we established with Death Row, and they wouldn't let us use the name.

What were you doing before you were part of the LBC Crew?
I was just finishin high school in Long Beach. I was rappin. Snoop had dropped the album with Dre, The Chronic, and he was very popular in the city. He always let us know that when it get to the point where he could put out artists he was gonna come talk to us. It got to that point. I lived around the corner from one of Snoop's good friends, C-Style. They hit me up, told me they wanted me to come to the studio and I been recordin with 'em ever since.

When was that?
That was middle of '94. Snoop had dropped Murder Was The Case. He was workin on the LBC project and The Dogfather. I really started workin with him in '94-95. Then in '96 I got my deal with Priority, put out my first album NAME '98. '99 I started workin on my second LP, Personal Business.

How did your first album do for you?
The album did cool. It didn't certify gold or platinum, but it was a real good first LP for me. Everything was cool the experience of steppin outta what I was used to. I was used to bein up under Snoop and acceptin a lotta his guidance. It was a chance to make my own way. All the experience is what made my second album come real tight. The first one was really good. It had features on there with Snoop and Kurupt. Supafly did some of the beats and DJ Pooh. And Gangsta from Tha Comrads, that's my label mates on Priority. It came out real cool.

In Southern California after so much Rap came outta Compton, we started seeing a lot of talent coming from Long Beach.
Long Beach is right next to Compton. If you drive outta Long Beach you see a sign that says: Leaving Long Beach, Welcome to Compton. You can walk from Long Beach to Compton. We all grew up together, we played sports against 'em and most of us had family in Compton. They're neighboring cities.

But the music is still a little different.
It's because a block away could be a world apart. Long Beach kids are little bit different. We carry ourselves different, we are exposed to different things. I don't really see a big difference in the music. If you look at LA as a whole, it's a bigger city and all the artists don't know each other. But all of us in Long Beach, we know each other. It's tight knit, it's a small city.

What was going on in Long Beach with Rap when you were growing up?
By us not having any rappers comin outta Long Beach, we listened to other Rap. We listened to Brooklyn. We listened to LL Cool J, we listened to the Fat Boys. Back then in LA they had King T and Coddy T and Mixmaster Spade. We vibed off those cats. And early Ice T. Then once NWA came out, that was what we listened to.

Do you still live in Long Beach?
I live like 30 minutes from Long Beach. But my mom still lives in the area. I got family and friends there. I got my son in Long Beach.

How different is this new album from your last one?
I got different artists, I got different producers, I got different flavor. My flavor hasn't changed to where you can't relate to it, but it's just the growth of Bad Azz. It's Bad Azz a few years later. I'm rappin a little better, I'm rappin a little smarter, I'm rappin a little harder. I got better beats this time. I'm improving every day. You can listen to my album and learn a lot about LA, learn a lot about California, learn a lot about Bad Azz.

> "LONG BEACH IS RIGHT NEXT TO COMPTON. IF YOU DRIVE OUTTA LONG BEACH YOU SEE A SIGN THAT SAYS: LEAVING LONG BEACH, WELCOME TO COMPTON. YOU CAN WALK FROM LONG BEACH TO COMPTON. WE ALL GREW UP TOGETHER, WE PLAYED SPORTS AGAINST 'EM AND MOST OF US HAD FAMILY IN COMPTON. THEY'RE NEIGHBORING CITIES."

Which producers did you work with on this album?
I worked with LT Hutton. He's a long time Dogg Pound affiliate. He worked with us in the LBC days. He produced stuff on Snoop's Dogfather album and on Game Is To Be Sold and Not Told and one Top Dog also. I got Battlecat on this album, he did like three tracks. We got production by Jelly Roll, he did "Shining Star" for Snoop on his last album. Then his brother Blaqtoven and Lil Bo Dosier, who's Lamont Dosier's son. Blaqtoven, Lil Bo Dosier and Jelly Roll make up Heat Chambers Production. My album was produced by Heat Chambers. DJ Don did one on there, that's the first single.

You had a lot of guest artists on the album?
For sure, everything is so fly. Me and Ice Cube have a song together called "Streets Illustrated". Then me, Silky Fine and Ras Kass have a song on there called "2000 4-Door Cadillac Let's Roll". I got Xzibit on the album, I got Kurupt on the album. Got Butch Cassady from the Eastsidaz project. This album is so fat. I got the Lowlifes, that's my group, I been down with them for years. Cocoa, Little J, Shorty K, Tip Toe. It's just live, man. This album is gonna be big. •

ZION-I INTERVIEW

BY BLACK DOG BONE

It seems like you are taking your music in a different direction on this new Zion I record.
What we've been doing over the last 10 years is every album is a little different. We put a different texture on what we do, but the message is pretty much consistent. In that way, this record is in the same tradition as what we've been doin. It sounds a little different, but what's behind it is the same. It's still Hip Hop music with an uplifting conscious type of message. It's still something we want people to party to and have a good time listening to.

I think Hip Hop is stagnant at this time because people are not taking risks. So many times I read about a project and get excited, thinking the music is going to be something new, but when I hear the music I'm disappointed.
I feel you. That's what this record to us is kinda vibing on. If you listen to the lyrics, what we're talkin about is trying to get people to listen to their own inner voice. Fuck what you hear on the news and in the media. Don't get caught up in living the "dream" that they sell you in the commercials. The world is going through a lot of changes with the "recession", and there's people on the planet who can't get good water in a lot of different areas, resources are drying up, there's a lot of war and conflict that's not being resolved. At the same time we've got people up here talkin about how much bubbly we can pop, what kinda car we riding. You understand. It's not paying attention to the reality of the world we live in. You're living in a video fantasy world. It's cool to go into a dream world sometimes, but there's a more powerful component to it. You can create a dream in your head that you can actually manifest in your life that will make change in the world. That's the kind of stuff we're talking about. Bring some foundation into this.

In every civilization when things get really bad the people try to escape into a fantasy. I see that more and more in this culture at this time, especially in the Black community. Because conditions in the Black community are worse than ever.
That's always been the case though. Talib Kweli said something in one of his song where he's talkin about the recession, that it's not nothing new. Black folks always been struggling. I feel like really it's an opportunity for people. Even in the music industry where the majors don't have the same control they used to have. It's a great time for us right now if you know what to do. I feel like it's the same in anything you do. There is a recession going on and it's hard for people, but that should make family stronger, it should bring us together closer. It shouldn't be something where you get more into alcohol and dope, because the problems ain't gonna go away like that. The reality's still there once you come down. Or you can really start changing yourself and your environment. And I feel like it's an opportunity right now. That's why a lot of the music on this record is talking about loving yourself and real positive uplifting shit. That's what I'm needing right now in my life, and that's what I'm attracted to. It's so easy to get caught up on the bullshit or get depressed or get unmotivated because of everything that's going on. We're trying to push in the other direction.

People need to turn off the TV and the internet and all those outer voices and tune into their inner voice. The more we soak up from the media and the system and our education, the more we lose our true selves. It takes us over.
You might lose yourself but yourself never leaves. You might forget about it, your connection to everything, but that's the only real thing in this world. It's more about remembering and going back to the real. Like, "I see that dude suffering; I'm actually connected to that fool." We're all connected. It's just a matter of reminding yourself. The media at this point in time is very subversive. It really effects people. You gotta say, "That advertising and marketing don't effect me. I don't go and buy a Big Mac every time I see a McDonalds commercial." But it does affect you. Regardless if you think you're making a conscious choice or not. People value Mercedes and BMW's and Gucci for a reason. Cause it's marketed in a way that impresses us. We all fall into it. I'm not saying I'm better or I'm above all of this. But I realize. I don't watch TV like that. I watch movies. I listen to a lot of music. But I made a decision not to watch too much TV. It just fills my mind with a lot of nonsense and I waste time instead of being creative.

What you're saying is that even if people know it's wrong or not good for them, they still buy into it. I see people who talk like they know, but then they keep eating McDonalds or buying designer clothes.
You come to the point where it's really about what you value. Do you really and truly respect yourself? That's the question we all have to ask ourselves. One out of two, if they answer truthfully, it's not gonna be the answer that they would answer without thinking deeply. We have to question ourselves. When you question yourself truthfully you're gonna get an answer. When you get an answer from within yourself you can trust it as generally true, at least for that moment. If you never question yourself and go about like it's all good all the time, what everybody's doing is all good, you get caught up in the wave of being a sheep. You're following the powers that be. There's a prescription they write for you and most of us are just reading that prescription and fulfilling it without never thinking, Damn, did I just drink the Kool-Aid? Am I that muthafucka in Jonestown sipping the Kool-Aid? We've gotta question that. The technology that we're dealing with and the psychology and the social programming is at an all time high right now.

Sometimes when I talk to people I feel like I'm talking to machines. They're so well programmed. I feel good talking to you.
It's scary, man. When they did the terrorist thing with 911, and the Amber Alerts with Afghanistan and Iraq, basically we've been in war ever since then. Now the economy is

> "YOU MIGHT LOSE YOURSELF BUT YOURSELF NEVER LEAVES. YOU MIGHT FORGET ABOUT IT, YOUR CONNECTION TO EVERYTHING, BUT THAT'S THE ONLY REAL THING IN THIS WORLD. IT'S MORE ABOUT REMEMBERING AND GOING BACK TO THE REAL. LIKE, "I SEE THAT DUDE SUFFERING; I'M ACTUALLY CONNECTED TO THAT FOOL." WE'RE ALL CONNECTED. IT'S JUST A MATTER OF REMINDING YOURSELF."

tripping, where war is supposed to stimulate the economy. It's not working right now. They're really freaking now trying to balance all this shit out. At the same time, they're programming people to be really closed minded. American society to me in the last 8 to 10 years has shut down. Growing up in the eighties and the seventies, it felt like there was a lot of ideas out there and you could basically think and express how you felt. There were some crackdowns, but it felt more open. Today it feels like everything's been boiled down. Like Hollywood is dumbed out, except for independent movies. The ideas that come across on TV and the radio, nothing is challenging. I feel like that's a result of all this fear of terrorism, and corporations dominating the media. They back these weapons manufacturers. It all becomes this one big circle of: keep American stupid, so you can continue to play like the police of the world. Like you're above everybody else. But America is just another piece of land. Once that mentality goes away, we can be more like world global citizens. That's what this world is moving toward eventually. We can't help but do that.

As a result of all this control and closed mindedness, music and art in America has become stagnant and uncreative. When you hear music from other parts of the world like M.I.A. or K'Naan, it's way more innovative than what's happening here.
Right. I see a lot of artists here that are pushing boundaries, especially with their message, but I feel like being an African American is not edgy no more. It's played out. Like society is saying, "OK we know your story. It doesn't interest us that much anymore." But now an artist from Sri Lanka or Somalia or Nigeria, that's interesting. You need to go deeper into the ethnic regions now to get the authentic versions of what reality is or what struggle is really l like. People are struggling everywhere. Just because you live in the United States don't mean you don't know struggle. But I feel like people have heard the same shit too many times. It's blasé now. Maybe it's because some of the lead artists in Hip Hop don't talk about reality no more. They're just about swag, bein real cool. That's the most popular theme in Hip Hop rather than social consciousness.

Zion I always brought that message forward. That's why you have survived and will continue to survive. You have a deep understanding that comes out in your lyrics. And AmpLive is a unique and innovative producer. But still I'd like to see you push it more and do something outrageous.
I feel you on that. Sometimes I'm like, man we need to go crazy like! It's funny though, cause once with Hip Hop creativity and originality was so heralded, it was an important aspect of the culture. Nowadays it's like if you don't act like a fool then you ain't cool. A lotta people just mimic each other. One or two three artists will find themselves and are actually authentic. Then everybody else clones after them. Out of those clones two might come through as real. And it just goes on and on in a recurring cycle. I would like for Hip Hop to get back to being daring. I want people to appreciate that you're trying, you're being creative, you're doin some ill shit. Maybe that is still in Hip Hop, but we're not all paying attention.

I don't see it. I'm listening to new artists all day long and trying to find the next. I've been with Murder Dog for 17 years, and I'm always looking for the new. I'm not stuck on the old early Hip Hop. I love it, but you've got to move on.
Sure, but there's something for everybody. To me the new thing would be a street cat who has an understanding. A person with a political social understanding but also is recognized and graced by the streets. That for Hip Hop would be magnificent.

You're saying what we need is a real street ghetto rapper with a deep understanding like you have in Zion I.
Yeah. I feel like our crowd is the college kids, we've got a lotta White kids. We've got all kinds of people, but our audience ain't a hood audience. Hip Hop is based out of the hood. I feel like if Hip Hop would swing a different direction, cats in the streets would have to respect that new voice. Someone who's bringing more than just "my money, my hoes, and the trap". What about the spirit? I'm not talking about a preacher or what the church is talkin about, but a true understanding of what it is to be on this planet in the times that we're living in. Connect all those dots. I'm not saying you could grab somebody and create this person, but in my mind that would be the high potential of like Tupac. Because he bridged all those different elements, and that's why he was so respected and loved. He linked all those people, while in Hip Hop now the separation is vast. You have cats from the streets talking about what they do, and then you have cats who talk about issues. There's definitely a gap between those two. There's nobody bridging those two worlds.

Do you feel like you are doing that with this new album?
We're bridging a bit, but we didn't just make the most street record we could make. We've got songs like "Don't Lose Ya Head" which is a much more street type of vibe. That type of energy isn't on this record. I like that kind of energy. With this record we went in a more organic musical direction because we had a lotta live instrumentation. That's just what we felt like doin, because we've been touring a lot with Reggae groups like Rebelution and it's been great for us. This is the environment we're in at the moment, so we created something that reflected how we're living right now. The more street edge will come back or the more electronic and experimental. But right now this is where we are.

Do you bring that influence into the group or Amplive did?
I grew up listening to Reggae and I love Reggae. It's been in the lyrics even since the first album "Mind Over Matter". That's how I come with it. With Amp, being on the road with Rebelution, I think he opened up more to the Reggae sound and vibe. We learned all their songs, and just being in that environment you soak it up. Then you start to see the crowds going nuts, how big the crowd is, and how they're so peaceful and accepting of certain messages. Where with Hip Hop sometimes they're like, "You're talkin that peace and love shit, I'm outta here." They can't relate to it. This Reggae audience, they're all about that, just smokin weed and chillin. That's a beautiful thing, man. It's like you get in front of people

> "IN MY MIND THAT WOULD BE THE HIGH POTENTIAL OF LIKE TUPAC. BECAUSE HE BRIDGED ALL THOSE DIFFERENT ELEMENTS, AND THAT'S WHY HE WAS SO RESPECTED AND LOVED. HE LINKED ALL THOSE PEOPLE, WHILE IN HIP HOP NOW THE SEPARATION IS VAST. YOU HAVE CATS FROM THE STREETS TALKING ABOUT WHAT THEY DO, AND THEN YOU HAVE CATS WHO TALK ABOUT ISSUES. THERE'S DEFINITELY A GAP BETWEEN THOSE TWO. THERE'S NOBODY BRIDGING THOSE TWO WORLDS."

YUKMOUTH INTERVIEW

BY BLACK DOG BONE • PHOTOS BY MARCUS HANSCHEN

who've never seen you before, but after the show they love you. All these different things influenced this album. It's a different sounding album once again. Our true fans know our next album is not gonna sound like this either. Every time we come we're gonna flip it up.

I love how you allow yourselves to change from one album to the next. Your last album was more of a Techno dance record, and it was a classic. I'm sure This next one will be great too. How did you meet up with Rebelution?
We did a show in Santa Barbara with a promoter who kept bringing us down. So our booking agent, who at the time was Tim House, told him that Rebelution is a lot like Zion I. Rebelution lives in Santa Barbara. I was like, who's Rebelution? I went and checked 'em out and they were tight. Then like 6 months later we heard that they wanted us to go on tour with them. We met 'em and the cats were hella cool. Low key, laid back cats. Real music lovers. People who love music have a mutual respect for each other. It's not about your ego. It's about the vibrations you're creating. Now we're back on the second tour with them. It's a good relationship. When you meet people that you connect really cool with, just build them bridges and continue to work together.

Where are you in the tour right now?
We're actually driving right now to Tucson, Arizona. We did a show last night in Flagstaff. It was sold out. I think tonight's sold out too. We'll be gone for almost a month, then we come back and do a bunch of Zion I record release shows for another 3 weeks.

How different are you and AmpLive? Is there a lot of push and pull when you work together?
We're really different people. I'm very emotional, I'm very expressive. I'm pretty sensitive about a lotta stuff. I feel a lotta stuff before I can see it. I think Amp is more of a heady dude. He doesn't talk as much, but he focuses really well. He's in the studio a lot, he has a lot of ideas. It is definitely like a push and pull, but what makes it work for us is we started out as friends and we respect each other's space. I know how he is now, and he knows how I get down. When stuff starts happening we just holler at each other and figure it out. You gotta be patient. We've been working together for like 20 years. He's like a brother. You gotta respect your brother, but at the same time you might do something that your brother doesn't like. But you can't take it too serious. We've built a foundation of what the relationship is. That's the most important thing. •

You have a new solo album coming out. What can we expect?
The name of the album is "The West Coast Don"; it's a tribute to the West Coast as a whole. On the album besides T-Pain I got nothing but West Coast artists on there. It's taking the listener on a ride throughout the West Coast. It's back on that story-tellin Gangsta shit! It's like when you would listen to an old DJ Quik or NWA album and they let you know what part of Compton not to go to. The nigga would warn you about shit ahead of time before you made a mistake and got caught up. It's shit like that. It's back to the informational thug shit, that street shit. It's just me going back to that street story tellin shit, man!

That's what the game needs right now!
Yeah, I think so too. I mean there are a couple happy songs on the album but other than that it's all grimy shit. It's the shit that people want to hear. I just got off of that ballin shit! I don't want to talk about that shit right now. Too many niggaz are talkin about shit like that. I'm back to talkin about street life experiences and it's on that level.

It sounds like you got time to really think about your life.
That's all you have time to do anyway. I wrote about 90% of the album in jail. I wrote about thirty songs while I was locked up for the three months. This album "The West Coast Don" came straight from fuckin' L.A. County jail. This I street shit, straight up!

It's good that you decided to just make what you feel and what your fans want from you. I wish more artists would stand up and do the same thing.
That's what it's all about man, the fans! I make this music for them and at the end of the day I want to be happy about the shit that I make. I don't want to flaunt no shit in the faces of people who are strugglin' to fuckin' live.

A lot of rappers were flaunting these stacks of money, fancy cars and diamonds in our faces. I don't know what it is like to pop bottles of expensive champaign and I don't even care. I just want to take care of my family; forget all that bullshit!
You feel me? Everybody don't pop bottles of champaign and drive Benz's and shit all day. It's time to get back to that reality Rap!

love.

It sounds like "West Coast Don" will have more of a serious tone than your previous albums.
Definitely, that's what it's all about. I got a song on there about being locked up in jail, I got songs about the West Coast, and I got songs that are territorial to the West Coast. Like I got songs about Portland, about Seattle, about Vegas, Phoenix, L.A., Oakland and all of that in between. I'm saluting the whole West Coast period A lot of people think that the West Coast is just Cali but it's not. I'm bangin the whole West Coast from top to the bottom. A lot of cats will only salute Cali like it's the whole West Coast. The West Coast is bigger than Cali, man.

Who is all going to be featured on your new album?
The only artist that is not from the West Coast on the album is T-Pain. In addition to him I've got Keak Da Sneak, Dru Down, Glasses Malone, Jacka, Mistah F.A.B., Sky Balla, Turf Talk, C-Bo, Crooked I, and Tech N9ne and the Regime. And last but not least I got Mac muthafuckin Dre on the album! I had to pull one out of the vault.

How does "West Coast Don" compare to "Million Dollar Mouth Piece"?
Rap-A-Lot kind of did a sabotage move on "Mouth Piece" where they mixed and mastered it all fucked up, so this one is way better than "Million Dollar Mouth Piece". The album is some dope shit and it is Yuk being back on his shit!

Does it feel good to be in control of your own destiny?
Yes it does! I have always been very hands on. I have always done this with every album. On every Rap-A-Lot album I never had an A&R nigga tell me what to do. At the end of the day I have put my albums together. Now I'm getting to reap the benefits of being able to be hands on. I have been doing this shit too long for me to not get paid and to not be owning my own label.

> "I WAS ALWAYS AN INDEPENDENT MAN DOING SOMETHING. I HAD DANGEROUS MUSIC AND I HAD $HORT RECORDS, THIS IS JUST ANOTHER VENTURE FOR ME. I HAVE A LOT OF MUSIC THAT I WANTED TO PUT OUT. I WANTED TO COME A NEW WITH A FRESH START. I WANTED A NAME THAT REFLECTED MY WORK HABITS."

What made you change your direction?
I did three months in L.A. County and that woke my game up, homie. I was all flossed out with jewelry and shit on every song. When I went and did the three months that shit made me realize that niggaz don't wanna hear that shit, cause really there are way more people that don't have shit than the ones that do have shit. My cellies who were coming in and out of jail didn't want to hear that shit. Niggaz wanna hear about what they're going through. That experience made me want to re-do the whole album. I wanted to give back to the fans and let them know that I got love for them.

What did you have to do 3 months for?
I had to do 90 days for some bitch-ass drive with no license shit. They really gave me six months but I had to do three out of the six. I had plenty of time to think and formulate all of my plans for the future and shit.

Of course I do have a couple ballin songs, I did before I went to jail. Before I went to jail I was on every song talking about money. Now I know it ain't about that.

A lot of people go to jail, but they don't always change the way you did.
Before I went to jail it was all about that ballin' shit with me. When I first came to LA I got thrown off living out here in Hollywood with everybody spending money and having money. That made me want to rap about money. There is other shit than just having money and other situations in the world that I would rather talk about. I was always an artist that tells stories, and having people who felt my stories more than anything made me want to come back. I ain't been the nigga that had a top hit single, but I had the top storytelling song. I had the top song about your momma passing away or some shit that moves you. At the end of the day that is the Yuk that they

Being from the Midwest I always looked to cats like C-Bo, Spice 1, Too Short, San Quinn, Mac Mall, and E-40. They give you a glimpse of what the West Coast is like. You have always been one of those artists to put people up on game. Has that always been important to you to be so informational?
That's how I came in the game. I told stories about my life while giving information about what is going down in the streets out here. On my last album "The Million Dollar Mouth Piece" I kind of got off of that for awhile. With that album it was all about money and shit.

That was almost 90% money related but the new album is the opposite. That was the last album that I was doing with Rap-A-Lot. It was the last album for me on the label so I really didn't want to give them my all. This new one is on my own label Smoke-A-Lot Records, with me as the executive. I just took it back to the beginning. how I started with the "Thugged Out Albulation". That's what the people want to hear! It's different when you get people saying, "I Got 5 On It is a fuckin' classic, man!" And then you get a muthafucka coming up to you crying saying, "That song you did about you losing your parents made me cry because I lost my parents." When you touch somebody's heart like that it makes you feel good and lets you know that you did your job, because you're touching people that are going through some pain.

When you can make songs like that to me it's deeper than making a hit. I don't know what to say! The shit is legendary and it is timeless!
That's why I listened to Rap in the first place. At first it was Run DMC and shit like that, but nothing is better then listening to "Fuck the Police" when you had cops kicking your ass in front of your parents. I like the shit that I can relate to the best.
Exactly! It's like when you used to listen to that old school Stevie Wonder music and you hear a song that you used to listen to back in the day with your parents before they passed. That song will bring the memories back of you with your parents. That song is timeless! That's the feeling I want to get with my shit. When you hear the songs you will think of the shit that you went through and it will bring it all back. That's what makes music timeless. It's emotional music.

When I think of Yukmouth I think of smokin' weed and actin' a fool, I also think of realness and hard times.
I like to give you all of that, but there's nothing like the emotional music. If I can hit you in the heart and make somebody cry then I'm going to stick to that. That's what I do the music for anyway. I don't do the music to do dance steps and all of that, I do music to hit the heart and hit the heart strong because I come from the heart.
You come from Oakland, which is similar to Flint, New Orleans, and many other cities across the country—that hardcore ghetto.
Oakland is real as fuck! Me, coming from a single momma who raised me in the projects on welfare and on section 8 and all that, walking into school with holes in my pants and shoes—seeing the dope dealers come up and being a dope dealer myself and living that life, to being a successful rapper—I have been through some shit. I was in and out of jail and I got shot and I shot muthafuckas too. It is what it is! It was some horrible shit, but I was able to survive and shake myself off and make it legit in the Rap business. I got stories to tell. I got a three or four episode movie about my life from beginning to end. Every album is just another chapter of my life that I give to the people. I give you a fuckin' glimpse of what it is like to be Yukmouth, to see where I have been through various stages in my life.

In a sense you are a reporter. You tell a real story and you inform people.
Everybody has a story and everybody is basically going through the same shit, it's just that we have different swag and different styles. I know a lot of people want to know about the life we live in the West Coast. I just

go in-depth about our OG's and our hustlers. I go in-depth about people like Tookie Williams, Harry-O, and many others. My shit is like an episode of "American Gangster" but the West Coast edition from beginning to end!

Which songs did you record before you went to jail?
I did a song called "They Like My Sawg" and I did a song with T-Pain and another song. I came out of jail with thirty songs wrote. I still got songs that I wrote for the "Free At Last" mixtape that I am doing too. You can see the mindset I was on before I went in. I still got those ballin' songs for the album but the majority of it is that real grimy street shit. I got hella music!

Didn't you write the "Ice Cream Man" in jail back in the early 90's?
I wrote "The Ice Cream Man" when I did a year in juvenile hall way back in the day. When you are locked up you got hella time. You have to use that time to think and to be creative about shit and to formulate plans of what you are going to do when you get out. Don't waste that time just sitting down and down just lookin at that TV and doing hella push ups. Especially if you are a musician you have to take advantage of the situation that you are in. In other words, do what you can to make the best of it.

I have a close friend who graduated from college when they were in prison. It's inspiring to see somebody get stuck in a situation like that and use it to their advantage.
Yeah, when I was in juvenile I got my GED. At the end of the day it's about being able to focus and gain control of your mind. I was in there, I didn't have no weed, no alcohol, and no females to disturb me and distract me. It was about me taking my music and imagining what type of shit I'm gonna bust over what beats. It's just lockin' in! It's also about waking up, because I was seeing the condition of other muthafucka that was in there with me. It made me think, "Damn, maybe I'm talking about this ballin' shit too much!" It made me go back to talk about the shit that these niggaz are going through in jail with me. That's what woke me up.

It seems like you also put the beefing aside. There was a time when you were known for your ability to assassinate the character of just about anyone. Are you done beefing for good?
Oh yeah, I am done with the beef shit man, even though I hear a few corny muthafuckas trying to do some slick shit. I heard 50 said some shit like, "Somethin' to make a loud mouth quiet," but I don't trip off that shit because I'm on to some other shit now.

It's been years since you came at them. Why do you think people continue to trip?
The whole 50 Cent beef thing was because of Rap-A-Lot and me being down with the family. The family was down with Irv Gotti and shit, and we was down with Ja and on his side. That's where my beef came in, just from being down with Rap-A-Lot. I didn't have no beef with G-Unit or any of these other niggaz. It's called loyalty, because when you're down with a label and you're down for the crew you're gonna do anything. You don't give a fuck if they are right or wrong; you're just going to ride with them. That's where the beef came from. When I left Rap-A-Lot I thought to myself, "Why beef? Why beef with some shit that I ain't got nothing to do with?" I'm not down with Murder Inc, and I am not down with Rap-A-Lot so why should I continue the beef. I shook that shit.

It's good you got perspective on that. All this beefing gets carried away. It's unnecessary.
True! Even before I came to that conclusion me and Game talked and we squashed our beef, and me and Spider Loc met personally. The beef was pretty much squashed before I even got off of Rap-A-Lot. After the last album "Million Dollar Mouth Piece" I was like "Fuck this, I'm not beefing for nobody else, and the next time I beef it will be for me and my crew and not for no other record labels or no other niggaz that the label is trying to protect." It's going to have to be for me and for what I live and I stand for and no other muthafuckas.

You and Master P were beefing for a long time. How did you finally resolve that?
He came at me and said "I never had no beef with you, it was you who had beef with me, man! I made the Ice Cream Man as a tribute to the Bay because in the Bay we were calling the dope boy the Ice Cream Man after you guys made the hit. I made it in tribute to that and not to bite." And when he said that I fully understood what he was saying. He said, "What if I dissed everybody that said 'Bout, it, Bout, It'?" When he broke it down like that I was like, "You right my nigga, and I appreciate the love!" We took it totally wrong back in the day. The moral to the story is that me and Master P was a great look and he was cool as fuck. It was way different from what I expected. I thought it was gonna be some fighting shit and I would have to swing this pool stick at this nigga a few times, but he was real cool. Situations like that let you know that beefin' is bullshit! You could be feeling one way and the other person could be like, " I don't even know this dude, why he is trippin' like this?" There's a flipside to everything.
all I needed to do was to holler at the dude and it would have been all good a long time ago. I was never able to holler at him directly face to face, but once we hollered it was squashed! I'm done with all of the beef shit.

> "IN MY MIND THAT WOULD BE THE HIGH POTENTIAL OF LIKE TUPAC. BECAUSE HE BRIDGED ALL THOSE DIFFERENT ELEMENTS, AND THAT'S WHY HE WAS SO RESPECTED AND LOVED. HE LINKED ALL THOSE PEOPLE, WHILE IN HIP HOP NOW THE SEPARATION IS VAST. YOU HAVE CATS FROM THE STREETS TALKING ABOUT WHAT THEY DO, AND THEN YOU HAVE CATS WHO TALK ABOUT ISSUES. THERE'S DEFINITELY A GAP BETWEEN THOSE TWO. THERE'S NOBODY BRIDGING THOSE TWO WORLDS."

Something stupid could lead to some serious shit, even death. I am happy to see Yuk still here!
Thank you, Scott. I'm done with all of the beef shit. I'm not saying I will never beef again, but I have no use for it. At the same time I hope niggaz don't want to try to test me right now because I have survived. Shot out to Ja that's my nigga but he is struggling to get his career back right now after the beef he had with 50. I'm still here and I am still droppin' albums and I am not struggling. I still have my fan base and I'm still doing hella shows out there. It's still poppin! A lot of careers get ended over some beef shit. I have survived the biggest beefs with 50 Cent, The Game, Master P, Too Short,

and I even had a beef with Scarface who was my label mate at the time. I had the beef with the biggest of niggaz and still survived, and that's why I say that I am a veteran at this shit.

Even without the beefing, you've proven yourself as an artist. You have longevity in this game.
I'm still here and that shows what type of nigga I am with my music and what kind of fans that I have. My fans hold me down. My fans are the best fans in the world! I have been doing this shit since '95, many moons man! It's 2009 and I got a solid fanbase for The Luniz and Yuk. They can't stop me!

Even longer, because I first heard you back in '93.
I have been doing this shit since '93 since I got out of juvenile hall with C-Note. We did the deal with Virgin back in '95.

I was 15 myself back then. When I saw the first Luniz "Operation Stackola" album cover I was like "What the Fuck?" It was a logo of a dick with a forty and a gun!
I drew that shit, man! I drew that logo in jail. The whole original name was the Looney Tunez and I wanted to draw a type of cartoon that was comical. It was a guy nuttin' up with a gun and a drink! He was a lunatic. That was the logo I drew and when I came out of jail we rolled with that. We had to change the name from Looney Tunez to The Luniz because of the Warner Bros shit.

It's crazy because it seems like yesterday I was bumpin' that shit and here we are over fifteen years later. It's gotta make you feel good to still be in the game and to still be relevant.
It's a blessing from God and a blessing from the fans because without the fans you are not relevant. The fans make you relevant because they buy your albums and keep your buzz out there and keep talking about you. I love my fans. And I don't just have fans in one region who are loyal, I got fans around the world who are loyal. I gotta shout out to all of my fans because they're the reason that I'm doing this shit. If they weren't buying it or requesting it or hitting me on myspace telling me the type of shit that they like, then I wouldn't be doing this. Thanks to the fans who have been with me and The Regime and the Mob Niggaz! I have to thank all of the people who have been down with me over the years like C-Note and Rap-A-Lot and the people who would push me.

You have made classic albums with The Luniz and solo and with The Regime. What made you want to go into the solo direction?
I wouldn't even be a solo rapper if it weren't for Rap-A-Lot! I would still just be The Luniz! J Prince came in the studio and literally said, "You do all of this shit by yourself. You need to have a solo career!" He said, "Let me sign you to Rap-A-Lot as a solo artist." That's how I got signed to Rap-A-Lot, with Num not being at the studio with me there recording by myself. I would just leave Num's part out and when he comes through from whatever party he was doing he would lay his part. I'm laying the hooks and all that shit, constructing everything on the fuckin' album and J-Prince saw that. He was working on Scarface's shit next door and they came into my session. Shot out to J-Prince for even making me want to be a solo artist. I was always with the group shit like: Me and Num forever!

It worked out good for you. I loved The Luniz but I also love your solo shit. Also when you pair up with somebody like C-Bo it's amazing. I loved the Thug Lordz album.
We're working on the Thug Lordz 2 right now called "Thug Money". That should be out by the end of this year or the beginning of next year. The whole C-Bo shit is amazing to me because I grew up as a fuckin' fan of C-Bo. When I was in jail I would listen to C-Bo and Brotha Lynch Hung back in '92 and '93. When I was the local rapper in the hood singing my "Ice Cream Man" shit people were like, "You can't fuck with C-Bo!" He was my competition in the hood, little did he know. I would be rappin my shit and niggaz would be braggin to my face about his shit. I was just the nigga in the hood rappin. To actually meet my nigga and do an album with him is a dream. I never thought I would be doing the music, let alone be doing a fuckin' album with C-Bo. Who would have ever thought that would happen?

What's amazing about C-Bo is that he has literally been in jail half of his life and he has still managed to put out more product than anybody.
Him and Mac Dre are going at it with them albums. They got hella catalog!

How far along are you and Bo with the Thug Lords album?
We are almost finished with it. We were finished with it before I went to jail, but since I went to jail the material got old and we're re-doing a lot of shit. It will come out on West Coast Mafia/Smoke-A-Lot Records.

You've released some great DVD's in the past. Are you still doing film?
I'm filming "Eye Candy Part Two" and "United Ghettos Part Three" right now. My next album which is called "J.J.; Based on A True Story" will come with a DVD documentary about my life. I talk to the people who I used to hustle with and all types of shit. It's going to give the niggaz more insight about my life and what they don't know and what they didn't hear on my records. That next album is gonna be off the fuckin' hook! That album is going to be a very personal album with my real life story and how it went down in the hood. It will be out some time in 2010.

Do you still do a lot of shows overseas?
Hell yeah! We are overseas all of the time. I was supposed to go to London in April but we ended up doing some other shit. Our last trip was to the Netherlands in Amsterdam.

What do you like to do when you are just kickin' it in your free time?
I'm a skinny nigga, but I just started working out. I added that to my list of things to do a couple months ago. I work out, hit the studio, do shows, travel, and smoke hella weed. That's what I do all day. I smoke weed, hit the studio, book shows, and travel! •

AN INTERVIEW WITH HI-TEK
BY DAVID FRIEDMAN

Your career in Hip Hop dates back to at least 1992. What's it like for you to be releasing your first solo album after all these years?

It feels real, real good 'cause it kind of happened out of nowhere, really. It wasn't supposed to be an album. It was supposed to be an EP. But I kind of turned it into an album myself just from cats wanting to get on some tracks and showing me love. I made it happen and then Rawkus had to roll with it. It was like why turn an LP down if retailers aren't going to buy an EP anyway?

It seems like you mix R&B with Hip Hop on "Hi-Teknology." What made you decide to go with that?

With this album, it ain't truthfully the album I would have done. But it's songs that I like that I've done. So it's not the real 'Hi-Teknology' album that I would have done initially if they had been like, 'Hi-Tek, yo, we're givin' you a budget. Let's do an album' instead of giving me bits and pieces and giving me all these different deadlines. And then initially it wasn't even supposed to be an album. Now it's an album. So it's not really the album I want it to be, but it's still joints on there. I try to make it to where if Rawkus doesn't give me an album deal or production deal, I want to make sure this album's displaying all different types of talents that I do – different flavors. So if I ever stepped to another label, I'd be like 'Yo, I do this, I got this R&B, I come with the street shit, from New York. It was like a childhood dream and shit.

You're from Cincinnati. What is the Hip Hop scene like there? I haven't heard of too many Hip Hop producers from Cincinnati.

Definitely, I'm putting it down – the real foundation shit. A lot of people come from here, but it's like nobody stays here. The scene is dead really, but it's growing. It's slow, but the era I come from – I come from the breakdancin'. I was always one of those dance cats. I was young, always hangin' with people older than me. So I kind of learned from the cats that stopped doin' it. I'm like the last of the Mohegans and shit, you know, the real b-boys in Cincinnati. 'Cause I learned from the best.

Who are some of the people you learned from?

J-Fresh, one of the dopest deejays from Cincinnati and one of the illest breakers. He was crazy with the breakdancing; he was just a b-boy. My man, Greg, he's dope of the scene. He's the one who actually taught me how to work the MPC. And my man Ravi T, him and J-Fresh taught me how to get on the turntables and work on the beats in the studio and stuff like that. I was a shorty. Those cats were like five, six years older than me. Right now, they ain't really even into it no more. But I'm kind of keepin' it alive for them. So when

> **"I MEAN, IF IT WASN'T FOR THE GHETTO I WOULDN'T BE THE PERSON I AM NOW. SO I DEFINITELY THINK THE GHETTO'S WHERE IT STARTED AND THAT'S WHERE HIP HOP COMES FROM."**

I've got the jazzy whatever Common-type shit.' So that's basically what this album is – just a display of all the different styles. I'm just trying to showcase the talent so I can move on to the next shit. I feel the joints off of the album, but it ain't really the album that I want it to be.

You've had a success with your album with Talib Kweli, "Reflection Eternal: Train of Thought." How did you meet Talib and what do you like about working with him?

Lately, the more we got into the business, we're trying to be more perfectionists and we're learning. We come together. I've always wanted to work with a New York MC. So when we hooked up in '96, it was like, 'Damn.' I already had beats. I always had catalogs of beats. I ain't gonna say I never had a real MC, I just always wanted to work with somebody

they see me, I know they definitely feel good.

I noticed that "Hi-Teknology" features the Cincinnati Hip Hop crew Mood on the songs "Suddenly" and "Breakin' Bread." You've been working with them since the early '90s, right?

I've been working with Mood ... I entered the business with Mood. We got a deal. We were doing demos here, shopping our shit, driving back and forth to New York all the time. They were kind of my road dogs going to New York, too. We went to New York and got the deal puttin' out our own video. We put out one single and video called 'Hustle On The Side." Actually, that was featurin' me and my man Vicious Lee. We were in a group called Vicious Lee and Hi-Tek and we teamed up with Mood. They were like the other dope group in

Cincinnati. So we teamed up and did a video and single and we had it running on The Box. We had a good response. We went up to New York, got with TVT and they signed them cats. Basically, I'm glad I never signed 'cause they got a bad deal. But I just did the beat that got them the deal. My man was rhymin' on it. So it was a collaboration. But I continued to work with Mood from there.

Do you have other artists from Cincinnati on the "Hi-Teknology" album as well?
I've got the girl doing the R&B stuff. Her name is Jonell and she's from Cincinnati. I started working with her this year. I met her a couple of years ago. She let me hear some stuff at a club one time. Actually, her solo joint that's on the album is a song she had sung to me in the club. I was just like, 'Yo, let's record that tomorrow.'

> "I DON'T JUST COME OUT OF BEING IN THE STUDIO ONE DAY. I'M MAINLY A STUDIO CAT."

I once read a quote where you said, "Don't fuck up the youth" when it comes to Rap lyrics. Do you feel like Gangsta rappers and others with offensive lyrics are a threat to young listeners?
Man, I wouldn't say messing up the youth as long as I could say it's the difference between glorifying the truth and exploiting it. I think it's cool to exploit the truth, but don't glorify it. If you're saying that's the cool shit to do… I would never be the type of person to rap about how much shit I've got, but I definitely would buy nice things. I like the bling-bling, but I never rap about it. I wouldn't never throw that in nobody's face 'cause I ain't that type of person. I think there's a difference in teaching people how to get money and giving them enlightenment and rapping about it. If you're telling stories from the hood and making people feel it instead of just glorifying it like that's the place to be. I mean, if it wasn't for the ghetto I wouldn't be the person I am now. So I definitely think the ghetto's where it started and that's where Hip Hop comes from.

In addition to your solo work and the Reflection Eternal project, you worked with Talib Kweli and Mos Def, producing six tracks for their "Black Star" album that came out in 1998. Who have you toured with over the years with the different groups you've been a part of?
Dilated Peoples from the West Coast. That was a dope tour; that was my first tour. Actually, my first tour was an overseas tour. We went to London, Amsterdam – Black Star's promo tour before the 'Black Star' album came out. It was me, Mos Def, Common and Kweli. We had a good time, man. That was a big introduction to the whole show stuff, but we went over to have fun. We went to Japan, Amsterdam, London, Paris. This is before the Black Star situation. We were doing songs from the new 'Black Star' album before it came out. I haven't been over there since, but I definitely had fun. I've been on tour with De La Soul, Common and Biz Markie. The last tour I was on was the Okayplayer tour with the Roots, Slum Village. Right now we're on tour with Erykah Badu, but I haven't been on all of the dates. I've been in the studio working on 'Hi-Teknology.' The only reason, truthfully, I haven't been on tour is 'cause I wanted to continue to work and not put all my eggs in one basket by touring and missing out on production. Plus, I'm working on remixes for the album. I don't just come out of being in the studio one day. I'm mainly a studio cat. I never initially wanted to be a tour person, but I like touring on some days if I'm comfortable with touring, my projects are right and my situation is right.

What are the projects you're most looking forward to completing in the next year or so?
Man, just continuing my own label, starting my own label. I'm gonna work on this R&B stuff with Jonell, and she's got her project comin' out. I'm just looking for production deal situations, to continue to work out of my own studio and to just do music like I used to. And whoever wants beats, they're more than welcome to get some from me.

One last question since I know you're busy in the studio. Could you share with Murder Dog readers what your favorite Hip Hop albums of all time are?
Definitely the Erik B. and Rakim. KRS One, 'Criminal Minded.' Tribe Called Quest, 'Low End Theory.' The first 'Chronic.' And I like Slum Village's album that never really came out big like it was supposed to. A lot of albums. They're some of my favorites of all time. And our album – Kweli and Hi-Tek. •

Last year was on of your biggest years. You left Jive, got with BME Records and had one of your hottest records ever. You always step out there and take risks. You have shown everybody where you can take it when you don't just play it safe.
When I first entered the Rap game, when I came with "Mr. Flamboyant" I felt that was one of the most unique songs every put together for a rapper. I've always figured if you come different—innovators do what everybody else don't. Everything that I ever did, even when I played baseball back when I was a youngster I used to pitch so unorthodox. My style, the way I batted, everything I did. When I was drumming in school I had my own unique style. When I was in the marching band at Franklin Junior High and Hogan High School I would flip my snare drum over, turn it on the back and take the stick and scratch. Make it like a turntable. That's the type of shit I used to do.

It's not like you really tried to be different. It's just the way you naturally are.
That's just the way I am. Everything about me is just different. God put me on the earth for a purpose. He blessed me with a cold-ass mouthpiece. No matter how people take me out there, whether they think I'm selfish or whatever, it ain't none of that. Basically what it is is I work harder than most. That's why I poke out like nipples, because I work extremely hard. Nowadays cats don't just want me to help 'em, they want me to also think of a way to help them. I just feel like at the end of the day the reason I outshine cats is first of all I'm a godly dude. I never done anything skanless in my life. I never fucked nobody out of no money. I never have, I never did that. Even before Rap I never did, I've always had a clean slate and I was solid.

There's always somebody who wants to see you fall. I wouldn't even listen to any of that negative shit.
I don't let a lotta people in my business. Whatever negative shit people hear out there, it's wrong information. When somebody fails that used to be part of you, that used to be part of your crew, if they didn't accomplish what they shoulda accomplished, they wait years later and look at themselves and they know they blew it. The only excuse they can think is to blame it on 40. That's the only thing they can think. They can't say, "40 was good to me. It was all my fault. I should've really been payin attention to how he was getting down and I coulda took his energy and did that with my career." You gotta have energy in this. You gotta stay focused, you gotta stay keepin your relationships with people even when they're not hot. That's me, cause you never know where that person's gonna be at next. You hear a big executive or an A&R person or a rapper not on this label, then the A&R person gets laid off or they companies merge. Next thing you know you might see them years down the line a bigger and better position. And they're gonna take care of you cause you kept it real with them even when they wasn't the shit.

People can say what they want, but when it comes down to it the reason that they failed is because they were not creative, they were not original, they were just following the trends. People who are unique, even if they don't sell a lot of records, they still get respect from everyone. You can hold their hand and put their record out, but if they're not creative with the music it's not gonna happen.

And if they wasn't motivated enough. I'm gonna give you a primary example. In 1995 when Mike Tyson returned from prison he had his first fight and I went to that fight, me and a whole bunch of tycoons. We was all there, my partner was a boxer and he invited me to Mike Tyson's house. I went to Mike Tyson's house, he threw a big party. It was me, Gary Paten, JR Rider and a whole bunch of people. When I saw his house instead of hating, because I'm not a hater, I admired that man's house and the way he had it laid out and the way he carried himself. I'm like, "I'm gonna really observe this and take what I've learned from him. And I'm gonna go for that gold. I want me a big-ass house like that." I had a house but it wasn't nowhere near as big as that and it wasn't on that level. About a year later, sho' nuff did it! I look at things and at the end of the day you know you can learn from a little baby. All that about cats blaming this one or that, come on man, we're grown. Don't wait till years later like that. We're grown folks. I'm not in nobody's way. I ain't never blackballed nobody. I ain't talkin to one particular person here, I'm talkin to the public about me overall. I've had a lotta artists on my label, some just kinda faded away, some wanted off the label. Now I got a whole new generation of rappers, I got a whole new squad. There's some old schoolers in there still, that's the ones who chose to stay around and fuck with me. Those in the past who wanted releases from the label, I let you go. You made your choice so don't get mad at me years later because I'm poppin right now. Just cause I'm hot and doin my thang and ain't bothering you or nobody else, don't get to talkin that shit like it's my fault. That's what cats do. Don't try to blame me when I'm stickin and movin and groovin. I'm grindin, I'm a hard worker. I've been a made man. I already done carved my identity into the history books. It's engrained into the muthafuckin history books in this Rap game. I am a true legend. I was a legend even before I put out "My Ghetto Report Card".

You were. What this record did was, more than taking you to another level, it took the Bay to another level. You took the Bay out there when we were just struggling here. People should not be jealous but grateful to you.
To every one hater there's a hundred thousand that love me. It's real. When I ride the streets and slidin and scootin through the Yay Area on different soils and whatnot, it ain't nothing but love. Basically when all that hate was poppin off it was rappers that was hatin, like bitter rappers. It's like, I ain't in your way! Why y'all wanna hate on me? Please love me! I broke the levy. I opened the floodgates for the Bay with this thing. I knew what I was gonna do, but I didn't know it was gonna be from Hyphy music. When I first signed with Lil Jon in late 2003 I was like, "I'm just gonna make good music." But you know what? At the same time I ain't never moved from the Bay Area. I'm right here reachable. I ain't been under no rock hiding. I got kinfolks, I got people from all the different hoods, I seen what was goin on. I see the Hyphy movement. It ain't like I been behind a rock all these years. I'm payin attention to my surroundings. I tell Lil Jon, "What we're gonna do is mix this up.

> **"IT WAS LIKE A MAGNET. "MY GHETTO REPORT CARD" ALBUM WAS A MAGNET FOR THE BAY. IT HAD PEOPLE CALLIN FROM ALL OVER THE PLACE, FROM LA, FROM DOWN SOUTH, TRYIN TO CONNECT WITH BAY RAPPERS. AND THEY DID IT. THAT PUT MONEY IN BAY RAPPERS' POCKETS. IF THE BAY RAPPERS DIDN'T TAKE ADVANTAGE OF THAT, THAT'S ON THEM, BUT IT'S OPEN SEASON. THEY LOVIN IT. THEY'RE LOVIN OUR MOVEMENT AND A LOTTA PEOPLE HAVE BEEN EATIN SINCE THE FLOODGATES BEEN OPENED."**

We're gonna put a little bit of everything on this album." I say, "I'm not gonna desert my soil. I'm gonna let it be known that we go this Hyphy thing goin on out here." I wanted to take it to another page. It so happened that that song became one of the biggest songs that ever came out the Bay Area.

That was THE song of this era. That's what woke the whole country up to Hyphy.

That album, bein a 100% complete nationwide album, it provided ways for rappers and everybody else out here to eat. It drew the attention to the Bay. It was like a magnet. "My Ghetto Report Card" album was a magnet for the Bay. It had people callin from all over the place, from LA, from Down South, tryin to connect with Bay rappers. And they did it. That put money in Bay rappers' pockets. If the Bay rappers didn't take advantage of that, that's on them, but it's open season. They lovin it. They're lovin our movement and a lotta people have been eatin since the floodgates been opened. People got deals. It's up to us to take advantage of this thing.

A lot of people are saying Hyphy is over already. What do you say?
I'm not gonna say Hyphy is dead cause it's gonna be here forever. It's a culture, it's a lifestyle. As far as the music thing, Bay Area rappers need to follow up. It's not over because we're so talented out here that we're gonna continue to make great music. Hopefully the world will embrace it like they did with "My Ghetto Report Card". Is it gonna be up to me this time around on "The Ball Street Journal" to keep that levy open? I don't know. I'm gonna do my part, I'ma play my position. Sure I'm an ambassador.

You've been signing a lot of new artists to Sick Wid It?
I reached out to several rappers in the Bay Area and I've helped a lotta them. I done got down with them on music. I done offered to see if they wanna roll with me, put the Sick Wid It chain around their neck. But some people think they can do it theyselves, some people just don't wanna roll with me. Everybody says, "Well he just signs his family..." and woo wopty woo. It ain't it. First of all, I come from a big family. My mother had 7 sisters and 3 brothers. It was 11 of them in the family. The same momma and daddy—CW Thurman and Euralee Thurman. Eleven kids and all of them had kids, which is all my cousins, I got a bunch of 'em. They all come from a talented background, from a church background, musical. We're just like everybody else, but we're a big family.

You see their talent and naturally you're going to take care of them.
Yeah, this is my blood. If they got the talent, why not take care of 'em? Why not put 'em in the mix, put 'em in the game. And we've been successful. I was just talkin to somebody the other day about The Click, how we are the only family ever to go gold with Rap besides TRU, Master P and his brothers Silkk The Shocker and C-Murder. We the only ones and we're all cut from this Bay cloth. I feel like that's an accomplishment. We sold 750,000 "Game Related" Click albums.

And that was a long time ago.
Way back then. I feel like it's a reason why E-40 is still current and still poppin and still have his buzz. I stay consistent over the years, regardless of what was going on with my career. It was a gap in between 2001 and 2004 where it wasn't a lotta support out here in the Bay for Bay rappers period. Radio wasn't fuckin with it. Then when things changed over there, things got better. People don't even know, for a minute I was so happy to be part of the Summer Jam in 2003. I was blackballed from the Summer Jam for like 10 years for something I never did. People don't know the struggle I've been through. They don't know I was out there battin, holdin up the Bay, lettin em know the Bay Area does exist. I'm not gonna say I'm the only one, don't get it twisted, but I was the main one. I ain't never turned my back on the Bay. I've always been Bay Area'd out. I know where the fuck I'm from. I'm from Vallejo, California, the 707. Magazine Street, one of the most popular streets in California besides probably Crenshaw and Foothill. Everybody know Magazine Street, that's where 40's from. I've always represented the Bay.

Last year was a great year for all of us in the Bay. For years all of us were just holding on and surviving, but everything turned around and it was because of your work. It was because of you bringing MTV and all of that attention here.
That's right. I brought that. If it wasn't for my record label, BME and Warner Bros, and me being an incredible and reputable, good solid genuine guy, MTV wouldn't have been out here. We put together a great single, a great album. Much love to Keak Da Sneak and The Game for bein part of the classic "Tell Me When To Go" single. Originally when we did that song nothing was preplanned or nothing. That song came outa nowhere. A hit, that's one thing about it, a hit is like a hit on the street—it'll come outa nowhere. You can't plan it. We started out, I knew I was gonna do a song called "Muscle Cars". Jon put the beat together. I knew I wanted it up-tempo, I knew what we wanted to talk about, and we put that together wonderful.

> "BUT WHAT I'M SAYIN IS, A CLOSED MOUTH DON'T GET FED AND A LAZY RAPPER DON'T GET BREAD. YOU SMELL ME? PEOPLE NEED TO STOP MAKIN EXCUSES AND POINTING THE FINGER. THIS IS LIFE IN GENERAL. FUCK RAP! STOP BLAMIN OTHERS, BLAME YOURSELF. LOTTA TIMES YOU COULD BE IN THE WAY OF YOURSELF. YOU COULD BE YOUR OWN WORST ENEMY BECAUSE YOU'RE IN THE WAY OF YOURSELF."

On that same day when we did "Muscle Cars" me and Keak and Dang did "Tell Me When To Go". That came that same day. It was amazing. That's what you call bein in the zone. After that other songs started comin, just winners! The album was already in motion. I had already done "Yay Area", "White Girl". The album just started becoming more of a classic album every day the more I stayed in the studio. But what I'm sayin is, a closed mouth don't get fed and a lazy rapper don't get bread. You smell me? People need to stop makin excuses and pointing the finger. This is life in general. Fuck Rap! Stop blamin others, blame yourself. Lotta times you could be in the way of yourself. You could be your own worst enemy because you're in the way of yourself.

When you first came out you just came out of nowhere, with no support, no lift or inside connections, and you just made it happen. A lot of people think as soon as a rapper gets big that he can put you on, but it's not that easy.
Exactly. It ain't about that all the time. With me and my family, we got it ourselves. We didn't have nobody to back us with money. We was our own executive producers: me, D-Shot, B-Legit and Suga T. My uncle St. Charles had the know-how and we paid him for everything that he did. He taught me a lot. I love him to death, he taught me a lot. But he made sure that we paid him for everything that he taught

me. I'm not mad at that cause it's business. Sometimes you have to separate business from family. St. Charles, we always gonna be family, but when we do business he charge you. He taught me a lot overall just being a man growing up. He was the dude I looked up to. But basically what I'm sayin is we, The Click and Sick Wid It Records, we didn't have not executive producers. We built ours from the ground up. We didn't have nobody with big long money to back us up. We put our own woo-wop in it.

There was nobody to endorse you, right?
Nobody to endorse us. We didn't come up under no big time rapper or nobody that was our name before we called ourselves The Click. It was 1987. We've been out for many moons, we just didn't get no radio play until like 1993. But regardless of that, when they heard our music we saved a lotta people's lives. Our music circulated through the YA system and through the penitentiaries, people bumpin it while they in the yard. That was our distribution and promotion. We spit the kinda music that the street hustler or a person with a regular job could relate to, cause we hit it from all angles. We are true legends, way ahead of our time. I was the first muthafucka ever to talk about a triple beam in a Rap history period. A triple beam scale, 1989, "Mr. Flamboyant". First one talkin about throwin a whole unit in a fan base besides his older fans. Let me tell you something, Hyphy's been around. It just didn't have no name for it. Just like poppin yo' collar. C'mon man, our granddaddies popped their collar but it wasn't no name for it. Me personally, I was the one that was able to get out there on TV and showcase how it's done because it was natural like an afro for me to do it. It's embroidered in me, I'm from the Bay Area. I was the first rapper ever sayin the word on wax. Then me, Messy Marv and San Quinn did a song called "Pop Ya Collar". As far as sayin it on wax—I see you up in Tupac's video poppin your collar—maybe somebody can bring it back before that, but I ain't never heard that on wax before I said

> **"I WAS THE FIRST MUTHAFUCKA EVER TO TALK ABOUT A TRIPLE BEAM IN A RAP HISTORY PERIOD. A TRIPLE BEAM SCALE, 1989, "MR. FLAMBOYANT". FIRST ONE TALKIN ABOUT THROWIN A WHOLE UNIT IN A GUMBO POT. FIRST ONE TALKIN ABOUT A DROUGHT. YOU KNOW WHAT I MEAN? THE FIRST RAPPER TALKIN ABOUT "WHITE GIRL". WHITE GIRL AIN'T NEW! I BEEN SCREAMIN THAT SINCE 1995. I SAID, "I SEE SOME HUSTLERS ON THE CORNER TRYNA HAVE THEIR MAIL, ON THE CORNER TALKIN ABOUT 'WHITE GIRL FOR SALE!'" THAT'S ON A SONG CALLED "IT'S ALL BAD" WITH LITTLE E, WHICH IS NOW DROOP-E, ON THE SONG WITH ME. THAT WAS ON THE "IN A MAJOR WAY" ALBUM. DROOP-E WAS 6 YEARS OLD."**

already established. We did it all. It was all from the grassroots. We are the pioneers. Anybody that got the audacity to try to say something about E-40 and try to erase this history is dang-near retarded. I'm the one, for real. I showed the world, that's why the South love me to death. If I could have a cameraman come with me and show how people from the South, Midwest, the East Coast, or course the West Coast, just the whole damn world accept me and love me. I'm talkin about airports. I'm talkin about sittin in the car in the passenger side, people pullin up with my CD in their hand, bumpin my music and talkin about, "Man can you sign this?" with the cover. That kinda shit. I'm talkin about worldwide. People really adore how I got down. I showed them how to sell records without no radio play in the early nineties. And for the record I want all them youngstas out there and everybody that's reading this to know that my first album—me, B-Legit, D-Shot and Suga T—came out in 1987. We put '88 on it cause we knew it was gonna take a while to get around to the rest of the country. On "MVP", the name of the group was called MVP, Most Valuable Playaz, Most Vicious Performers, that was gumbo pot. First one talkin about a drought. You know what I mean? The first rapper talkin about "White Girl". White girl ain't new! I been screamin that since 1995. I said, "I see some hustlers on the corner tryna have their mail, on the corner talkin about 'White girl for sale!'" That's on a song called "It's All Bad" with Little E, which is now Droop-E, on the song with me. That was on the "In A Major Way" album. Droop-E was 6 years old.

You have moved with the times and stayed current. A lot of artists get stuck with a certain style of music, but kept moving forward and responding to what's going on in your environment.
A prime example: R. Kelly. R. Kelly started in the early 90's with a group called The Public Announcement. This dude all these years he stayed up. Despite problems outside of the music world that he's been encountering, as far as the law suits and all of that, that man has been staying on top of his game. He keeps adjusting with the times, he stays current. This dude revised Ron Isley's career. With R. Kelly getting with him and doin music with him, it gave him a whole new that. That was on the "Hall of Game" album in 1996. We been poppin our collar. You can go back to our old videos. "I Practice Lookin Hard" and "The Mailman" and all them old videos way back in the day you can see us poppin our collar. That's the same with Hyphy. Hyphy been around, just didn't have no name for it. We been at Dan Foley Park smokin up the block and hangin out the window and showboatin and showcasing. We been wild like that there. I been havin up-tempo, dumb-ass knocks. You smell me?

Go back and listen to your old records and see how fast you were rapping and the up-tempo beats. It's not like you just jumped on the bandwagon. 40 was doing that, you were just doing it naturally.
Been doin it. Been talkin about gas breakin and dippin. Been doin all that shit. Talkin about slangin 'em and gettin sideways. Had a song called "Sideways". We've been on that page, we been showcasing. Back in those days instead of stunna shades it mighta been Gazelles. I took my graduation picture, I'm talkin about my high school graduation picture, with some Gazelles on. Mustard and

mayonnaise, old school mob cars, Cutlasses and Cougars. Been fuckin with all that! Been doin it. We been Hyphy, we just didn't have a name for it. What is the big deal? It's like what? Everybody else can talk about the shit, but when 40 do it it's a problem? When did this lil' hatin-ass shit come about?

You've been doing it big for many years, but this year was different. You really took over the nation this time. You know how people are, they get jealous. At a time when we should be celebrate and be joyful, they turn negative.
And ride the muthafuckin wave! Muthafuckas didn't bring out their surfboards. They didn't wanna ride the wave. Some did, some didn't. Those that didn't got lost in the muthafuckin sea.

We got so many calls and emails from all over the world at Murder Dog, people asking about Hyphy. Everybody should join with this and blow it up big.
First of all my album was one of the most solid albums ever put out. Any time you have an album where you can bump multiple songs on the radio—I'm talkin about 7 or 8 songs on the radio—come on man, you got you a cold-ass album. I'm not gonna say it's like a "Chronic 2000", but it's right there in the same company.

This one is better than any "Chronic" to me. I'm serious.
I appreciate that. That's a big complement. People don't realize the impact that that album made. I mean "U and Dat" had more radio space than I ever had in my whole entire life. Probably it had more space than the whole Bay put together. As far as the audience that it reached, it reached billions. Not millions, it reached billions. Because it was radio play on Pop stations that we'd never had in our whole life. Not just Pop, but Urban, Rhythmic, everywhere. It took the world by storm, the whole album.

What it did was turn eyes to the Bay. They started all focusing on the Bay to see what else was hot here.
Man, major labels started comin out. It reminded me of 1992-1993 when the Click was doin our thing, "The Mailman" was poppin. Back then we was sellin the most records independently. We was independent at the time and I always said, "I'm not gonna sign until it's the right time." Every label started comin out here. I was in a serious bidding war. I was on the cover of Rap Pages. And let me explain this 3.5 million dollar thing right quick. When I was on the cover of Rap Pages, that was something that Jive didn't do or I didn't do or nobody in my crew did. That was something where that number just popped up cause that's how big of a demand it was.

Priority was tryin to get at me, Def America, Def Jam, MCA, Jive. Every record label there was that was doing Rap music was tryin to sign E-40 and The Click. Nobody gonna get no 3.5 million dollars up front. If they do, that's spread over the years. It's like a football contract or a baseball contract. They'll say, "He just got a 80 million dollar contract." First of all they gonna take taxes off the shit, and they're not gonna give it to you all up front. And when they do give it, it's an advance. I didn't want shit from 'em. I took bare minimum. I barely was 6 digits, cause I already had money. Me and my crew, we already had it so we didn't do that. We wanted to see our money. See, when you take them big-ass advances—people don't know this shit; I know this shit like I know my dick—when you take the money in advance it's gonna be hard for you to see your money when your royalty statements come 6 months later. You gonna be, "OK, I'm un-recouped by X amount of dollars." But when you take bare minimum just to the get the album done—that's all I wanted to do was get the album done. I proved myself when I came with that muthafuckin "In A Major Way". I proved myself. It sold a million records and I seen all my money. I got my shit on the backhand. Fuck all that up front shit. That's how I get down. I didn't take no money.

You always managed to keep an upper hand when you played with the majors.
You wanna know the only rapper that I made me money that I put out on Sick Wid It Records? Cause my brother had his own situation with Jive, and B-Legit. We all had hybrid deals. We had unique deals. B-Legit's deal was very similar to mine and D-Shot's was. Celly Cel's was similar. We was paid on a certain amount per unit as a P & D, pressing and distribution. Then it kicks into high royalty, that was an unheard of situation. That's how we was paid. Now the only person that made me money over all these years was Celly Cel. Nobody else made me money. Celly Cel sold just as many records as any-fuckin-body in the Bay Area. When he put out that muthafuckin "Killa Cali", the one with "It's Goin Down Tonight" Soundscanned like 4 digits. Anybody that got access to the Soundscan, y'all make sure you go and look up Celly Cel on his album in 1995 and you find out. You pull up that Soundscan and you will see that that boy sold 450,000 records. Cel love me to this day. Cel's loyal, that was my friend before this Rap game. Straight from the Hillside. Right around the corner from each other, played baseball. We family, to this day. It was one of those things where dude, he listened to me. He went and got property, he bought houses. I hunt him down to pay him, cause he's makin me money. I would do that anyway. Everybody else wanna pitch the bitch, act like I owe them. Muthafuckas couldn't accumulate enough. Everybody on that label was good. Even if they didn't sell I'd still give 'em the shirt off my back. That's just how me and B-Legit was. B-Legit was definitely my business partner with that. What I'm sayin is, I ain't never fucked nobody ever.

What I see with you is you're a creative person, a true artist, and you put your energy into the music. Business is not your biggest focus in life. Someone like Master P is not creative, but he puts more into the business.
I love making music. What people don't understand…somebody told me at the time when the hate break was up on "My Ghetto Report Card", when certain muthafuckas was hatin, somebody told me, "They feel like you hoggin up the spotlight." How the fuck am I hoggin up the spotlight? I ain't in the way of no-muthafuckin-body! I'm out here givin dap and showin love to everybody here in the Bay. Lettin it be known that this Bay is here. The way I got my money was because of me, my albums. People forget, I wasn't just some damn CEO. I rap. And I'm one of the coldest rappers in the whole muthafuckin world. I'm

> "HYPHY'S BEEN AROUND. IT JUST DIDN'T HAVE NO NAME FOR IT. JUST LIKE POPPIN YO' COLLAR. C'MON MAN, OUR GRANDDADDIES POPPED THEIR COLLAR BUT IT WASN'T NO NAME FOR IT. ME PERSONALLY, I WAS THE ONE THAT WAS ABLE TO GET OUT THERE ON TV AND SHOWCASE HOW IT'S DONE BECAUSE IT WAS NATURAL LIKE AN AFRO FOR ME TO DO IT. IT'S EMBROIDERED IN ME, I'M FROM THE BAY AREA. I WAS THE FIRST RAPPER EVER SAYIN THE WORD ON WAX."

> "BEEN DOIN IT. BEEN TALKIN ABOUT GAS BREAKIN AND DIPPIN. BEEN DOIN ALL THAT SHIT. TALKIN ABOUT SLANGIN 'EM AND GETTIN SIDEWAYS. HAD A SONG CALLED "SIDEWAYS". WE'VE BEEN ON THAT PAGE, WE BEEN SHOWCASING. BACK IN THOSE DAYS INSTEAD OF STUNNA SHADES IT MIGHTA BEEN GAZELLES. I TOOK MY GRADUATION PICTURE, I'M TALKIN ABOUT MY HIGH SCHOOL GRADUATION PICTURE, WITH SOME GAZELLES ON. MUSTARD AND MAYONNAISE, OLD SCHOOL MOB CARS, CUTLASSES AND COUGARS. BEEN FUCKIN WITH ALL THAT! BEEN DOIN IT. WE BEEN HYPHY, WE JUST DIDN'T HAVE A NAME FOR IT."

the coldest rapper in my own category.

Believe me, not in your category. You're one of the coldest period.
Thank you man. I honestly do feel like I'm one of the coldest, if not the coldest, in the world. I really do feel like that, man. If people just pull up my catalog and really listen they'll hear some shit. If all this was a fluke and I was just some one-hitter quitter, I wouldn't be here 20 years later in this Rap game still current. I'm still rappin circles around muthafuckas that call they self the shit. I'm am the shit. I'm like contaminated spinach. I'm the shit!

When you were with Jive for all those years, I could be wrong but I felt they weren't doing it for you. They could have taken you to this level at that time if they had put more money and energy behind you the way BME and Warner did.
You're right, man. That's why Lil Jon loves me to this day. Everything we've done has been successful. Even before I signed with Lil Jon. People act like I signed with Lil Jon when the Hyphy movement was going on. I was already fuckin with Lil Jon and we already had shit in motion. I had a song on my album in 2002, the album was called "E-40 The Ballatician, Grit & Grind", and I had a song called "Rep Yo City" with me, Petey Pablo, Bun B, and 8ball. Lil Jon produced the beat. The song "Rep Yo City" was a smash, not just in the Bay but in the nation. But with Jive Records they never pushed it. We had BET asking for that video. They were callin up, "Where's that video? I love that song." They didn't wanna do it. That's Jive. Right now if you look at Jive today, if you look at their Rap department it ain't handling. They don't push stuff. They put one single out and call it a day. They never push it after that. If your first week's Soundscan is fucked up, they're gonna drop the ball on you. They feel like it's over after the first week. They're good with their R & B section, but as far as their Rap department? No disrespect to the rappers, they have a lotta talent over there. It ain't got nothing to do with them. Jive always had talented rappers up on the label, but they never pushed us.

Different people have played a major role in shaping this Bay Area Hyphy sound. The way I see it is you came up with the fast rapping style, Rick Rock came up with the up-tempo beats, Keak came up with the name and Mac Dre came up with the style with the dreads and colorful clothing. Do you see it like that?
I think if formed itself. Mac Dre was definitely an innovator and a character. I ain't got nothing bad to say about dude. He's not here represent himself, everybody else wants to talk for him. The ones who wanna talk for him are the ones, if anything, who would disrespect his name. Not me. I never did nothing to the man. Me and dude, he even know, even when we had our lil rappin back and forth shit I never really entertained that shit. Even when he was in the penitentiary we had talked and we was straight. That's why, if you could find a song that he did after he got out the penitentiary about me—put it out! If he got a song where he's talkin bad about E-40, where is it at? People talk about Mac Dre and E-40 wasn't cool. I'm not sayin we was best friends, but dude had respect for me and I had respect for him. Like I said, this the thing that happens when a person blossoms. Ever since I done started makin a lotta noise with the new album "My Ghetto Report Card", it comes with the package. Haters come outa nowhere. They gotta target somebody. It's cats from different little soils that made songs about me. I ain't never heard them, but they don't know me and I ain't never did shit to their ass! They just wanna feed off somebody else's negativity, which is silly. All they doin is hurtin themselves, cause at the end of the day only the strong can survive and only the real gonna stay alive. I'm alive in this Rap game. What I mean by that is my music is very current and I ain't never fell off in this Rap game. •

WHORIDAS
BY DAVID FRIEDMAN • PHOTO BY BLACK DOG BONE

A few years ago you had a deal with Delicious Vinyl. What happened with that?
After the second album they didn't pick up the option for the third album. It was Delicious Vinyl/TVT and TVT didn't go with the third album. High Times was the last album we had out with Delicious Vinyl. So basically we turned to free agents. We set up our label Military Entertainment. We signed with Hip Hop Hall of Fame Management, and that's goin well.

You just released your third album, Corner Store. What else is in the works?
We still got like two more Whorida albums. Then I got my solo album. I got some other artists I'm gonna put out on my label—Niggarachi, and Mahasin from Hobo Junction.

What about your album?
My shit is straight fire. It's bangin. It's stupid-bangin. It's fourteen/fifteen tracks on there. We got a few features on there, but mainly it's Whoridas. We got a lotta shit to say, so I wanted to make sure they heard it. It's not no big names, but I'm tryin to give some people a chance to get on.

The Whoridas have a different sound from a lot of groups in the Bay. You have more of a Hip Hop sound with street/Reality type of lyrics.
That's exactly right. It's because I got a Hip Hop background and my brother Saffir, he wanted to groom me basically and then just let me loose. He's runnin with Aftermath right now.

and make it bang. I'm not one-track minded when it comes to expressing myself. If the track's bangin it don't matter. It's just about feelin the music and makin something outta it. Like Outkast, I love them. They take whatever and make it slap. That's kinda like how we attackin it.

What kind of music were you listening to when you were working on the first Whoridas albums?
I was listening to everybody from Dogg Pound to Bone, Alkaholics, Too Short, East Coast… everybody influenced me. I listen to all kinds of music.

Who or what really inspired you to want to do this?
I was at my brother Saffir's record release

> "YEAH, IT'S THE MUSIC THAT WE CHOOSE. IT'S NOT THE NORMAL BAY AREA SHIT. I TRY TO TAKE IT TO A WHOLE 'NOTHER LEVEL. SEE, I'M THE BAY AREA SHIT, BUT THE MUSIC GONNA COME FROM FOUR/FIVE DIFFERENT ANGLES. I'M GONNA HAVE SOME SHIT FOR THE SOUTH; I'M GONNA HAVE SOME SHIT FOR MY CATS IN LA; I'M GONNA HAVE SOME SHIT FOR MY DOGS BACK EAST. IT'S LIKE MY EAR IS UNIVERSAL. I CAN FUCK WITH SOME COUNTRY SHIT AND MAKE IT BANG. I'M NOT ONE-TRACK MINDED WHEN IT COMES TO EXPRESSING MYSELF. IF THE TRACK'S BANGIN IT DON'T MATTER. IT'S JUST ABOUT FEELIN THE MUSIC AND MAKIN SOMETHING OUTTA IT. LIKE OUTKAST, I LOVE THEM. THEY TAKE WHATEVER AND MAKE IT SLAP. THAT'S KINDA LIKE HOW WE ATTACKIN IT."

Just getting with a couple people and try to get they ball rollin for them so they can fly.

This record is coming out on your label with distribution through Bayside?
That's right. This is our first project with Bayside. If this works good we'll continue doin business together. Just smash on. I'm tryin to be a young Black entrepreneur out here like Master P, E-40, Richie Rich, Dre, the list goes on of successful independent bosses. I got enough examples to follow and I got my own tenacity to work with, so thing's look promising.

What do you think about the situation in the Bay right now? There's a lot of good product in the streets right now, but it's not selling like it could.
I can't really speak on nobody else's music, but I think a lotta people just ain't makin it for everybody. They just makin music. There's a difference between makin music for yourself and makin it for other people too. You can't be scared to expand your horizons artistically.

Saffir is your blood brother?
That's my oldest brother. I'm the youngest in my family. Then my other brother Niggarachi is another artist that's comin out on Military. But I come from that background—abstract, real Hip Hop—that's how I came into the game, up under that. But then I'm from the turf, I'm fresh off the block. What I talk about and what I think about from my experience is all street. I ain't been to college—I been all over the world, this Rap shit took me around the world—but before that I'm straight from the block.

You probably had a hard time fitting into a category though…
Yeah, it's the music that we choose. It's not the normal Bay Area shit. I try to take it to a whole 'nother level. See, I'm the Bay Area shit, but the music gonna come from four/five different angles. I'm gonna have some shit for the South; I'm gonna have some shit for my cats in LA; I'm gonna have some shit for my dogs back East. It's like my ear is universal. I can fuck with some country shit

party when his first album dropped, I was like nineteen. We got on the mic, me and Mr. Tay, and we just started spittin. I looked down at the crowd and everybody was lovin it, rockin and swayin. When we finished doin our thing, everybody was screamin and showin their love. I've been getting down since I was twelve. I was with the APG Crew when I was 12-13 years old. I came up in this. Then the streets messed me up and I went through the whole street thing until my brother snatched me up. That's how Whoridas came about. Then when I got down at the record release I knew this is for sure. Up until then all I was doin was freestylin. My brother told me I should write that shit down, so I started writin my shit down.

How did you meet your partner? How did The Whoridas come together?
That's family. We both from the town. We been knowin each other from before this Rap shit, before puberty. Like eighteen years. That's family. That's how the name came about—Whoridas—from us just bein

stupid and wild, young bg's or however you wanna say it. People would be sayin, Y'all be whoridin. So when it came time to name the group we said, Fuck it, we be The Whoridas.

When did your first album come out on Delicious?
We signed in '96. Our shit was supposed to come out in August, but didn't come out till that next year. Business just wasn't real tight with the label. They promoted it, but then when it was time to put out the album muthafuckas started trippin. That's when the faulty shit came in and that's how the bullshit with the first record happened. They didn't drop the album on time and that fucked up the whole momentum we built. Before that we were sellin tapes on the streets. A couple labels came for us, but we went with Delicious Vinyl cause they came with the most cheese.

I remember how all the Hobo Junction people used to sell their tapes on the street. Now I don't see them out there. You were part of Hobo Junction?
Hell yeah, I'm a Hobo Junction for life. My shit is imbedded in blood. I was like the young hitter in the crew. They was more Hip Hop, and I was the wild street shit.

Is this new Whoridas album a big departure from your old albums?
This shit is just more slappin, it's matured. The old shit my voice was all high, I sounded like a youngster. I'm older now. You gonna hear The Whoridas when you put it on, but you're gonna hear the maturity. The beats are never the same, the producers I worked with on the last one ain't on this album except for a couple like Lev Berlak. I got my nig Tone Capone, he laced me; B-Bumble, DJ Rectangle from LA, The Dotrix from the Mechanics. It's not really as different sound, it's just bangin. It's way harder, cause I'm the A & R on this shit. Ain't nobody in my ear.

Harder in what way? Lyrically?
Lyrically it's still chaos. I'm still talkin this street shit from a West Oakland point of view. The album is called The Corner Store; it's basically everything that happens at the corner store in every ghetto from here to New York. I'm just talkin this ghetto shit, some real shit I had to get off my chest. You know when you go to the corner store you gonna see everything under the cherry moon. You get a little bit of everything off the corner store and you get a little bit of everything off the Whoridas. •

BIG MOE
BY MATT SONZALA

How many Screw tapes do you think you have appeared on?
It's a lot, probably about 30 or 40. I don't know. I been lost count a long time ago. I did a Screw tape that did real good. If the underground sold this tape here for a dollar a piece, I think it went platinum. It's called June 27th. So many people have the tape. I'm on there, Pokey on there, Yungstar on there, to this day people ask for the tape. This tape for $10, this boy offered me $50 for a tape. That's another tape that people know too.

> "I WANTED TO BE LIKE A SCREWED UP PRODUCTIONS, BUT SCREW PASSED AWAY SO, BUT ME AND HAWK HAD TALKED ONE TIME AND SCREW WAS LIKE HE DIDN'T WANT TO DO A CEO THING, HE JUST WANTED TO DJ AND I RESPECTED THAT."

Do you remember the first time you ever heard your voice Screwed?
When I first heard Screw, I really didn't like Screw. I ain't gonna lie. My voice wasn't on there, but as like I grew old that's what everybody listened to and I listened to it so much and it started sounding good to me. That was like '92 - '93. When the majority of the Screwed Up Clique met Screw anyway. I kind of like hooked up with him in '92, but I really hooked up with him mostly in '94 when we really started kicking it. That's when I heard my voice on a Screw tape. It sound kind of fly and I liked it so I stayed with it. I hopped on his album. The album came out and the album did great. Featuring Keke and featuring me. Album did good and we all got paid. The album made our name big, you know Texas sized around here and it got deeper than that, it got around everywhere. Everybody know about it.

What was the first Screw tape you appeared on?
The DJ Screw 3 In the Mornin tape. Underground wise on a tape called RIP T-Lee, a dude that passed away. It was a RIP tape. He passed away and Screw wanted me to come sing on it. Some RIP shit, miss my potna or whatever. So Screw called me.

Do you ever make songs with the Screwed version in mind? Do you think about that beforehand?
I sing a lot. I'm more r&b than a rapper, but I rap too. I'm so used to doing straight up singing I feel that's where I sound good. And singing, got some good singing, slowed down, that'll always sound good. Yeah, I be thrown by how it sound slowed down. I'm so used to listening, I just started listening to the radio. I guess it's cuz I want to hear myself on the radio, but at first there was no radio. Straight to Screw. Straight Screw.

Your new album "Purple World" follows the syrup theme of your first album. Would you say that syrup use in Houston is really as big as the music and media makes it out to be?
It just really started getting big because of these teenagers. Me, I ain't a old dude or whatever, but I got a mother and she raised me, she really was a cool mother. She said "you want to get drunk, get drunk right here. You want to smoke weed you smoke weed in the house." She didn't want her children outside. "You want to have sex with your girlfriend? Go in your room." That's the kind of mom I got. So it's like that kind of mom she supervised us and that was my deterrent. I'm 20 something, she 47 she drank it before I was born. Police and all of them, they done it. What I done for it? There's a lot of old people I know that drank. They done it for a long time. But now since these laws, they got big cases and laws came up in it, and you just can't do it if you don't want to go to jail, cuz it's not legal.

Being that it's not legal, but it is a prescription drug, how do people get so much of it?
Well it's for bronchitis. That's what it's really for. It's a downer, and people like that feeling. I can't lie I done been on it. I talk about it a lot because it's what's going on. I don't talk about it and say I do it like that. I talk about it cuz that's what's happening. If I was talking about chronic right now, why not write another song about chronic? That's gonna sell you know what I'm saying. So I write a song about syrup.

But is it really a big thing here like it's made out to be. Is it really such a phenomenon?
Now I don't knock 3 6 Mafia, I cut for them. But I know where that started from. They came down here. Matter of fact, I kicked it with MJG and 8Ball, they from Memphis you know what I'm saying? They used to come down here and that's what everybody was doing. You wasn't no player if you wasn't doing it. Shit's crazy, but that's what everybody was doing. And we didn't make it no better cuz we said it so much on tape, and then people look up to us already. People ask me what it taste like? You want to ask me what it taste like, I ain't your parents. I'm not trying to tell anyone what to do basically it's on them.

So you can just get it on the street in Houston? Or do people go to their doctors and get prescriptions?
Well there's crooked doctors and there's the streets too. The hustles. I been around all that before but God blessed me to get away from all that. I don't have to sell. It's dudes that will hook up with something and they on the block just like selling grass. I'm from 3rd Ward, there's a corner in 3rd Ward folks call the Million Dollar Corner, you go get anything you want over there. And they all know each other so somebody pull up wants some drank, there's probably drank over there so they call him over get the drink. Cuz this dude here he probably sell weed. This how this works. They had a couple doctors that was doing it too much. Just giving scripts out. And we saw that same old doctor in handcuffs. Cuz that's illegal how they do that right there. The doctor will give it to you if you really need it.

Is it a cheap drug?
It's cheap but it's high. I mean a pint will go for, at a pharmacy it'll go for like $12 or something. Out here it cost $225. So that's where the money at there. If they got the inside hook up or whatever, they can go in there and man. I been around when the price is high and I been around when the price is low. It's laid back and relaxing but it ain't good for you. You gotta drink a lot of water, you know what I'm sayin'? It'll dehydrate you. I done been to the hospital for it. It was just dehydration though. You have to drink a lot of water.

If you buy some syrup on the street how do you know you're not buying NyQuil or Robitussin or something.
You don't. For one thing you gotta know somebody. Some of them do it. Actually one time I gave this boy, when a pint was $275, I gave this boy an unopened Snapple container. Grape. I'm laughing, man. I said MAN!

How much of "Purple World" revolves around syrup?
I mean, purple, that's the color of it. Purples my favorite color, it's a pretty color. I feel I'd just change it up a little bit. Do something a little different. Like on a Kool Aid level.

But is it a subject that comes up on the record a lot this time around?
Naw I kind of slowed down cuz I talked about it a lot on the last one. This one here it's more deeper.

Can you tell me a little about the new record? Who are some of the guests and producers? What's you're favorite song?
Well I ain't named the songs yet. But the album done though. I got a song called "Drop the Top." I like that song. It's about coming out on the boulevard on a day the sun out, drop the top, ride around, that's what it's about. Drop the top, ride through the wind. I ain't really got too many features. Last one didn't have too many features. This album here I got my best friend Toon on the album. I got Pokey and Z-ro. The producers are the Platinum Sound producers which are Wreck Shop Producers.

So you don't have a lot of features on your album? Is the Screwed Up Clique as tight now that Screw is gone as they were before? Do you still get down to do music?
On my album I got all the people on there. I got Hawk on there, I got Pokey on there, I got Keke on there. I got my people on there. We all sticking together it's just that we all signed with different labels. I wanted to be like a Screwed Up Productions, but Screw passed away so, but me and Hawk had talked one time and Screw was like he didn't want to do a CEO thing, he just wanted to DJ and I respected that. So it made me look and I made a decision and went with Wreck Shop. I think I made a good choice.

Who would you say is doing a good job of keeping the spirit of Screw alive?
Everybody representing him. Everybody miss him you know what I'm saying? I'm always going to, at a show or anything. I miss my boy. •

TECH N9NE

INTERVIEW & PHOTO BY BLACK DOG BONE

We talk a lot about music, Tech, but people wanna know about your women.
I got one girlfriend straight up 41 years old. I don't fuck with bitches! I got one lady. I am still legally married and my Wife and me are really good friends. Other than that just my girlfriend and my wife.

What about your kids?
I got three kids, 2 girls and a boy. My girl goes to college now and my son is trying to get into college. My fourteen year old girl Rainbow is still going to school. I try to keep my life simple. Back then I had a lotta girls but I can't trust bitches these days. Everybody is out to get something and I got something that a lotta people want. It takes a lot of time and money to take care of women. What I take care of with my Wife out in LA is enough because to live in LA it costs a lot. It don't cost much for me and my girl because we kick it together. To have multiple women takes multiple dollars. I got multiple dollars but I don't feel that I should trick it off like I use too. I would spend $3,000 in a strip club and I know all the bitches in every town. Me going to the strip club is ass backwards when I got artists that need radio campaigns and video campaigns and shit like that. I am just looking at life a little bit different now and trying to simplify my life. Bitches ain't gonna help me simplify my life although I love women to death.

You have been doing music for a long time. How do you feel about the business side from the time you started and the whole thing right now?
I think when you have muthafuckaz like Macklemore blowing up independently and BET and MTV making millions of dollars and the same thing with Tech N9ne being in Forbes over and over again I think it is a beautiful climate. I think there is money out there for everybody still, and I think there is money out here in the streets for rap music or music period. It is out here everywhere for the youngsters to come up and Technology is making it easier for you to be heard and seen through youtube, Facebook, and twitter. A Muthafucka can just click on your link and be able to buy your shit. Technology is making it easier for people to get paid and I think that is a powerful thing because there is a lot of poverty and where ever there is poverty there is gonna be pain and crime and all you gotta do is watch CNN and everything is poppin in a bad way. It is not really going in a way that it went on something else. It went from bad to good, and from hell to heaven. It is not going from heaven to hell in this world and wherever there is poverty there is going to be crime. Music is making a way for people to get money and I think that is positive even if the message is not positive.

After all these years how do you feel about your dreams?
I am still reaching for world domination but I am not there yet. Things are happening in my life that I say "Wow" because they are calling em in India and Africa now. All these places I half to go like Japan. I still got a lotta work to do and that is why I am still doing music. I don't have the world yet, there are many places that I have to reach. I don't have the world yet but we are getting there. My dreams are steadily coming through. We just won the Caraboo Lou battle, I am not suppose to talk about it, but I am happy about it because it gives me the ability to capitalize on something else. It allows me to use the music to get out there and to use the music to get there. I'm gonna just keep going and going and getting my life right for my children so they wont have to worry about anything. They still work but they wont have to worry about too much of nothing because we set it up for them. If man don't blow this muthafuckin place up like it is looking like if we do anything with Syria which breaks international law. So if man don't blow this muthafucka up then we can build shit for our children. I have not near made it to my dream yet, me or Travis. It is a beautiful thing to be able to do what we are doing this late in life but when I can go to Barcelona for five days off and nobody knows me there, then that means that I am not doing my job all the way. That means I got more work to do. I will let you know. You will know because you will see me on that TV and see me everywhere. You will hear my music and see my movies everywhere and all those things are coming.

Certain artists throughout history when they do something people don't recognize them right away because they are doing something so new that people can't understand it. It takes a while!
I know!

You are moving forward so fast that people cannot catch up with you right now.
I see exactly what you are trying to say because it is being ahead of your time and when you are not doing the norm people that are normal can't see that. When you're strange people will never remember your name and I get it but we shall make it to where everybody remembers my name. Even if you don't know Tech N9ne's music

> "THAT'S A CLICK THAT ME AND ICY ROCK AND MY BROTHER DYNO MACK WERE IN. THAT GROUP TAUGHT ME HOW TO THINK DIFFERENT. TAUGHT ME TO NOT GIVE A FUCK WHAT A MOTHERFUCKER THOUGHT AND TO NOT GIVE A FUCK ABOUT WHAT EVERYBODY ELSE IS DOING. DO WHAT YOU WANT TO DO. I BECAME THE CLOWN TO THESE MUTHAFUCKAS. I HAD TO."

you know the name. We just gotta put a face to the name and keep on pushing to where we have global world domination. I feel like Krizz Kalico is on the same wave length, Ces Cru is on the same wave length, Stevie Stone, Rittz, Prozak, Mayday, Kutt Calhoun, Krizz Kaliko, Brotha Lynch, Big Scoob and all my artists are on the same page. I know we are on the same page and keep pushing forward.

I come across rappers all day and I see what you are doing is amazing. I remember the first interview when we did the Kansas City thing when you had the hair, and now I think "Wow, Tech N9ne did it!" I am so proud of you!
It is a blessing! I just got that will power to keep going. After they knock me down I keep getting up. There are a lotta obstacles where we are wanting to go because world dominance is humungous. Everybody can't get that and I have the ability to do it because I have a passport and all I have to do is infect all these places just like we infected all these places. It is gonna take time and you have to take a pay cut in order to spread love. You can't go over there and say "I want $100,000" for a place that holds 200 people. You gotta take a pay cut. You gotta be able

to do some shows over there for $3500 like you did when you first started but it is worth spreading it to grow it. A lotta muthafuckaz won't do that!

If you can get big in some African countries it will spread!
I am trying to go everywhere. They are trying to call me from Iran. In Dubai I missed the show because I was on tour. They wanted me for a big amount too and we had to pass it up because nothing over my fans. Yeah it was a lotta money but there were two Seattle shows I would have to miss to do Dubai. I can't do that to my fans so Dubai is gonna have to wait on me. Hopefully it will come back because world dominance can't happen without Dubai. It can't happen without Africa, China or Japan, it can't happen without Spain, Turkey, Bangkok, or Istanbul. I went to Kuwait in the middle of the bullshit and I did my shows even though I broke my ribs. I was born to do this. I was born to be on the road and spread love through songs. I want to do it all over the world like Quincy Jones did.

People don't realize how big places like Africa and Asia are. They are huge and people like Bob Marley broke through there.
To me my face paint looks like my ancestors from over there.
When you go there the people will be like "That muthafucka is one of us for real!"

I would like to see man!
When I go over to New Zealand and Australia I see a lot of Ethiopian girls over there and they are all on my music. Music is incredible and it can spread. Thank god for the internet.

Your new album is a landmark album and I feel like it is a new beginning!
It's like a movie!

It's a different Tech N9ne! You and Seven did something different on this one!
His beats take me to a higher height lyrically. I am axioms to see what we are gonna do next. We are mixing a rock project right now and I got about 7 songs about to come out November 5th. Some of the guys from Limp Bizkit came to play and people just came in and really helped.

Is it an EP?
Yeah, it is 7 songs and it is an EP called "Therapy."

Is this like a rap-rock album?
Yeah, it is! It is a rap-rock album. It is full on rock. I am rappin; on a lot of it but it is live music. It is another level of Tech N9ne. I always have rock orientated music like "Riot Maker" and "Tormented" and other songs that I do with the Def Tones, but this is the full on. We went outside of our box. It is just me rappin but everybody is coming on to play. Seven constructed some beats and we took it out to Venice Beach and wrote out everything at Ross Robinson's house. I was sitting on the beach just writing a song and we are just coming off of "Somethin' Else" and I am wondering when the demon is gonna come. There was too much love around me so I wrote a song on there called "When Demon's Come Around Me" and a lot of people that dislike me back in the day are now suckin' a dick so there is another song on their called "We Don't Need No Head Now" it is like saying "You didn't like us back then, but we got enough head right now, we don't need head right now!" We are good so keep that shit over there. All these songs came off of my experiences with something else thus far.

Did Seven have anything to do with this record?
Yeah he did! He constructed the beats and we went out to Ross Robinson and they reconstructed them with live instruments. They added these instruments to Seven's beats.

With the Doors and being on Venice Beach they were into that in the 70s!
Yeah that is what it was like. That is what it felt like. I was livi9ng on Venice Beach. It was like back in the day. I met so many wonderful angels going up and down the strip. I was sitting out there on the beach writing and people were passing by like "Are you Tech N9ne?" and I was like "Yeah I am writing my Rock project" and people would want to take pictures. A lot of people wanted to take pictures and I had to go back inside after awhile and write my songs but a bunch of it I wrote right on the beach with the water right there. I even recorded with the water right in front of me. With the way Ross Robinson's house is, it is all glass. So he put the mic in his living room of this big ass mansion on Venice beach and you can see the beach right there man. I was just recording looking at wonderful water.

When I se a lot of rappers they want to copy what is going on and the difference with you is you don't give a fuck about what other people are doing!
I still don't! I pay attention! I bought Kanye and Jay-Z's new album and I paid attention to what they were doing. I don't copy though because what is going on this year won't be going on next year. I stick to 501s and original Jordan's. I stick to things that will never go out of style to me. I don't think Dickeys, Jordan's, or 501s will never go out of style. I wear original shoes like Chuck Taylor, Adidas and Puma and other original things that will never go out of style. My style morphs all the time but I can do anything. It is not gonna be whatever they call "swag" because next year it might be something else. I am gonna always be something else period! Something else is gonna always be relevant.

No one can be Tech N9ne!
It is real hard to be Tech N9ne. You can take things that I do and apply it to you like "OK, he tours relentlessly so we are gonna do the same thing, or he has merchandise so we will do the same thing. His business we love it." I get that kind of love and I do it because young people will prosper. We don't hold that game back. As far as my style my fans try to do it and a lot of them get close but I am always rappin; so I can say "Ahhhh you can't do this!" I am gonna always challenge myself and never try to do what everybody else is trying to do. That is why I hate when my fans will say just cause I did a song with Wiz Khalifa and B.O.B. that I sold out. This is a beat that I chose from B.O.B. and Drumma Boy. There is a song called "See

> "I AM TRYING TO GO EVERYWHERE. THEY ARE TRYING TO CALL ME FROM IRAN. IN DUBAI I MISSED THE SHOW BECAUSE I WAS ON TOUR. THEY WANTED ME FOR A BIG AMOUNT TOO AND WE HAD TO PASS IT UP BECAUSE NOTHING OVER MY FANS."

Me" and it is bangin' but people are just not use to seeing or hearing me on the radio. This lady that I met at a meet and greet said "It's weird hearing Tech N9ne on the radio that belongs to me it is not suppose to belong to everybody else!" Then I said "Well it does belong to you but it is suppose to belong to everybody!" Don't get selfish with Tech N9ne because it is suppose to spread like a disease. I hate when my fans get locked into one style that I do "I just like the dark shit!" This was way before K.O.D. I did music way before I did my dark album. If you came in at K.O.D. and that is what you love cool but that is my only fully dark album and I will never be able to do that again. If you like my gangsta shit then you are gonna always love the stuff that I did with the Rogue Dogs talking about the hood. That is only one part of me because I am three dimensional. That is why I wear those 3-D glasses because I am three dimensional. My fans sometimes get locked into one thing that I do. I do everything but I guess I have to accept the fans are gonna like what they like but don't come to me when you hear something on the radio and say that I sold out muthafucka, it's Tech N9ne/Strange Music on the radio. That's Strange Music on the radio. That's that Strange shit coming through on the radio that you ain't never even heard.

People like certain eras and they want to box you in there but you are a free artist to do whatever you want!
Yeah, just like Outkast! Urban radio would have never played "Hey Yaaaaaaah" but they pushed it and I loved that shit. "Fragile" that song I did with Kendrick Lamar and Mayday was picked up by the radio. That is not even the single that we are pushing right now. I didn't make that record to be on the radio but good music is gonna always find its way. Don't get mad when you see me on the radio or the TV because its gonna happen. That good shit always shines.

The people should be happy for you!
A lot of the original Technicians are! A lot of my fans are.

We are always screaming for Tech and we know that you are the biggest!
God is keeping me young man. God is keeping me young for a reason. My brain is still producing the shit that the youngsters wanna hear. This shit is happening for a reason.

When I did my first interview with you I could feel like you were not the normal rapper!
Naw, not even in my hood. My hood niggaz like Big Scoob knew when I was in school I was a weirdo nigga but they loved me. They are the reason why I wear these colors. To this day I wish Scoob was here with me now but he is close by. They knew me as the music muthafucka. None of this is surprising to my homies in my hood.

You have taken Strange Music to a level as an independent label that I have never seen before, so what is next?
I am battling myself to the point of where if it will cost each artist $150,000 to get a radio campaign, would it make more sense to buy Mayday on a tour with somebody bigger. Or Kutt Calhoun on tour with T.I. or Ces Cru on tour with the Roots or Talib Kweli? Does it make more sense to take those radio campaign dollars to put into tours because back in the day I did it. I bought onto Jay-Z and 311's Sprite Tour back in 2001. That was when we first dropped "Anghellic" and I would do "This Ring" and after every show the crowd would get greater. Even Jay-Z and all of them were hearing about. When we got done with the tour we went back to those places and they remembered our show and that is how it happened. We paid to get on that tour. We bought on and it worked. We are trying to go back to the old style of doing things because radio is a hard thing and I am just talking with Travis right now because we don't know what to do because every artist deserves a shot. Stevie Stone deserves a shot and all the artists deserve a real shot. Yeah, we put out 11 projects this year and 8 of them charted on Billboard. We are moving but I am thinking of other strategies to build these guys and make them even bigger than me. They are gonna always be good on my tours and people will come to see them on m y tours but I want Mayday to be able to be on Jimmy Fallon or something. I want them to be seen by 1000s of different people.

A different crowd!
Yes! The people I sign I am a fan of them. I see them humungous. Stevie Stone is incredible and people need to see that shit. Kriz Kalico is amazing and he could be on tour with Lady Gaga. He can open up for Gaga that is how good he is. I am always thinking how I can make them prosper and their families.

That is a good idea to open up Strange Music so they are on their own with other people!
That might be the strategy real soon. I would put all my money into my artists, I would! That is how much I believe in them! •

A CONVERSATION WITH ICE CUBE

BY ALLEN GORDON • PHOTO BY MARCUS HANSCHEN

First off, let me preface this interview by saying, you are the among the greatest rappers of all time: Ice Cube, Too Short, Scarface, KRS One, Rakim, Kane, Brother J, E-40, Chuck D, Jay Z and Melle Mel. But WC is my all time favorite.
For real. Thanks for the compliment. But man, I been telling people for years that they sleeping on Dub. When I say for years, I mean years, homie. Like since 1989. Since Low Profile through WC and the MAAD Circle to his solo albums. He's one of the best out there, and he's doing it all these years later. Why do you think I still fuck with him? You know I don't really hang with too many people as it is, but me Dub and DJ Crazy Toones, Brother Ron. That's been consistent for as long as you've known me.

What is it about WC that you find most intriguing as a rapper?
What do I find most intriguing about his flow? Where do I start? First off, he's got a crazy flow that he switches up, but you know that signature WC sound when it comes out. Then he's smart as hell, so he can give you a ghetto ass rhyme and you don't even know he just hit you with some brilliant gems, like they say in New York. A song like "This Is Los Angeles" has some deep meaning too, but it is straight up West Coast Gangsta music and we don't apologize for it. This is where we are from and how it goes down.

What is the chemistry between you two like? Sometimes when people link up, the stronger media personality tends to dominate the other rappers flow. Like Turk and Lil' Wayne started doing more of a BG type flow at some point during the Hot Boys day.
I don't know much about that but I think I know what you are asking. Dub and me are two different rappers from the same neighborhood. We don't sound nothing alike and we were never in the shadow of each other, so nobody can say that he's riding my coattails or some bullshit like that. He's a successful artist doing his thing. I mean since 1989! Come on that's almost 20 years on stage, in the game and he is still a major factor. Shit when we went on the road for "Laugh Now Cry Later", some niggas wanted to see Dub-C more than me. Asking about his new album, spitting they favorite lines, just showing love. That alone says it all. Still here making hits and in demand to a fanbase that is loyal. And after this new record on Lench Mob comes out, he'll have some new fans.

How long have you known each other? How far do you and he go back as friends or musically?
I've known Dub since we was little. He stayed right around the corner from me.

Did you know he rhymed?
I knew he rhymed. I think he might have been rhyming before me. I can't remember. He was doing his thing back in the day when I was doing my thing with Jinx, K-Dee and Dre. Then Dub got hooked with Ice T and Rhyme Syndicate. I was happy for him when him and DJ Alladin got signed to Priority in 1988 or 89 as Low Profile. So we saw each other more often than we had when NWA started taking off. We always kept in touch. I was in his first video "Pay Ya Dues", if you remember.

Yeah! You and Brother Ron. He was getting his Stanley on back then too.
Man, what it all comes down to with Dub is, he's just a real friend. I don't call too many people that. He's just a real nigga. He don't want nothing from me. He don't ask me for shit or try to pimp our friendship. We're just alike in that manner. He's not trying to be all up under me or take advantage of being down with Ice Cube. He's his own man, my homeboy, and it just so happens that we work well together.

So what does the future hold for Lench Mob? When I interviewed you for the last Westside Connection album, you said you would never do another label. Too much of a headache.
Lench Mob Records is the future. I know I said I would never do another label deal, but I had to rethink a few things. I just don't want the headache of dealing with the attitudes or disposition of artists. I'm not trying to juggle, struggle or babysit personalities. That's not what I do and I don't have time for that shit. Right now, the label is me and Dub as far as artists go. He has full creative control over his project and we have our team pushing all the buttons. Being independent, we are going to do this album like HE wants to. At the end of the day, I know I can trust Dub to do what is needed, so I don't have to worry about him. He's all about the work. Crazy Toones is all about the work. Tony Draper is all about the work. Brother Ron is all about the work. If I do decide to start signing acts, it will have to be cats that are like me and Dub. Not the way they sound, but with a real work ethic, hella talented, and just polished as a person. I'm not taking on no whiny ass, begging-ass, headed for trouble, "I want a million dollar advance" wannabe artist no matter how talented they are. I can't be bothered.

What has been the biggest thrill or relief recording "Guilty By Affiliation" and being independent? What are you looking forward to?
To tell you the truth, being independent has made this shit fun again. When I go to the studio, cats are ready to work or are already knee deep into something. There are no overhead headaches, niggas calling in the middle of the night needing something, no label politics. We just make good songs and share a lot of ideas. As far as what I want to see. . . I want to see my homeboy Dub do well. When he hits the road it will be the Dub C show and I'll be the hype man. I want to see people gravitate to this record and realize that WC is an incredible artist. That is for the people who don't already know. Most of all I want his supporters to enjoy something that they never have before, and that is WC doing what he wants to in a creative space where he can. Lench Mob is what it's all about.

What else are you working on film wise or soundtracks.
This album is the only focus right now. If we are going to talk about me and what I'm doing, you can call me back in a few months, this all about Dub and "Guilty By Affiliation".

You still have your platinum plaque right?
We did the damn thang and it was fun. Who knows if there will be another album somewhere down the line? What we're talking about today, tomorrow and any other time me and you chop it up is Dub-C and Guilty By Affiliation. In stores now. What did you think of the record?

I think it is the best WC record since "Curb Servin". I actually like it better than "Curb Servin", because I'm 10 years older than that album today. "Guilty By Affiliation" is where I am now. Teaching high school kids in Oakland Public Schools and this album feels grown and young at the same time. I'm only 37 years old, but it caters to my sense of responsibility without removing me from the element that I'm so a part of. I'm not out in the suburbs away, I'm here assessing the damage and working with the casualties. That's what the album means to me lyrically. Beat wise, the shit is ridiculous. Toones went bananas. Every track has life of its own and sets a mood and atmosphere. The music is like a score to film. This is the Los Angeles version of "City of God".
Damn! I was expecting you to say that you liked the beats and the rhymes were cool, but its good that you analyzed it like that. I

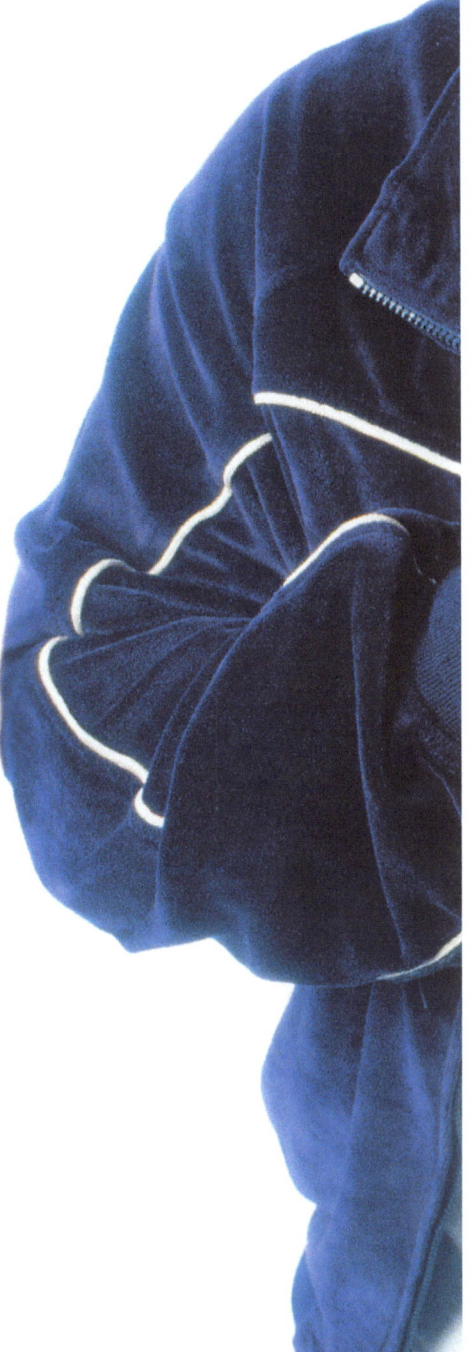

> "MAN, WHAT IT ALL COMES DOWN TO WITH DUB IS, HE'S JUST A REAL FRIEND. I DON'T CALL TOO MANY PEOPLE THAT. HE'S JUST A REAL NIGGA. HE DON'T WANT NOTHING FROM ME. HE DON'T ASK ME FOR SHIT OR TRY TO PIMP OUR FRIENDSHIP. WE'RE JUST ALIKE IN THAT MANNER. HE'S NOT TRYING TO BE ALL UP UNDER ME OR TAKE ADVANTAGE OF BEING DOWN WITH ICE CUBE. HE'S HIS OWN MAN, MY HOMEBOY, AND IT JUST SO HAPPENS THAT WE WORK WELL TOGETHER."

A businessman to the end.
Got to be.

I would like to talk about the Westside Connection and Mack 10.
The Westside Connection served its purpose for the time. Niggas spoke on some things in the music game and in the world. We put it down for the West Coast and Hip Hop, twice.

hope you do some reviews and let people see it from that perspective. That was a pretty interesting look at it. It's good that you ride for the West Coast like you have and are intelligent enough to argue things like that. Magazines need that these days for music period. •

BEANIE SIGEL

BY BLACK DOG BONE
PHOTOS BY MARCUS HANSCHEN

People you grew up with are probably surprised to see you signed to one of the biggest labels and doing all this.
A lotta my friends, they ain't even believe it. Not too many people even knew that I knew how to rap. When I was growin up in the streets in Philly if you was a rapper you was a sucker. You gotta look at who was in the Rap scene in Philly before people like me was comin out. It wasn't cool to wear no Gumby hairstyle. To have a Gumby hairstyle, sneakers and suits to match. I don't know nobody who wore sneakers and suits. When I grew up, as far as the people I was around, if you was a rapper you was a sucker. You was a weirdo. Them people from Philly who was rappin at that time was weirdoes. If you was a rapper you was a character, you was funny. And it wasn't no jokes where I was from. Ain't nobody laughin and smilin.

When did Philadelphia get opened to this type of Rap--the street stuff?
Philly got opened up to this typa Rap when Beanie Sigel stepped up. The only people that was holdin Rap down that I'd give it to was the Roots, and they was a Alternative band. They was more Alternative with the live music and stuff like that. But as far as the straight flat out street Rap, the only person out there that was keepin it Gangsta that I can think of was Black Thought from The Roots. As far as the MC period. One of the best freestylers I ever heard.

How did the doors open up for you?
I met this cat Murder Mil, he's signed to Jive right now. Me and Murda Mil became partners. And we met Philly's Most Wanted, and Philly's Most Wanted had a situation with Atlantic Records, and they was tryna get signed to Roc-A-Fella. They asked me did I wanna go up, take a ride to New York. I took that ride with 'em and I ended meetin up with Damon Dash and Jay. The rest is history.

They liked you right away?
From the door I was signed. After I met Jay Z I was doin the Hard Knock Life album with him, I was doin that album in about 5 days.

Since that time what's been goin on with you?
I been doin everybody's albums, Jay-Z to Biggie Smalls, Puff Daddy, Cisco, Foxy Brown, various soundtracks, Eve's album, the Roots. I done made a movie. I'm workin on a clothing line right now called Versatile. I'm into the real estate business, I'm buyin properties right now. Startin this apartment complex. I'm tryin to get this community center in Philadelphia so the kids can have something to do after school instead of just bein in the streets. I'm opening up restaurants that sell good, clean, food.

What are the neighborhoods you have in Philly and what part are you from?
I'm from South Philly. The heart of Philadelphia! The most segregated part of Philadelphia where you got your Italian neighborhood. You got your Irish neighborhood. You got your Black neighborhood. Your Oriental neighborhood, the Hispanic neighborhood.

Is that where most of the Rap comes from? Where do The Roots come from?
Straight outta South Philly. Black Thought's from South Philly. Freeway's from North Philly. Oshino & Sparks is from West Philly. Different parts we from. North Philly, West Philly and South Philly.

How is Philadelphia different from New York?
In New York it's just a lotta lights, that's how I look at it. Real bright. Ain't nothing bright like that in Philadelphia. It's a lotta glitz and glamour and all the glitter and gold. And Philadelphia is gray, it's gloomy.

Your music has a real dark, grimy feel.
That's what it is, it's dark. When you look at New York streets, them big wide city streets. And on these blocks people can double and triple park in the streets--you barely got enough room to move one car a block. The houses in Philly are so close and tight together and everything is real close and all one-way streets in South Philly. No two-way streets. That's a real concrete jungle where I grew up. It's a box.

You really got the whole mood captured in your music.
Come to Philly and you'll understand what I'm talkin about. I'm talkin about New York and Philly. New York's the city that never sleeps. 24 hours of clubs--from 8 o'clock at night until 7 in the mornin. Then you got Philadelphia, a city that shuts down at 2 'o clock, and there ain't nobody in the streets but killaz, murderers, crack heads, dope dealers and trouble. That's all that's happening in the streets of Philly at night. You can party in New York, ain't nobody partying in Philly. You out after 2 o'clock, you out there tryna make money any way you know how--whether you're sellin drugs or you stickin up the drug dealers or you trickin the drug dealers, that's how it go on in Philly. After 2 o'clock it's lights out.

Lyrically you talk about the streets. I'm sure you talk from your life experiences. What kind of life did you have growing up in Philly?
I probably had the normal average life for a young man comin up in Philly. I didn't complete high school. I dropped outta school in between the ninth and tenth grade. I left home when I was 14-15 years old. Been in and outta every juvenile institution. On the streets sellin drugs. Locked up numerous times. I been shot, been mixed up in a shoot out with the police. I done touched it all. I'm just blessed to be here. I'm your average cat from the street. I been stabbed, shot, rocked and chopped. I'm nothing new under the sun. I'm like one of the last dinosaurs right now.

When you were growing up what were you listening to?
My mother had all kindsa music in the house. I listened to all types of music. I bounced around from my mother's to my grandmother's house. I was raised up in my grandmother's house a lot. I grew up listening to people like the Temptations, Stylistics, Four Tops, Otis Redding, the Delphonics, all kindsa music. I just love music period.

Did you ever dream it could go like this? How did it feel for you when your first got with Roc-A-Fella, to be working with people like Jay-Z and Damon?
As far back as I could remember I always wanted to be a gangsta. I never knew I was gonna rap and fall in line with the music business. But Roc-A-Fella was on the top, there was no choice but for me to be on Roc-A-Fella. That was a given. I wouldn'ta fit nowhere else but Roc-A-Fella. I never looked to get signed. I knew something was special, I knew Allah had a plan for me to do something great.

Who are your favorite lyricists out there doing it right now?
Of course you know I'm gonna give it to Jay-Z. I'm a have to say myself. Then you have to go back to people like Scarface, Biggie Smalls, N.W.A., 2Pac.

What's the main difference to you between this new Beanie Sigel album and the last?
I feel on this album I stepped up a lot. I feel real comfortable with this album right here. What I did on this album came straight from the heart. On the last album I think I tried too hard. I like to be natural. On the Truth album I sat down and really thought about the songs that I was writin. This album I just went in the studio and just gave what people know me as--the rawness and the flows and the style of my delivery. I game 'em a lotta hard Hip Hop tracks, a lotta club bangers. Shit you could knock in your jeep, every club gonna be bangin it, and the street rhymes and flows that you couldn't even imagine. My word play on this album is ridiculous.

I think you gained so much confidence from the first album that you just did exactly what you wanted on this album.
That's why I named it The Truth. There's always a reason behind the truth. This album is just backin up the first album. When you hear The Reason, you're gonna feel like it's

> "NAW, I'M ON THE BEANIE SIGEL TIP. I'M GOIN TO BE ME, AND THAT'S STRAIGHT OUTTA THE EAST AND SOUTH PHILLY. ALL I DO IS SPEAK THE STORY. NOT JUST PHILLY--ANY GHETTO, ANY STREET YOU FROM YOU GONNA FEEL THAT. IT'S NOT JUST MY STORY, IT'S YOUR STORY TOO."

part 2 of The Truth.

Who did you work with for production? Do you pick your own beats?
Yeah, yeah. When I worked on my first album it was a cat named Just Blaze who I think did the hottest songs on my album. He did the song that I did with Memphis Bleek called "Who The Fuck Want What." I wanted to work with Just Blaze on this album, cause we got chemistry. I know what to expect from him and he know what to expect from me. And when I did The Dynasty album with Jay, A cat named Rick Rock did a lotta tracks on the album. And I used a guy named Kanye West, he did some tracks on my first album. Those are the main producers I worked with on this album. I did a track with 88 Ki's, I did a track with No ID and a cat from Philly named Big Demi (he was on my first album). I didn't go out and look for the big producers like Swizz and Timbaland and Primo. There's new cats comin out just like me. You're new until you get your name. I'm new in the game and I want to give folks opportunity to get on. As I grow, they grow. Judgin from the stuff that Just Blaze doin, he's bananas right now. He's gonna be getting into Timbaland money soon. That hundred thousand a track. That's what I'm tryin do right now, build a relationship with my producers.

Of all the songs you've done which is your favorite?
Every song. Every time I give a part of me, that's my favorite. In every song that's what I'm doin, I'm givin you a part of Beanie Sigel. When I do something I'm givin you the whole me. I feel that I put the best into everything I do.

For this album did you record a lot of extra songs and just pick some?
No, every song I did on this album, I'd come in the studio, I'd listen to the beats--the whole album I did in the studio, I never had to prepare for no songs. When I heard the beats I wrote everything on the spot.

You wrote the rap and then recorded it?
Not even writin it down, cause I don't write with an ink pen no more. I write in my head. When I'm sittin there listenin to the music, I write. That's a trait I picked up from Jay Z. I've never seen him use an ink pen. He comes in the studio, he listens to the beats and he writes in his head. Why write it down? It's just like exercising the mind. Keep that thought, think of what you want to want to say next, then you know you wanna add that to the paper, but just add it to the thought in your brain. Just keep sayin it. That's how I do it.

Jay Z is a cool person to work with?
Jay Z, he's like a big brother to me. Especially when it comes to music, when we be workin on things, he's a like a big brother. He's gonna show you what he needs to show you. You take it from there. He's gonna show you what you need to know, and he's gonna take it from there. That's what I like about Jay Z. He's not gonna just put it in your hands, he's gonna put it on a platter. He tells you only what you need to know and it's up to you to take it and run with it. I've learned from Jay Z without him teachin. Just from bein around him and watchin and observin. Same thing he does from me. Like with steel, when you run two pieces of steel together, one don't get sharp, they both get sharp.

Of all the Roc-A-Fella artists you have the darkest sound.
You have to look at the world today. It's not about champagne and the diamonds and how many cars you got and all that. It's really about maintaining and keepin your family in order. Havin a foundation and structure for you family. Cause you not gonna be here forever, that's how I look at it. I lived my life, I done my dirt in the streets. I'm makin progress in tryin to change my life. I can build corporations and businesses so my family can be alright. This is what I had to go through. They don't have to go through what I had to go through, not knowin how I'm gonna feed my kid or how I'm gonna feed myself. Have to go out and rob and steal for pamper money, to feed your child. I don't want them to go through that.
A lot of people rap about all the cars and jewelry they have, but that's not the reality. I think that's where a lot of rappers fall off. Once you get in the game in this Rap business, for a person that's on the street hustlin, he's used to havin his money hands on. He used to seein his paper. He can't put that money in the bank. That money's under the bed, in the mattress, that money's somewhere safe in the wall. So when you change over to that lifestyle when you a business man, people don't know how to separate their life from havin paper money. They're not used to the checks and money bein in the bank. That's why a lotta rappers fall off. When you get outta that stage of havin to see paper money, then you do better. There's a thing called credit, and that's what I learned to do when I'm in this business, it's about buildin credit or building equity. That's what Roc-A-Fella teach you, they teach you how to be a businessman, not only as an artist. If you in Roc-A-Fella you not gonna just be a rapper. You gotta have some kinda company. Right now I'm doin a movie. You got to look forward to all that with Roc-A-Fella. A lotta rappers talk about the cars--anybody can lease a car or a house, but to maintain the payments and them bills when you out there flossin every night with the champagne, buyin the $150,000 watch and all that. It took me two years to buy jewelry. Right now I have a 5-bedroom crib, I got land, I have no neighbors, I got some Bentley's parked in my garage, I have a Suburban and a truck. And I only dropped one album. It's about not just doin rap, when you make that money you have to spend that money to get into that other money. That's why I got into this real estate business. I had bills and I bought property and the rent that I got from there pays for my lifestyle I'm livin now. You got to learn to be versatile.

Roc-A-Fella is owned by Jay Z and Damon Dash. What's Damon like?
When it comes to business, Damon is--how can I say this--he's an animal. He's a very determined man. When he believes it, he's gonna get it accomplished. He's the typa guy, when you sign with Roc-A-Fella, he's not gonna let you just be an artist. He's gonna make sure you own a home. If you have hard times when things don't go too well, one thing Damon's gonna make sure is that you do own a home. You gonna have some kinda money in the bank so you can maintain your lifestyle. Nobody wanna got back from a 6 bedroom house, 4 car garage, to workin at the gas station, livin in a 2 bedroom apartment. You don't wanna make that transition. You wanna maintain that lifestyle. Damon Dash is gonna make sure you set up to maintain that lifestyle. He's not gonna let you just be a rapper. You're gonna be a business man. And he teaches you. I done heard him ask artists to fire his lawyer. Like you have a lawyer come in to negotiate your deal with Roc-A-Fella, they go to talk to Damon. And Damon'll let you know if your lawyer ain't shit, he's not fightin for you hard enough. Damon is the fairest person that I know. He's out to win, but he wants you to win too. He don't make no money if you don't make no money. I got to sell records. That's why I do my best, cause I know Damon's gonna do his job as far as promotin the album and all that. I know he's gonna put his all into it, so I wanna give him the best project and the best songs that I can.

Is he a young cat?
Young. He's young in the game. And I feel sorry, cause he's gonna be there for a long time, for all the upcomin people and the people that's already in the game. Damon Dash and Roc-A-Fella Records is on a rise right now and it's really about to be a dynasty like no other.

Damon doesn't do music, he's just into the business?
No, he doesn't do music. But he comes in and listens to the music. He has an ear for music. His ear for music is phenomenal.

I heard you started your own label?
A lotta these Philly artists that's signed right

now, these are the guys that came up under my wing. I think it's time for me to get some of that paper. I'm puttin out my camp. I got these young cats bout to come out right now. One dude, you heard him on the Dynasty album, named Freeway. He's incredible. We did a song together on DJ Clue The Professional Part 2. You can look forward to Freeway, he's gonna be comin out soon on my label, Criminal Records.

Who's going to do the distribution for you?

I'm stayin with the Roc, I'm goin straight Roc. Not cause I had to, that's a choice from me. I'm dedicated. I'm always gonna be with Roc-A-Fella. I'm gonna be a Roc-A-Fella artist forever. •

ACE HOOD
BY BLACK DOG BONE • PHOTO COURTESY DEF JAM

There are rappers coming out of every town in the country now. What makes Florida rappers different from artists from California or New York or Houston?

Unity, man. Unity. We got something down here in Florida we call The Movement, that's what separates us a lot from every other area. The way we bond together and the way we help each other out. The Movement is powerful. Like me and Ricky Ross, Flo-Rida or DJ Khaled or T-Pain—everybody willing to help each other out in order to get to where we need to get to. Everybody greet each other as brothers. Our Movement is what separates us from everybody else in the game.

What about musically? How do you stand out musically? Are you more into club music or lyrical music?

We into both, that's what separates us. We lyrical and we hit 'em with swag records, whatever we wanna do. We just make great music. We are serious artists. We can get on an international record and get passionate on the rap if we wanna. That's the thing about bein an artist. When you a rapper you can make records forever and ever, but an artist is an actual perfection of your craft. When you an artist you paint pictures for people. You can hit 'em with lyrical or you can hit 'em with that swag or we can hit 'em with that that gun talk, we can hit 'em with lyrical assault. We can flip a Jay-Z on 'em, we can flip Biggie on 'em. Or we can come down and flip swag on 'em.

What about Ace Hood? What is the key sound of Ace Hood?

The key sound of me is just me. I hit you with that gritty talk. I got them hard lyrics on that hard beat. You gonna know when you're listening to Ace Hood. It's just that stamp, that future. You can hear it in my music.

What was it like growing up in Broward County, Florida?

Born and raised in Broward, grew up there. I just was basically growin up and trying to be this big time ball player, doin what I do in my city. Just tryin to come from nothing, get something going. At the end of the day, just trying to make a way. I'm from the city and we grew up lookin up to the dope boy. People ridin big rims and flossin and gettin money. That's the things we looked up to. Me bein a young knucklehead on the block tryin to do what I do and stay focused at the same time, I was playing ball. But due to an injury, I hurt my knee playin football.

How old were you when you got hurt?
I got hurt in like tenth grade. Once I hurt my knee one thing lead to another. Music was always a part of me, it was always in my front pocket, that's something I kept with me. After I got hurt and tried to come back and play ball again I found that the love for it just wasn't there no more. That's when I decided to take it to another level, take it to a different aspect, do this music full time. Lotta people thought I was crazy, kickin ball to the side and pickin up music as my full-time grind. But at the end of the day I ended up doing music, met up with DJ Khaled, it changed my life.

Is your city big?
Naw naw, it's not big at all. We only have like two exits to my city, that's it. I stayed in a small city, Deerfield Beach.

South Florida is so different from other parts of the US, with the tropical climate. It must have been different to grow up down there.
It's different down here. It's different everywhere you go. I've travelled to a lotta different cities and every city is different from where I'm from definitely. I'm proud of where I came from.

What makes Ace Hood different from other rappers out there?
One thing about me, let me tell you, I come from a different family. I was raised by a mother who had to provide for five siblings. She worked two or three jobs in order to provide for her young. She had to be ruthless. That's where a lot of my inspirations come from, that's why I named my new album "Ruthless". By naming my album "Ruthless" I'm bringin you back to my life and what I've been through. That's why I'm working overtime. With the recession and the important point in time we're living in right now. This other record I got, my second single that's out, is called "Champion". When you grow up without nothing and at the end of the day you come out victorious, that's the sign of a champion. And the name "Ruthless" represents my actual life and my mother's inspiration.

You grew up without a dad?
No, I had my dad. But my real father wasn't always around, I had my stepfather. He came in and did what he did, but my mother is the one that made sure we had what we needed. Even if she had to work overtime. She was important in my life. Ruthless describes my life. I'm in this music game right now. I grew up listening to the Jeezy's and the Weezy's and the Ricky Rosses. Those are the people that was in my time. I'm 21 and I'm young, so I grew up listening to them. Now I gotta think about who's listening to me. At the end of the day, what I do is what I do. I'm moving into the future now. My starvation and my hunger is different from everyone else. You don't see this starvation anywhere anymore. That's why I go so hard, why I do it like this, cause nothing comes easy. I got a ruthless mind frame, that's why "Ruthless" connects everything I do in life.

How does it feel to go from struggling to getting all this press, travelling, touring, this different lifestyle. To be signed to one of the biggest labels, it's like a dream a lot of people have but never reach.
That's big. It's a big blessing. Me being with the biggest distribution company out there, Def Jam, it's a dream come true. I know millions of people would love to be in my position, that's why I go as hard as I do. I don't take anything for granted. At the end of the day, I give thanks to the almighty high man. That's what allows me to maintain my humbleness. At the end of the day, I just gotta get it, so I'm givin thanks.

In your family are you one of the youngest or oldest kids? What are your brothers and sisters doing?
I'm the youngest. My brother's in college, he does a little fighting. My sister's in college right now, and my other brother's in college, my little sister's in college too. Everybody is doin them.

What made you go in the direction of music? Why is your path so different from your family?
Music was always a part of my life. My original father and my stepfather was involved in music. I was always doing something with music. When I was in middle school I used to play around and write little rhymes. I did that for a while and people always told me you're a dope writer and you can write real well. When I was in high school I just continued writing, then I started making music. I started puttin words together, then I started putting pictures behind what I was speaking of.

You started writing when you were pretty young.
I was young, like sixth grade: skittle, riddle, little. Just puttin words together. To me back then rapping was just rhyming, not even having a clear vision that rapping can be like painting a picture. You have to paint a picture for them. I didn't experience that level until I got a bit older.

When you were growing up were there a lot of other people in your town who were doing Rap?
No, I'm pretty much the first out of my city. I'm the first to be holding it down for my city on the international level. You had other people aspiring to do their music, but I was the first to blow outa my city. Now I'm working on a couple of other situations, snatch a couple of people up.

In your town are they a lot of African Americans or is it mixed?
Yeah, it's African Americans plus a lot of Haitians as well.

Do you have any island roots?
No, no Haitian roots. I'm Black African American. I got a lotta people that I roll with that are Haitians though.

Do you think being around Haitian culture influenced your music? Did you hear a lot of Haitian music when you were growing up?
No, not at all. The music I listened to? I grew up listening to Ricky Ross, Jeezy, Lil Wayne. Those are the musics I came up listening to. That's what I stayed focused

> "NO, I HAD MY DAD. BUT MY REAL FATHER WASN'T ALWAYS AROUND, I HAD MY STEPFATHER. HE CAME IN AND DID WHAT HE DID, BUT MY MOTHER IS THE ONE THAT MADE SURE WE HAD WHAT WE NEEDED. EVEN IF SHE HAD TO WORK OVERTIME. SHE WAS IMPORTANT IN MY LIFE. RUTHLESS DESCRIBES MY LIFE."

on.

What kind of music did you hear at your house growing up?
I heard a lot of older music. There was a lotta music in my house—Teddy Pendergrass, Luther Vandross, The Temptations, Patty LaBelle—just great music.

When you first met DJ Khaled, was it in Broward?
No, I was down at the radio station in Miami 99-Jamz and I ran into him. I gave him a little demo. He heard it and called me back. One thing led to another. I dropped that CD off to him and everything, we worked out some business and that led me to be the man I am today.

Before you got with DJ Khaled you were signed to Dollaz & Dealz Records. Who is behind that label?
That was my local label, Dollaz & Dealz. That's my own label. "Money Over Everything" was my record that came on that label.

Why would you say money is more important than everything else?
Money is the key thing. Money gets you what you need. Money is life. Money is what you need in order to have. That's why I put money over everything. At the end of the day we gotta get those dollars. You need money to get it poppin. You need money to get your album promoted and in stores. You need money to make the CD's. Bottom line, "Money Over Everything" was just a record that went crazy in the hood. It got me to this day right here.

Don't you think the humans in the world or the animals or the trees are more precious than money? Isn't your family more precious than money?
I feel that way, at the end of the day it's music. It's what the people wanna hear. "Money Over Everything" is just a hustler's mentality. If you're a hustler then that should be your mentality. Of course family and God and other things are just as important, but "Money Over Everything" sums up the mentality.

Did you think this way when you were growing up or is this something you realized later in life?
I always felt like this. Money is it.

If I listen to your record is that the overriding theme?
When you get a record from Ace Hood you gonna get motivation. That's why I put out records such as "Overtime". I put out records that give people hope. I put out real life records. I'm showing different the different aspects of a hustle. You gonna go overtime in the streets or you gonna go over time in sports or whatever you do to get money. That's why I drop records like my second single "Champion". Just showin that you can do something, that you able to do something. When they think of Ace Hood they gonna think of a hood motivational speaker. He's a person who reps the hood. He's young and he's the future of this street shit. His album drops June 30.

Basically you got this rare opportunity and you're working as hard as you can to make it.
Yeah. I'm workin overtime to be the champion. When you think of Ace Hood just think of a person who goes harder than the next man. My hunger sets me apart from the rest. Ace Hood's gonna always goes hard. He's always gonna be that cat that goes extremely hard. Making that good street music, that music for the knuckleheads, that motivational music. You gonna respect me for that.

How is this new album different from your previous album?
This album is phenomenal. On this album I'm definitely in the position I wanted to be. I'm happy with the whole situation, I'm happy with everything. This album is more me. I show more of my personality, it's about my life. I'm proud of it. My first album "Gutta" was the introduction to Ace Hood. "Ruthless" just takes it deeper, more into me.

Musically what is different about the second album?
The "Gutta" album was the introduction to me, the "Ruthless" album is more of who I am—why I'm in the state of mind I'm in, why I go so hard. It's a celebration of my hard work.

There's a lot of dance music going on in Atlanta and Baltimore and Philadelphia. How do you relate to that scene?
That dance music definitely has nothing to do with me. I'm an artist. That's what I do. I don't make dance music, that's not what I do. Dance music is good for some, but it's just not the type of music I want to create. It's not the type of music my crowd wants, it's not the type of music I want. I just speak what I know.

But you know gangsters like to dance too.
That's all cool. I'm not saying anything against it, but as far as me creating that music it's not what I do. It's not what matters.

Who made the beats on "Ruthless"?
I got to work with many phenomenal producers on this album. The Inkredibles produced my single. DJ Nasty on the album. I got my brothers straight outa my city, The Runners. He's a local producer and he's hot. As far as features I got Jeremiah, he's got a crazy record out. I've got Baby on there, I got Ludacris on there. Jack Sullivan, Ricky Ross, I got Shawty Lo.

The album is just phenomenal. What are you doing now, you're touring?
Yeah, I'm on the Ruthless tour right now. I actually got an "I Am Ruthless" campaign. I'm on my tour right now. It's hot.

How did you get your name Ace Hood?
Ace is a name that I used to have when I was young. Ace is the name that I feel was always on me. I always felt that I was ten people in one, that's why I chose "Ace". Then when I had my situation, once I got with Khaled, being where I'm from, being what I was reppin and what I was speaking about, I just attached the "Hood".

What made you name your first album "Gutta"?
"Gutta" just represented where I was from. That was just my style, that's my swag, that's the way I talk and the way I walk. It's the way I swag. I gave them that gutta swag. That was just extremely hardcore, that's why I hit 'em as hard as I did. Now with "Ruthless" it's more of what I've been through and what I'm going through. It's me portraying it in my music. Lettin 'em know that I'm still gutta but now I've got this ruthless mentality. •

> "WHEN YOU GET A RECORD FROM ACE HOOD YOU GONNA GET MOTIVATION. THAT'S WHY I PUT OUT RECORDS SUCH AS "OVERTIME". I PUT OUT RECORDS THAT GIVE PEOPLE HOPE. I PUT OUT REAL LIFE RECORDS. I'M SHOWING DIFFERENT THE DIFFERENT ASPECTS OF A HUSTLE."

INTERVIEW WITH FAT KILLAZ

BY SCOTT BEJDA • PHOTO BY CHE PATTERSON

Do you have a new album out?
Fat Father: The project is called Guess Who's Coming To Dinner. It's a bunch of good songs. I look at it like a motion picture because we got songs that will make you cry and we got real songs about real life issues. We also got songs about party life, females, gettin drunk and gettin high. It's a collage of all different kinds of music that puts you through different kinds of feelings.

On Tech N9ne's DVD he was sporting your shirt from your solo album. Did you think your album would get out there like it did?
King Gordy: You never know, so you have to put it out there and see what happens. The people that did respond to it means that they were open minded people. If I could just open the whole world to the music that I want to do and I respect that.

Is this your first project as a group?
Fat Father: We released two mix tapes called 2 Fat 2 Furious and FK Radio and they did pretty good on the streets and the internet. We got a nice response to them and of course King Gordy had a solo album released last year.

What is the meaning of Guess Who's Coming to Dinner?
Fat Father: Dinner is a metaphor for the industry. Guess who is about to come to the table and eat with all you multi-platinum artists?
Bang: The concept to me is kind of like we are coming to dinner and the rap game is the dinner. We are hungry and we want everything that the rap game has to offer.
King Gordy: It is what it is! It is our introduction to the game! We are coming to eat and get the money and respect. We are coming to feast and appeal to the masses.

What are your plans as a group?
Fat Father: We are what the game is missing right now. D-12 and a few other local groups I can see doing it as a group, but we have the vibe. When we get together it is just magical in the studio. We hear the beat and put a song together in an hour. I love working together with these guys and I believe we can bring something to the game that is missing right now. A lot of what the game is missing is originality. Everybody is following everybody and they are using the next man's formula to get on. We created our own formula! Our mission is not to give the people what they want, but to make them want what we give them.

How did the Fat Killahz come about?
Fat Father: It's a real name because we are fat and we are killaz lyrically. That was how the name came about. The group started when I met Marv-Won a few years back outside of the open mic at the Lush Lounge. We were kicking it and hit it off real good. Somebody was like, "Ya'll should be the Fat Killahz." I was always going around saying I was a fat killa but I never meant it as a group. We were coming up with all these ideas about doing a project. We knew Gordy was a dope MC and I'm King Gordy's hype man already anyway. We put it together with Gordy and Bang was another MC in the open mic community. We are all solo artists, but it is beautiful as a group.
Marv-Won: We were all MC's in the same circle and we all respected each other. It just so happened that we all are of a larger stature. We came up with the idea of the fact that the game hasn't seen nothing like us in a long time. So, we got together and formed the super group The Fat Killahz.
Bang: I was in a squad back in the day and Gordy and Fats was together on some shit and Marv was in the picture. Fats came up with the idea doing the Fat Killahz and being in open mic I was down with it. We have been down ever since like brothers.
King Gordy: Me and Fats was in this group called the Teamsters back in '99-'00. We were going to open mics from east to the west side doing our thing and eventually we got with Marv and Bang. Fat's was like one day joking around saying "We are gonna be the Fat Killahz." That was how we came about! We are the four fattest MC's in Detroit, and lyrically we are unstoppable. We are like an all-star group.

> **"FAT'S WAS LIKE ONE DAY JOKING AROUND SAYING "WE ARE GONNA BE THE FAT KILLAHZ." THAT WAS HOW WE CAME ABOUT. WE ARE THE FOUR FATTEST MC'S IN DETROIT, AND LYRICALLY WE ARE UNSTOPPABLE. WE ARE LIKE AN ALL-STAR GROUP."**

Do you sound like a lot of other Detroit artists, or do you have your own flavor?
Bang: We have our own sound that is our very unique. Each individual in the group has their own style. You are not listening to the same nigga rap on the whole album. Back to the food reference, but that is what we are cooking. I bring my own ingredients, Gordy brings his, Fat Father and Marv bring theirs. We put it all together and it is something incredible.

How is the group project different from your solo album?
King Gordy: What I do as far as a solo artist is totally different from what I do with the group. The group is its own separate entity so it has its one sound.

How has the response been for the group so far?
Marv-Won: We have been real blessed! It has been all love regardless of where we have been, or what we are trying to do. The whole fat concept hasn't really been used besides the Fat Boys back in the day.

Why do you think that is?
Fat Father: A lot of people look at the music game and say "Well, he is doing it like this way." When 50 gets on stage 50 can take his shirt off and you have to dress a certain way. We don't care about none of that! We will take our shirt off too! When I take my shirt off I'm not doing it because I'm a fat guy "Hey look at me and laugh," I'm doing it because Pac did it all the time and I want to show off all my tattoos too. Being fat all your life with people laughing and joking, so we flipped it and said, "Ok we are fat, but we want to be fat." A lot of people stray away from that because they are scared what people are going to say about them.
Marv-Won: The rap game got away from lyrics for a long time. I think it really became about image and how marketable you can be. There hasn't been a balance, but when push comes to shove we will step in the circle with any MC and give them the business.

Why did rap go away from the streets?
Marv-Won: Not to sound like a prick or anything, but I think it became too real for people. A group like NWA couldn't really thrive today, because they were hard with a political message. Nowadays people just want something to dance too. Now it's basically about "My chain costed more than yours!"
Bang: There is a void in the rap game and we are here to fill that void in the game.
Marv-Won: I ain't gonna say no names, but I met a lot of niggaz that is full of shit.

It's all fucked up because it is fuckin' up the culture of hip hop itself. It wasn't like that back in the day! I could listen to Rakim and know about what was going on in New York, I could listen to 40 and know what was going on in Cali, or listen to Face and know what was going on in Houston. Now everybody is telling the same goddamn story. Everyone is following the same formula.

Bang: There are so many rappers and not enough stars. Sometimes it is not even about who can rap the dopest, but more about the star quality. Honestly there are not too many muthafuckaz out here with hot albums.

Do Fat Killahz do a lot of shows?

King Gordy: We have done a lot of shows just paying dues. Some shows we would not even get paid and some shows we would get paid. It's all a struggle! The people love us. We have toured with D-12 and everything. Our biggest response was like we were headlining. We definitely did our thing!

What is your relationship like with Eminem and D-12?

Marv-Won: Those are our big brothers and I have a lot of respect for them. They showed us a lot about the game and took us on tour with them. We owe a lot of our success to them and people like Slum Village and AWOL for paving the way for Detroit artists. Hopefully we can go out here and try to carve our niche.

Who is featured on your album?

Marv-Won: We only got one rap feature and that is my man Guilty Conscious. We got the singers Phoenix and Niko Red. We also got different producers like BR Gunner who did Slum Village's last album, we got Kon Artis from D-12, we got Kidd who did BG's album. We also got these new cats called Silent Riot. The album will be out March 15th.

What if you all lose a lot of weight, then what will you be called?

Fat Father: I'll always be fat! Even if I lost two hundred pounds! Fat to me is not only the weight, but a way of life. I know skinny people that can eat a bucket of chicken. The way I live is fat! If I don't have a remote control then I'm not watching TV, or if there are stairs and an elevator then I'm going to take the elevator. That is the fat way! Fat is a way of life!

Marv-Won: We're using our weight in order to get people to look at us, but our talent will take over. Regardless of what size we are, we will still be four of the dopest MC's you have ever heard. Whether we all drop down to 150 and just be called The Killahz, we will still be the same people with the same talent.

How do you think the world will react to you?

Marv-Won: At first I think people will think that it is a gimmick until they are able to sit down and listen and know that we are really some skillful niggaz. They gotta except it, because you are gonna see it everywhere. We are gonna shove it down your damn throat. It is gonna be like we are Chingy, but just a whole lot better. •

BABY OF BIG TYMERS

BY BLACK DOG BONE • PHOTO BY MARCUS HANSCHEN

Last year was incredible. Cash Money took over everything.
We came in the game feelin that we was gonna be the best to ever fuck with the game. I been sayin that since we first did an interview with you a few years ago. Since we got with Universal we ain't dropped nothing but four albums. I'm tryin to get 30-40 albums under my wings, but we only did four albums. But we did what we had to do, we hard workin. Our hard work paved the way. It's nice, I love how it's goin, but we're goin take it to where we want. We gonna be the history to this game.

What's amazing about Cash Money is that you broke every market, from the West Coast to Midwest to New York. No Southern artists have done that before.
We go to New York and get mad mad mad mad love. I guess it's because we went to New York and took it to the ghetto.

supposed to be one of the hardest spots in New York. That's where we go every time we go, we been there like 4 times. It's a club called The Tunnel. We just take it to the niggaz' ghetto. We break our shit in the streets first. We go to any niggaz' ghetto and lay it down. We don't give a fuck where it be. Our whole motto is to the streets with this game. That ain't never gonna change. We just some street niggaz.

All the Cash Money albums that came out last year are platinum.
When we sell a platinum album we feel like that album just did alright, cause all our shit sell 2 million and better. It's cool for a nigga to sell platinum, that's a blessin, but a platinum for us ain't our status. We're platinum plus. When our albums sell a million we gonna think something wrong.

You're not happy with your sales?
I'm not happy with a million sales. Everything we do gotta do 2 million and better. It's a new era, niggaz can make more and do more, but they gotta be dedicated and work hard. We're gonna do our numbers. Everything we put out gonna do 2 million. Like now 5 million, new album might do 10 million.

How did Juvenile do?
Juvey's now goin on 5 million, but his new album comin out already triple platinum. I'm lookin for Juvey to do 10 million on this new album. Hot Boys, double platinum. Wayne's goin on double platinum. BG's double platinum. And they're still sellin, still scannin.

I see all the old Cash Money albums are also on the Billboard charts.
I've got 5 albums in the top 20 right now. One of my goals is I wanna break records in this game. I wanna be the history maker. Me and these niggaz I fuck with, the Cash Money millionaires, my dog Fresh, my brother Slim, Wayne, Turk, Juvey, BG. Throw in my brother Slim, the granddaddy, the brains and my shocks that I run with.
When Cash Money came up you basically wiped No Limit right out of the picture.
I look at it like this. I ain't gonna consider myself wiping them outta the game. I take my hat off to that nigga, P can hustle. I just came in this game and took it over from P, Puff and any nigga was in the game. I'm not tryin to knock them in what they do. I love what they do and how they hustle, but I come and did it my way. I come and changed this game and do what I wanna do with this shit.

I always knew you were going to blow up, but I was surprised the way you took the New York market.
New York ain't really no market. New York just like real niggaz. They like niggaz just like niggaz across the country. I knew it was no market I couldn't bust when it come to my people, cause I'm gonna take it to a niggaz's face. I'm gonna come to the muthafuckin projects and do it. They say niggaz don't never get no play in New York, I don't know nothing about that. I went to New York and did what the fuck I had to do and got mad love from everybody. They show me mad love. I can't complain about none of that shit dog. I give it up to all the stations, all the PD's, all the street hustlers, everybody in this game, cause they helped make us successful. And we did our part, we're gonna be here with this shit. I got the Rap game on lock. Can't nobody fuck with us.

What do you see for next year?
I'm goin into next year with big heavyweight shit. Lil' Wayne, I still got shit from '99 goin to 2 g--Lil Wayne's album, BG's album, Hot Boys' album, Juvenile's new album. I got the movie comin out, Baller Blockin, I got the Big Tymers' new album, I got the Hot Boys' new album. I'm straight, I'm gonna do my thing. I'm gonna change this game. I'm here to fuck it up, I'm gonna change all the rules to this game the way the White man been playin us for years and years and years. They got this shit situated like the sixes and the sevens. The way they workin the contracts and all that shit, I'm here to change all that shit. If a nigga do they homework after me he'll be just as successful as I was or bigger than me if he got his game tight. I'm gonna change this shit.

All anybody's talking about this year is Cash Money.
Muthafuckas was waitin for this here man, for some real street niggaz to come through. Just some real street niggaz, ain't no nigga bullshittin. Ain't no knock to no nigga that's doin their thing cause I jock seein my niggaz get their cheddar, everybody got to eat. I can only speak for my camp. I'm here to fuck the game up, change the fuckin way the White man got this shit formatted and make it easier for all my niggaz. We been gettin fucked over too long in this game. I can only speak for my peeps, we break bread together. Ain't no nigga over hear gonna cry about no check, we gonna get it. It's a fucked up game, but it's cool.

Since you signed the deal with Universal have you learned a lot about this industry?
Me and my brother, we had 7 years experience. If I were to come in the game naked it would be fucked up for me. By us knowin a little something and have our game on tight, we don't have a fucked up situation to be honest with you, we got the best deal in the industry--ever. A lotta niggaz don't be ownin their shit, but I'm here to fuck all that shit up. I play fair by my people, I don't believe in all that bullshit. Money ain't no thing to me, I wanna see my niggaz shine like we all supposed to shine. I've gotta kick big for a lotta muthafuckas in this game who been fuckin up this game, cause anybody who do business with Cash Money, we gonna overpower the decision. Anything dealin with us, we're gonna have a top notch part of it. The old school rules need to be broken.

What made you decide to approach it this way? You and Ron talked about it and decided it needed to be changed?
Far as the business part, I see a lotta fucked up shit. It's really fucked up the way they treat a nigga, the labels. Any nigga fuck with me ain't never had a problem. Any label fuck with me, I'm gonna fuck the game up. They gonna have to get me what the fuck I want or fuck 'em.

So many major artists are so unhappy and stuck in a bad deal with the label.
It's fucked up. I can't believe that shit. It took for me to get to this level to see this

> "WHEN WE SELL A PLATINUM ALBUM WE FEEL LIKE THAT ALBUM JUST DID ALRIGHT, CAUSE ALL OUR SHIT SELL 2 MILLION AND BETTER."

shit. Them niggaz be on TV, they hustlin, but their situation's so fucked. And they ain't got no strength to change that shit. I'm here to change that shit for the better for me and the nigga that come behind me.

I'm happy for you. I believed in you from way back.
If you quote my phrases from way back then, I've always said we can't be fucked with. I studied this game. A lotta shit went on, a lotta niggaz made fucked up decisions. I watched Master P, I watched Puff, I watched Sugg Knight and them, I watched all their good and bad decisions. I baked all they shit with the brains me and my brother got and I'll never make the same decisions they made. I'm gonna go through them same decisions, I'm gonna face the same things they had to face. My decision making is what's gonna bless me to be something bigger than the fuckin Godzilla in this game. •

INTERVIEW WITH GORILLA ZOE

BY GREG "GATE$" DAVENPORT

Where did Gorilla Zoe come from? I was talking to Block a while back and he said he had you on deck and then you just came out of nowhere.
You say you be in Atlanta all the time?

Yeah.
You know where Underground at?

Yeah.
You know where Peachtree at?

Yeah.
You know where The Funk Shop at?

Yeah.
Well there you go. You know that's a big weed trap, right? You know I use to run that, right?

No, I didn't know all that. I don't get into other people's business like that.
That's the history. That's where I come from – downtown.

So I just got to ask the cats in the streets, huh?
Exactly. We had The Funk Shop. I help rebuild Music Media. We put another music store downtown. We went in half and built this studio right there on Peachtree, where Grand Hustle was and where (DJ) Drama was. Muthafuckas just didn't take me serious with the music until I learned how

to work my own equipment and made my own muthafuckin' songs. The shit got in Block's hands and you know Block – he got that real press play button.

How long have you been doing music?
Professionally, a good two years. I've been on the retail side of thangs like SoundScan, promotions, marketing … I use to sell ya'll niggas magazine out the store. I know this game. I've been watching these artists. I did two thangs – I made money how I could make money and I made money through the music stores. I always kept two hustles and both of them were independent grinds. Wasn't no muthafuckin' check.

I like the fact that you actually know the business. Do you think that's going to give you an advantage over other artists?
I've already got an advantage over a lot of other artists because I've been making money and dealing with money my whole life, and dealing with business. Dealing with responsibility nigga, since I was shit, 13. I don't need nobody to tell me to get up in the morning and where this. I don't need a stylist. I appreciate it and I appreciate the people who help me. But, I got an independent mind myself, that's going to wake me up, that's gonna make me talk to whoever the hell want to interview me, thank them for taking the time out of their day for interviewing me. You could be goddamn kicking it with your bitch right now. But, you're interviewing me. Thank you my nigga.

Do you think a lot of rappers aren't appreciative of the opportunities they have before them?
It's gonna show. I did two albums this year – Boyz N Da Hood and my album at the same time. Also, I helped (Yung) Joc with his project. Produced for 8Ball and MJG. This my first year in the game and I'm on Screamfest on, to every hood club in the goddamn South.

What inspired you to do music in the first place?
Everything I take I take it seriously. And everything I got I take it. I wasn't never waiting on the music industry. I had done created a buzz for myself in the street so big before. Everybody already knew Zoe. Atlanta! Nigga, I can sell 100,000 records in Atlanta hand to hand out my muthafuckin' music store. I wasn't never thinking, 'Oh, I need to get in the industry.' It just happened like that. I just thank God that I met a street nigga like Block that knew how to handle me and teach me.

That's why I blew up like that because I'm humble. I don't know it all dawg. And it's niggas that's done been where I'm going and been where I'm at and can teach me. And a nigga like Block is one of them niggas. I listen to that nigga and he keep it gangsta with me. It's gonna be a crazy year. If muthafuckas don't know. If they think that "Hood Nigga" song was just a fluke … It's a movement. That's me and all my folk. Damn that song! My album is stupid!

> "I'VE ALREADY GOT AN ADVANTAGE OVER A LOT OF OTHER ARTISTS BECAUSE I'VE BEEN MAKING MONEY AND DEALING WITH MONEY MY WHOLE LIFE, AND DEALING WITH BUSINESS. DEALING WITH RESPONSIBILITY NIGGA, SINCE I WAS SHIT, 13."

When is the album coming and what is it going to sound like?
Sept. 25 and it's gonna be a classic. I mean classic like "The Chronic." I mean classic like "Me Against The World." I mean classic like Biggie first album. I mean classic like South Circle nigga. 8Ball and MJG "Coming Out Hard"

Who's on the album?
It ain't about who's on the album, man. It's Gorilla Zoe first album and ya'll gonna get to meet Gorilla Zoe. I go hard in the booth. The production on it – how about me and Drumma Boy got six songs in there together. And you know how hot that boy is right now. Me and Jazze (Pha) got two songs together. So, it's like a connection with certain niggas.

How would you describe your sound?
No one sounds like Gorilla Zoe and Gorilla Zoe sounds like no one.

How's it being part of Boyz N Da Hood?
It's been a blessing. That's all it was. We vibe together good and we work together good.

Did they embrace you as part of the group? You know the trouble they had with Young Jeezy situation when that went down. Did you feel like when you were coming in that people were saying "Oh, he's the guy coming in to replace Jeezy."
I felt like any real nigga would feel. I ain't trying to replace shawty. He is him. He's still got his lane. Jeezy do his thang. Big up to Jeezy. What I'm finna do is if ya'll don't fuck around and open the door up I'm finna make a lane for my goddamn self.

What about the people who are saying the music industry is messed up and street albums like the Gorilla Zoe album aren't selling any records?
What I have to say is – You're right. The music industry is fucked up. The reason the streets ain't selling no albums is because the streets buy bootlegs that be on the streets. It's real. But, what I got to say about Gorilla Zoe – Gorilla Zoe is a hustler. Gorilla Zoe is on the Screamfest Tour right now. Where I don't supposed to be saying hood nigga huh? Gorilla Zoe is on "Coffee Shop." Oh yeah, don't think I don't know what's going on.

Do you have any aspirations to be a CEO and doing what Block is doing?
That's what Block is building me to be – a CEO. He's building me for that right now.

Who are the people you plan on bringing out?
I'm finna tell you what's coming next – Block Boys. I'm finna grab from every side and trap in Atlanta. Not just one. I'm finna grab a nigga from every crevice in that bitch. And not just Atlanta. We finna go everywhere … It's more than music. •

INTERVIEW WITH JAY ROCK

BY BLACK DOG BONE • PHOTOS BY MARCUS HANSCHEN

You're the first West Coast artist to sign with Strange Music. How did the deal come together?
I had a couple of labels wanting to sign me. I was just weighing my options. Tech N9ne, a couple of years back he did a video back home in my city. I met Estevan, and we hooked up; since then we've been cool. I've always been a friend of Tech N9ne. He was always up on me cause he was in the underground scene, and he knew about my label situation. So he made a couple of calls to me like, "What's up? I'd love to fuck with you." I was weighing different options, and Strange Music gave me the best offer than all the other labels. So we took it from there.

Do you feel like your music is very different from other music at Strange Music? Do you feel at home there?
I feel like it's family. They welcomed me with open arms. No other label could offer me tours like this. That's what I like to do, I like to be on the road connecting with my fans. That's what Tech N9ne's been doin for years. It's a beautiful thing. They welcomed me and make me feel like family. Every city we went to, it's been all love.

When Tech N9ne first was coming out with the painted face and strange image a lot of the people in the hood didn't accept him. How did the hood react to Tech N9ne, his style of music and the face paint and all of that?
Usually the hood don't mess with it. At first a lotta my homeboys really weren't up on Tech N9ne. He'd been on the underground scene for so long. He's the type of dude who came up without no radio play, no videos, no major label. I always used to tell people they gotta check on him. When I checked out his show it just blowed me away. You just gotta see his live performance. He's one of the best live entertainers ever. A lotta people were sayin he worship the devil and all that. This guy is a wonderful dude. You can't never judge a book by its cover. I took a couple of my homeboys to see his show and that changed their whole mind about Tech N9ne. They like, "Wow, this dude really go!" Music is music. Doesn't matter weather White people love it or Black music. Good music is good music. Music brings everybody together anyway. Now all my niggaz is glad that I made this move. Niggaz in the hood back me up. They like to see the grime. That's what they love about it.

I was happy to hear that you chose to work with Tech N9ne. You come from the street level and Tech comes with the strange and dark. It's going to be good for both you and Tech to reach each other's fans.
Yeah, but you know what's crazy: I've been on this tour right now, the Independent Grind Tour, and I was shocked by how many of the Juggalos and Juggalettes already knew who I was. They knew my songs and they knew my music. It really shocked me, that so many of the Strange Music fans already was up on game for me. That blew my mind. Like I said, music is music, and music is what brings everybody together. When people find good music they love it and stick with it forever.

Juggalos and people who like weird stuff are sometimes pretty open, but it's the people in the hood who can be very closed minded when It comes to something new or unusual. Last year when I talked to you I thought you had another record deal and were about to drop an album. What happened?
I was on Warner Brothers for like 3 years. I thank Warner Brothers for the opportunity that they gave me. Me and my team felt that they weren't for my best interest, cause I had a record with Lil Wayne produced by Cool & Dre—it was one of the biggest records that I ever had. The label didn't have my back 100% for that record. They just let that record go down the drain like that. It was when Time-Warner was makin a lotta changes and it was all typa stuff going on. So my team went in there and got the release, got the walkin papers, and look at me now. I wanna thank Naim Ali for giving me the opportunity to do what I do. I appreciate him for that.

When is your album going to come out on Strange Music?
It's gonna be on at the top of the year. I'm out there coming up with new material. All my fans who've been supporting me since day one—the album is comin. It's comin! It's like 90% done. I'm still in the lab recording. I'm still working.

What does the title "Follow Me Home" stand for?
The title "Follow Me Home" basically means follow me home through my city, through my life. I'm gonna show you the ins and outs through my life, through Watts, the trials and tribulations, what goes on in the hood, in the ghetto. The mind state of a person living in Southcentral, in the gutter. Follow me home and I'ma show you. That's what that title stands for.

Who are some of the people you're working with?
Me and Neyo got something crazy on there. Me and Gucci got something crazy. Me and Yo Gotti did something. Shout out to my boy Kendrick Lamar, Black Hippy—we've got something crazy on there. Producers: Justice League, Tha Bizness, Neyo, DJ Quik, Cool and Dre, 1500, Focus, Sounwave, and possibly a couple big surprises. I've been workin with a lotta different producers.

A lot of artists I interview tell me that they're doing something different from everybody else, but when I hear the record it's not different at all. What about Jay Rock, what makes you different?
It's different when I'm chillin. Once I get at the microphone, that's when the transformation comes. It's a different person.

> "I FEEL LIKE IT'S FAMILY. THEY WELCOMED ME WITH OPEN ARMS. NO OTHER LABEL COULD OFFER ME TOURS LIKE THIS. THAT'S WHAT I LIKE TO DO, I LIKE TO BE ON THE ROAD CONNECTING WITH MY FANS. THAT'S WHAT TECH N9NE'S BEEN DOIN FOR YEARS. IT'S A BEAUTIFUL THING. THEY WELCOMED ME AND MAKE ME FEEL LIKE FAMILY. EVERY CITY WE WENT TO, IT'S BEEN ALL LOVE."

Who's the person that comes out?
It's me. It's the real Jay Rock. When you hear his music you know that's Jay Rock right there. Ain't nobody else like Jay Rock.

What are you bringing to the table?
I'm bringing hit records, that's what I'm bringing. Me and Top Dawg Entertainment, we're bringing hit records and good quality music. Anybody out there who know good quality music and that real shit, be ready. That's what's comin, straight up. It's real. No fake shit. On top of that I'm one of the first dudes outta my city Watts to ever be signed, especially outta my projects. I'm one of the first and the youngest too. That's a big thing right there.

Right now for you to sign with Tech N9ne is bigger than signing with a major. He's the biggest buzz all over the industry. Who is Top Dawg Entertainment?
Top Dawg, that's the label that I'm on. That's my big homey, his name is Top Dawg. He's the owner of the company. The other artists that's on the label are Kendrick Lamar, School Boy Q and Ab-Soul. We've also got a group called Black Hippy. Everybody is workin on their own individual projects too, and we've got a group project coming out. Black Hippy is us four in the studio doin what we wanna do on the microphone. Care free, like back in the days Hippies were able to say what the fuck they wanted to say, do what they wanna do. They spoke their mind. That's what we do on the mic. We go hard, speak our mind and we do what the fuck we wanna do on the microphone.

> "THE TITLE "FOLLOW ME HOME" BASICALLY MEANS FOLLOW ME HOME THROUGH MY CITY, THROUGH MY LIFE. I'M GONNA SHOW YOU THE INS AND OUTS THROUGH MY LIFE, THROUGH WATTS, THE TRIALS AND TRIBULATIONS, WHAT GOES ON IN THE HOOD, IN THE GHETTO. THE MIND STATE OF A PERSON LIVING IN SOUTHCENTRAL, IN THE GUTTER. FOLLOW ME HOME AND I'MA SHOW YOU."

A lot of people misunderstand what the Hippies were all about. What attracted you to the Hippy movement?
Basically that they spoke their mind. They'd get high and speak their mind. That's what I always saw about them when I'd watch it on TV back in the seventies. They do what they do.

What was it like for you when you were growing up and how did you get into music?
I was hardheaded when I was growin up. I had my good times and I had my bad times. Fuckin up in school, gangbangin, doin all this other bullshit. But I always had a talent for music. I don't know why but I always loved music. When I was about 15 all my homies used to rap, and I used to come around and play around with it. Just fuck around with it. But I was always in the street doin what I do. Until one day when my big homey Top Dawg—we come from the same neighborhood, we come from the same struggle—he made it out. I didn't know he was into the music business like that. He heard one of my poems and he was lookin for me. He used to always come through the hood and ask the young cats about me. I thought he was gonna lecture me about something I did, but all the time he was wanting me to do some music. He rolled up on me one day like, "Man, you've got a voice everybody likes. Not just me, but my friends, family. You've got the voice. You need to be in the studio doing this and that. Stick to the rappin." I just took heed. Went to my nigga's studio. He locked me in that muthafucka, and look at me now.

When did you meet Top Dawg?
I've been knowing Top Dawg all my life. He's a big homey from my neighborhood. He'd been through the same struggles and everything. Fortunately he was able to make it out and be successful with his company. That's what we need; we need more older cats like that to come and lecture to young cats and get 'em off he streets, make 'em do something positive. He took me off the negative and turned my negative to a positive.

In America the family structure is really getting broken up. If we don't have family or community we have nothing.
Family is everything. We've all gotta stick together. Straight up.

Did you grow up with your parents?
My mom and my pops separated when I was young. My mama remarried later. He was in my life for the rest of my years. Unfortunately, my real father passed away. But I always had a small family behind me. My family always supported me. That's a blessing right there.

Does Watts have a certain style of Rap?
Straight gutta, man. That's the sound comin from my area. Gutta. That ghetto sound.

Is it very different from the LA Rap we've heard before, people like Ice Cube, Snoop Dogg?
It's different cause it's comin from a new generation. Back in the old days that was their generation. The young cats got that new gutta sound.

What music were you listening to when you were growing up?
I grew up listening to all of them: Ice Cube, Snoop, Dre, DJ Quik, Spice 1, Scarface, Nas, Busta Rhymes, C-Bo. I listened to all them cats.

What are people in your hood listening to now?
They listen to Jay Rock! They listen to Kendrick Lamar. They listen to Glasses Malone. They listen to Black Hippy. They listen to the Lil Wayne's, the Waka Flocka's, the Nicki Minaj's, all that.

You're in the middle of big tour with Tech N9ne and E-40. How is that going?
The tour is going great. All love. We did like 24 cities. Every show been crazy. The energy, the people, it's been real great! No problems, nobody got hurt, nothing but love. We're in Anaheim today. It's my first time being back home in 20-something days. I'm gonna turn it up tonight.

What other tours are up ahead for Jay Rock and Strange Music?
I'm not sure. I heard Tech saying Snoop Dogg wanna do a tour with him. I heard him say Lil Wayne possibly wanna do a tour with him. Hopefully that goes.

Will other Top Dawg artists be coming out under Strange Music too?
No. Top Dawg didn't sign to Strange. We partnered with them. We joined forces, the two companies.

What were some of your earlier songs that got real hot?
When I did that record "Lift Me Up". Shot out to Julio G from out the Bay, he just took the record, cleaned it up and put it on his radio show. That's what did it for me. Julio G was one of the first to spin my record on the radio. I didn't ask him to play it or nothing. He heard it and he cleaned it up for the radio, and played it. That was one of the biggest records right there. After that it was the record I did with Lil Wayne, "All My Life". That was the next big one.

What were some of your favorite records that you did?
"All My Life", cause that's my whole story right there. That's my story, and that was an introduction and it's one of my favorite records of all time. •

How does it feel to be a free man?
It's a blessing and I feel real excited about getting out here and having a second chance to do this music and put it down out here. I'm feeling real good right now and I can't even explain it.

What was the first thing you did when you got out?
When I got out I got a haircut and went shopping. I had a guest appearance at a club in Atlanta that day so I had to get ready for that. When I got out it was like I hit the ground running. I started working that same day, so there has been no rest for me.

Sounds like it's been a hectic schedule for you?
I've been on the road from Tuesday to Sunday every week so that is about five days out of the week doing shows. It's crazy right now and they are feeling me down south so it's real hard work. Also I have been in the lab making new stuff for my new album so I can stay sharp and work at my craft. I'm a real hard worker right now and really I don't get to sleep that much any more.

Do you have a title for the new album?
I'm thinking about a couple of different things, but mainly I been thinking about calling it "Trapathon" like a marathon.

What makes you stick with the Trap music when a lot of cats are doing Crunk or now getting into the whole Snap thing?
I'm a fan of Snap music because of me being from Atlanta, but it's just not me. I like making Trap music for my hood to give the people something that they can relate to. The people from my neighborhood are really not too fond of hearing Snap music. Me personally I like it but I'm more on that Trap because that is what I know.

What is the main difference between the two?
Snap gets the club crunk and it's cool to get the females on the dance floor because I'm a fan of that, but me personally I'm going to keep it gutta at all times.

I commend you for that because I'm sure that being on a major there is a lot of pressure to make that hit single. Do they ever tell you to tone it down a little bit?
No, my label is behind me! I would say they are one hundred percent behind me but they are two hundred percent behind me. Whatever I do they are behind it and have my back at all times. They're like the biggest fans of mine and it's cool because I'll go to the studio do a song and let them hear it and they get so excited about each song. They love that shit!

I'm sure this time around you have a lot more to say about all that you have been through! Are you getting more personal on this one?
I'm going to put a lot of my personal life experiences on there and pull as hard as I can. Right now I have a lot of ears and attention and I plan to use that to my advantage. I'm going to be heard and respected and now I have a chance to show and prove what I'm about and I know I'm going to do this. I have the talent to do it, but I'm gonna come so hard this time that it will be a wrap!

When you were locked up did you meet any talent on the inside?
There's a lot of talent in there and a lot of guys that are tight because I used to rock every day with them. A lot of people will hear my stuff and say that they already heard that when they were locked up with me because I was rappin' in there. I was like "I'm one of ya'll!" There is so much talent in jail right now!

When will you release the "Trapathon" album?
My last album sold about 130,000 copies while I was incarcerated and I did no promotion on the album because I was locked up the whole time. I was released one time on the day that my album actually dropped but about a month later I got locked up for six months straight. I didn't have no time to promote the album and it did its numbers strictly on word of mouth. People just respect the way that I'm putting shit down! I'm trying to push "Trap House" to at least 2-300,000 copies sold once we drop the single to my new video called "Go Ahead" which is now blowing up. I would have to say at least the late summer before that one comes out because I still wanna promote "Trap House".

You want to make up for all the time you missed promoting the album.
I'm glad you feel me because some people keep saying, "Drop some new shit!" My album is hard as fuck and it's classic shit, but a lot of people didn't even hear it yet. We got to play our position and do it but I'm not mad at all because I like being the underdog. I've been an underdog all my life anyway and that inspires you to grind harder. I'm so used to struggling and making what I got to work for me. I got people that want to help me and care about me and tell me they are behind me and that is a blessing to me.

Pimp C is out, you're out, Project Pat is out, but what would you say to Turk and C-Murder who are still locked up?
I'm big fans of all those guys that you just named and my advice to them is to keep their heads up and remember that they can't hold you forever. It might have been over for me and look what happened. I got another shot and the doors can open for them too!

What kind of production are you working with this time around?
I'm fuckin' with Shawty Redd, Ice, Frank Nitty, and I will reach out to a couple other people. I have a couple more surprises, but I'm going to I wanna keep the same people that I had on my first album because they're the shit. I'm trying to reach out to a couple of big name producers but I like keeping it gutter. It ain't even about the beat; I can go crazy on any beat. Why go to a big name producer and spend all this money when instead you can save money and put it all in your pocket?

I think the production is better from the underground because those cats have more hunger!
And you have to have that heat though. If there are cats who got some beats who are hungry you gotta fuck with them if their shit is hard. Don't just run to a bigger name out there and get some bullshit because you could get tighter shit from a dude coming up. You have to fuck with the hungry cats! This is where Hip Hop started back when people didn't have no money. Now people are spending crazy money.

> "MY LABEL IS BEHIND ME! I WOULD SAY THEY ARE ONE HUNDRED PERCENT BEHIND ME BUT THEY ARE TWO HUNDRED PERCENT BEHIND ME. WHATEVER I DO THEY ARE BEHIND IT AND HAVE MY BACK AT ALL TIMES. THEY'RE LIKE THE BIGGEST FANS OF MINE AND IT'S COOL BECAUSE I'LL GO TO THE STUDIO DO A SONG AND LET THEM HEAR IT AND THEY GET SO EXCITED ABOUT EACH SONG. THEY LOVE THAT SHIT!"

What will be the major difference between "Trapathon" and "Trap House"?
I'm a better rapper and I have had more practice. My delivery got better and I have been writing raps over and over again and you can hear the determination in my voice when I rap. I'm just a better rapper! It will be a way more change from my first album.

It was looking bad for you for a minute.

How did you get out of that mess?
The people looked at the evidence and the evidence said that I was not guilty of the murder charge and they had to let me go. The folks done their job!

Do you think the prosecution jumped the gun in going after you so quick?
I really can't say why, but I look at it that I am glad that I am out. I got this behind me and it's time for me to push on and I don't hold no grudge with nobody. I'm just trying to stay positive and keep going.

You are very humble and honest. Have you always been like that?
Yeah, because I grew up in a small town in Alabama real poor! I grew up in Bessemer Alabama and that's like 20 minutes away from Birmingham. It's a real small and poor town!

How long did you live there?
I stayed there until I was nine years old and then I moved to Atlanta. A lot of cats will tell you they are from the "A", and I have been here in the "A" for fifteen years since I was nine years old. To me it's not about where you are from but how you come! I go to all kinds of towns and will do a show in a country ass town somewhere in Alabama, Florida, Georgia or Mississippi just rockin' that shit because that's where I come from. You have to do what you have to do! The "A" is where I get my slang from and everything, but being a country boy from where I was born is what keeps me humble.

A lot of rappers are real fuckin' arrogant but there is no need for that shit!
The only time that I'm arrogant is when I am on the mic. It's like a pro football player when they are on the field they are tearing each others head off but then they go home and play with their children! Even with a boxer, he uses his hands to punch someone in the face but at the end of the night he uses the same hands to caress his woman. If you think about it like I do then you will see, because I'm always a street nigga but at the same time I'm not a fool because I graduated from high school and went to college.

What did you go to college for?
I went to college for computer programming but they dropped me because I got caught with a whole bunch of crack. It ain't nothing to be proud of, but I have really been in the streets ever since then. They told me to get out or if I had the money to pay for the books I was supposed to have because they took the scholarship away. I could've continued it but I said fuck it.

Before the crack charge did you get a chance to learn about computers?
I learned a little but not a lot, because I was halfway in the streets and halfway in the school. I coulda done it if I had put my mind to it, but I was trying to make some money.

How much time did you get on the crack charge?
It was my first offense and I did about 90 days in the county and about three years probation and that was back in '97/'98.

> "MY ALBUM IS HARD AS FUCK AND IT'S CLASSIC SHIT, BUT A LOT OF PEOPLE DIDN'T EVEN HEAR IT YET. WE GOT TO PLAY OUR POSITION AND DO IT BUT I'M NOT MAD AT ALL BECAUSE I LIKE BEING THE UNDERDOG. I'VE BEEN AN UNDERDOG ALL MY LIFE ANYWAY AND THAT INSPIRES YOU TO GRIND HARDER. I'M SO USED TO STRUGGLING AND MAKING WHAT I GOT TO WORK FOR ME. I GOT PEOPLE THAT WANT TO HELP ME AND CARE ABOUT ME AND TELL ME THEY ARE BEHIND ME AND THAT IS A BLESSING TO ME."

It worked out though because now you got a major rap career going.
I'm doing it real big and when I go to the mall I run into the same people I went to school with and they ask me for my autograph. They tell me that their kids or brothers listen to my shit all the time and it makes me feel good. I could have been locked up or killed a long time ago. I was living a treacherous ass life and I'm blessed that I got a chance to do something like this because I won't let anybody down. A lot of people want to see me do good and I don't want to disappoint them. •

DROOP-E INTERVIEW

BY SCOTT BEJDA • PHOTO BY MARCUS HANSCHEN

You are one of the most promising new producers in the Bay right now. Do you feel a lot of pressure on you?
Yes and no. At the end of the day my main thing from the beginning is to be different. When other people in the Bay or anywhere in nation start using the same sounds that I use or the same drum patterns as I do then I will switch it up. The only pressure on me is to be different. If everybody else starts making what I am making then I ain't got the problem to take four months to a year off to make something new, because that's what I do. I am an artist.

You want to stand apart from the crowd.
Exactly! I'm trying to be a Vincent Van Gogh and not Michael Johnson. I want to be someone you will remember. The only pressure I have is to be different and to not keep coming with the same stuff.

How long does it take you to make a beat?
Sometimes it could take five minutes and sometimes it could take the whole day. It just depends on how comfortable I get. I am real grateful to be able to make music in my home or wherever I am at. I don't just sit there and pound my brain though. I might make something and then go chill for awhile a d then get right back on it. Sometimes it could take anywhere from five to forty-five minutes. It depends on what I am doing in between.

Do you think the Bay got its fair share of attention from the whole Hyphy movement? Or do you think the media just labeled it as a fad and moved on?
It could have got a lot more if everybody kept on doing different things. You know how they say the glory years in the Bay was between '92 and '96? I was born in '88, so I seen all that too. But my glory years in the Bay was between '03 and '05, because that was when we were the hungriest I feel. If you go back and listen you will see that we had our own shit. At one point I remember people in the Bay were doing some New York shit and one point there were some that was doing the South shit, but at one point they was like, "We just gonna do what we do, fuck it!" That was my favorite time in the Bay. Those are my favorite years! The thing that I like is when people switch it up. After the Bay blew up you had a lot of people trying to do what the next man was doing or try to do whatever was hot on the radio. That almost made the Bay look corny. When my Pops (E-40) did "Tell Me When To Go" you could hear in his verses and even in Keak Da Sneak's verses that they were still talking about street shit. My whole point is that song "Tell Me When To Go" was to paint a picture for the whole

world. I think that my pops painted a pretty good picture to the nation. It shows the real and it wasn't goofy, because we are really not goofy out here.

It's some serious shit going on in the Bay.
Yeah, because somebody might be going dumb and next thing you know there might be some gunshots. That song painted a great picture and it was necessary, but that doesn't mean everybody in the Bay has to talk about the same stuff. In the Bay we still can take it to the top, and I still support the Hyphy movement as long as people switch it up. Don't say, "We are gonna do a Hyphy song!" Just switch it up!

"ALL THIS SLANDEROUS TALK WITHOUT TEACHING ANYBODY ANYTHING AT THE END OF THE DAY IS KIND OF STUPID. YOU GOT ALL THESE KIDS OUT IN THE STREETS WHO DON'T HAVE NOTHING GOING FOR THEMSELVES AND THEY SEE THIS RAPPER ON TV WITH THESE CHAINS TALKING ABOUT HOW HE SLANGS DOPE ALL DAY."

E-40 really set that blueprint to be yourself and do your own thing. I think that is why he has been in the game for so long.
At the end of the day he believes in originality, even with his older stuff until now, because back then he didn't try to sound like anybody. As soon as he gets on you already know who it is!

Very few people can rap that long and still be able to speak to all the newer generations that are coming up like that. I think that passed on to you because you are a monster with the beats!
I appreciate that, man.

What about the rapping?
The last album I put out I was 17, I was a kid. I learned a lot in a few years. The way I feel right now I will keep rapping, but I just rap on what I want to rap. I just concentrate on Sick Wid It. There's only a handful of rappers that I even like right now in the whole nation. I got a lot of love for people, but as far as people who are talented and are doing different things the numbers are limited.

There are so many rappers. It's hard to see the fire for the smoke.
All this slanderous talk without teaching anybody anything at the end of the day is kind of stupid. You got all these kids out in the streets who don't have nothing going for themselves and they see this rapper on TV with these chains talking about how he slangs dope all day. They think that is how you get there! On that whole album they don't talk about the other side of things and what comes with that package. I will not sell myself out as a man and talk about the same bullshit that everyone else is talking about

Who are the few artists that you do bump today?
I got a list in no specific order. First I think that my Pops is one of the greatest rappers from the originality, longevity, delivery and all of that combined. I also like Lil' Wayne, Andre 3000, Turf Talk, Juelz Santana, Jay-Z and I also listen to a lot of other forms of music.

You are just musical period!
I listen to rap, but my whole perspective is always changing, because I can't sit and listen to the next man's craft all day if I feel I can do that. I listen to people that when you hear their voice you automatically know who it is and they don't try to switch it up as far as trying to sound like anybody else.

At what age did you start producing?
I was fifteen!

How big of an influence was your Dad?
He was about 95%. I was ready for my whole life. If it wasn't for music I don't know where I would be. This was a big influence on my life and seeing where music can get you and me being here from the beginning. What my Pops did was give me the opportunity. I wasn't just sitting in my room one day and said, "Hey can I get a studio?" When he got it for me it was because he saw me sneaking around playing on Triton keyboards. He saw I was hungry for it and he got me this damn TC-88 Keyboard; it's basically just a controller and he seen how I made things work. My main influence in general is god and my Pops.

How much of a factor does your spiritual vision play in your life?
You can work your whole life, but if you look at it, with global warming or if we get bombed, all that stuff you worked for is gone. You can do some shady shit and get some money and then suffer for eternity, You can't take your money with you. I have been seeing some crazy shit!

Seeing the crazy shit has to humble you?
By far! Right now scientists are really tripping out because they realized that we are made of energy. The whole universe is made up of energy, but where did that energy come from in the beginning? What holds the body together? A lot of Scientists are turning to religion because they realized that the energy had to come from somewhere and just didn't pop up. When people look at Katrina, and all these things happening it's like, "What else can I do but keep my faith?" He was there with me when I was bullshitting living the rappers life fucking all the hoes and doing that dumb shit and he kept me alive long enough for me to come back to him. I'm grinding and one day I would like to show people that you can grind to get to your goal and still keep your faith in him. Some people look at religion as rules, but at the end of the day it's not about rules. It all comes down to how you would like to love somebody and how you would like to be loved. I just want to show people that there is another way!

You were just a little kid when your dad put out "Federal", and all those classic albums. Do you ever go back and listen to that stuff now?
Yeah, and I understand that he was spitting the same stuff that they say nowadays. A lot of stuff he was saying back then people are just saying now. He was ahead of his time. If you go back to "The Element Of Surprise", that album is killing almost everybody right now.

Do you have any projects in the works?
I'm working on this "Sick Wid It Umbrella" compilation to showcase all of the talent that we got over here. I'm also working on the "Bay Bridge 2" compilation, which I got Yukmouth, Too Short and others on there. I'm showing the new generation and the older generation. I'm switching it! •

LIL FLIP

BY BLACK DOG BONE • PHOTO BY MATT SONZALA

You freestyle a lot. Do you freestyle more than you write?
It depends on the vibe. Some beats might be throwed, where I be like do I wanna write or do I wanna freestyle. It depends on what kinda mood I'm in. sometimes I might freestyle just to get the style I wanna rap. It depends on if I'm feeling the beat like that. I write half. I freestyle half. If I don't like it, then what I freestyle, I take pieces out of it and put it together like that.

The Freestyle King title, I understand there's been some controversy behind that?
I met Screw a couple of years ago, through one of my friends named Jason. He used to rap with me, but he died of cancer. When I hooked up with he was like, if you can freestyle, rap. Most people tell you they can rap and they be scared to rap on the spot. I was just freestylin' about stuff I was doin', what I did that day, what kind of car he had. It was like he put me on the spot and said if you can rap, rap. So I just rapped, and he was like man, you cool and I want you to come do some tapes with me. And I hooked up with him and he was like, man you freestyle for hours. The first Screw tape I did was called "Southside Still Holdin'". I had freestyled 10 minutes straight, just rappin' and Screw was like, man, you the Freestyle King. You don't never stop rappin'. After he told me that and gave me a plaque for it, he put me in the Screwed-up Click. I just kept the name.

I was looking at the Source article on you and the picture with you and KeKe has a caption under it that says, "Family Feud." What's that about; were they serious or were they just causing drama?
I don't know. They ain't tell us nothing like that. What they told us is this is an interview about the Screwed-Up Click. We need you and KeKe there. They ain't tell us the title or nothin'. I ain't know it was gon be no Family Feud and all that. I ain't got nothin' against KeKe or nobody. They did that on they own.

Everybody knows that recently you were shot. I just want you to set the record straight and tell everybody what happened.
They don't want me to talk about it much, but basically, I was leaving the studio and somebody just pulled up on the side of us and started shooting at me. I was on the passenger side. They were going fast. We was in a whole 'nother lane. We stopped and they flew by. It was hard for 'em just to, cause we went a whole 'nother way. They started shooting and I got shot. Like in the ribs. I was blessed because the bullet went through the door and it slowed t down, so the bullet ain't go through. I'm alright. It just fractured one rib

and that's it. I got out the next day.

I heard you still had a bullet in your chest. Is it out?
Yeah, it's out. When that happened, it just made me realize you just can't be out like that. If you on TV and people consider you a star, you can't just put yourself out there like that. I was just comin' from the studio going home. But some stuff you can't do cause you never know who's watching. It just made me realize, man, everybody ain't gon like you, regardless of how much you do, how much money you spend, whatever. We always got somebody who ain't gon like you. If you a star and all that, you gotta make it so people can't get to you that easy. It just made me open up my eyes. What I do, who I'm around, all that stuff. Can you tell me why you think they did it? Man, I don't know. I think it's probably some jealousy. I'm sellin' all the records. I got Jags, Benzes, all kind of stuff. I don't know what it was. You know, I don't mess over nobody. I don't mess with too many people, either, so I don't know.

I know you said it's changed how you do things. Has it changed your wanting to be a rap star?
It changed everything, like a whole 360 degrees. I mean, it was fun going on the road, doin' this, doin' that. Now it's like, alright, this is my job, you know what I mean? It just made me observe more. Cause it's like, bein' in the music industry, you got so much stuff comin' at you. You got girls, promoters, you got all kind of stuff comin' your way, just fast, boom, boom, boom. It's hard for you to weed all that stuff out. But now it's like I don't let nobody get close to me. It just made me realize you gotta watch everybody. That's the bottom line. You gotta get in the show go do the show, and leave. Just like that.

Do you think you'll ever get out of that mind frame?
It's like this, no matter what I do, no matter how much money I got., every day I get up I'm gon be like, damn, I got shot. You gon always feel more protective now. Like, you gon think that anybody could do something. It's just crazy. You gon think about it every day. No matter what you doin'.

I've heard that you were gonna get a label deal with Universal or with Loud. What's going on?
We signed with Sony. I mean, we was gettin' offers from everybody. We were gonna sign with Def Jam, but the way they work, they wanna take all, they don't wanna give nobody no money. They just do the artist bad. You'll be famous, but you'll be broke. Basically, Sony—everything we asked for, we got it. We got creative control. They not in it just to make money. They wanna make sure that we straight, we comfortable. It's a label deal and an artist deal. So we signed a $22 million dollar deal with Sony.

What's the next project to come out on Sucka Free Records?
My album, it's called Underground Legend. It'll be out in July. I got Lil Ron and Shasta. Shasta is my cousin; he sing all the hooks. They comin' out. Shasta and Lil Ron's album is called "Mind Ya Business" and we got Papa Reu now. He signed with us. And we're working on Papa Reu's stuff. Basically we doin' it all. I got a movie about my life, how I made it rappin' and all that. I'm almost finished with that. I'm finna shoot my video for my new single, "This is the Way We Ball" next month. I'm just doin' it all.

> "IT JUST MADE ME REALIZE, MAN, EVERYBODY AIN'T GON LIKE YOU, REGARDLESS OF HOW MUCH YOU DO, HOW MUCH MONEY YOU SPEND, WHATEVER. WE ALWAYS GOT SOMEBODY WHO AIN'T GON LIKE YOU. IF YOU A STAR AND ALL THAT, YOU GOTTA MAKE IT SO PEOPLE CAN'T GET TO YOU THAT EASY."

I keep hearing rumors about some beef between you and other members of the Screwed-Up Click. Are any of them true?
I mean, it's like competition and everybody gon compete to try to be the best. But we done squashed all that. Me and ESG squashed the beef, and me and KeKe ain't never had no beef. Basically ain't no beef between me and nobody, cause we all make money. We all doin' our thing, so we squashed all that.

How do you think the game has changed since Screw has passed?
Now, it's gonna be harder for some people. If you not an established artist already with a name already, like if you not a part of Swisha House, or Screwed-Up Click, it's gon be hard. It's even harder now because it's so many people tryin' to rap now. Screw's done mixtapes, I came out, doin' underground. I'm the first artist to do my underground, and put 'em out. I got 10 different volumes. I sold a lotta undergound records. Now everybody else tryin' to do undergound records. It's like what people see you do, they gon try to copy it. It's gettin overcrowded. It's so many people wanna rap. It's so many people tryin' to do undergrounds now. Everything has changed. •

KRIZZ KALIKO

BY BLACK DOG BONE • PHOTOS BY MARCUS HANSCHEN

Strange Music artists all stand as unique individuals. Krizz Kaliko is very different from Tech N9ne and Kutt Calhoun is different from you. All of you are original and have your own sound. I think that is one of the successes of Strange Music.
I feel the same way. I know I make a lot of sports references and I do that because of the science of the team. Tech is the quarter back, but you can't win the game with just a good quarter back. The wide receiver has to be talented, the running back has to be talented, and you have to have a good line to block. He is a great quarter back but to make a successful team everybody has got to be elite. I would consider myself either the running back or the wide receiver because my job for years is to support Tech and to help with making him as big as possible and making his music as elite as possible. I am not separating from him at all and I will always be a part of his show, but it's also time for everybody to see me not as the Tech N9ne dude. Cause forever they be like, "Oh, the Tech N9ne dude!" Now it's time for you to see Krizz Kaliko and for me to come out of his shadow and be like, "Oh, this dude can stand on his own two feet and show you some elite talent." Tech always says, "You guys were surprised at Krizz Kaliko but I always knew and that is why I always have him with me." He had influenced me so much that there would be no Krizz Kaliko without Tech N9ne. He influenced me so much, but not to the point to where I would have to mimic him. He is not an influence to copy off of, but more like a coach. He would say, "When you get on a song you have to annihilate them!" Before I was with him I went to his shows and I saw how super energetic he was and I was like, "I have to match his energy and even exceed his energy to keep his show going." It taught me in the process of growing as a company and growing as a Tech N9ne act, and it taught me when I do my own shows I have to keep it turned up the entire time. I can't wait for you to see my solo show. My solo show is like super energy the whole time.

When you watch artists like the Temptations, James Brown or the Supremes they were entertainers to the max the way they would dance and do the whole show. I always felt like in Rap that was missing. Strange Music brought it back.
We think the same way and we saw what was missing. I think that Strange Music was the missing link in Rap. There are a few people who are making their shows entertaining like Busta Rhymes, he is just giving it to them, and Black Eyed Peas are entertaining. I know some people are like, "Those acts are Pop," but they are entertaining. Run DMC and Public Enemy use to be like that back in the day. That's another reason why there probably won't be another label like Strange Music or artists like the Strange Music artists because we are entertaining. You don't even have to know our music to like the show.

That's right. Anybody can just walk in to a Strange Music show and they'll get blown away! I remember seeing Run DMC and Public Enemy a long time ago when I was just getting into rap; after seeing them I was sold on it. I would run to the record store and get all their records.
That's what people do with Strange. If someone invites them to a concert they watch me, Tech N9ne or someone else, and they go out and buy our shit. They're like, "I went to the merch booth and bought all your CD's because I didn't know. My friend told me it was the best concert I could ever go to and I didn't believe them, so I had to come. Now I went to the merchandise booth and bought all the CD's." I hear that every single night that we're on the road.

When Strange Music was first getting started a lot of people were closed minded and couldn't get into what you were doing. A lot of Rap fans thought Tech N9ne was too weird, not street or Gangsta enough. Now everybody loves Strange Music. Now Tech doesn't have to prove anything. He can just do what he does, and people know he can be street or gangsta and is a phenomenal entertainer.
What that is, Black Dog, is the imagery. I would say that the regular typical Black Rap fan wants to see what you look like. If it's not something that they are use to seeing, they reject it. I would have to say the White fans generally want to see wild and crazy and the Black fans typically like to see if you look like the last dude that they really liked. That is sad to say and I really hate to say it, but the bottom line is once they hear the music they are hooked whether they are Black, White or whatever. They are hooked! My new album cover is crazy; you might see it and think that it is not even Hip Hop. If you are the type that wants to see me with a big gold chain on in front of a car then you might be turned off, but if you listen to it you will be like, "That dude can for real rap!" The part that I think would scare your typical Rap fan is the imagery. That is one of the reasons why I named my album "Shock Treatment", because I have to have a shocking affect on everything. The shows are shock treatment, the music is shock treatment, the imagery is shock treatment. I felt like that is what we have been giving them for years and that is why I named my album that.

A lot of people feel like they're gangsta and tough because they carry a gun, but that is not gangsta. Gangsta to me comes from the inner. Any fool can have a gun and pull a trigger.
To me gangsta is being daring, being brave, and taking a chance. Anyone can have a gun, but are you really gonna shoot this nigga face to face in broad daylight? That's what our music is. I'm not saying we are killing people on the music, but we are brave enough musically to pull it out in board daylight. We're not just following conventions, we are stepping out there and doing what we believe. I think that the thing that associates us with being gangsta is one word and that is "fearless". Our music is fearless, our stage show is fearless and our imagery is fearless.

You bring something different! When you first started to hear NWA, Too Short, C-Bo or Ice Cube it was exciting because you hadn't heard anything like that before. Now twenty years later the ghetto stories have been told and retold many times. Let's hear the ghetto stories presented in a new way. I feel Strange Music is bringing that, and Krizz Kaliko is bringing that.
I say we are gonna tell a ghetto story over a different sound in music to where you might talk about something in the hood, but we are gonna talk about it over a whole Rock song. That is daring and something that is fresh. People have seen Rock and Rap merged together, but the way that we do it is the whole Strange Music sound.

When you first met Tech N9ne how long ago was that?
That was in late 1999. They were first getting ready to start up Strange Music and I met

Tech over at Icy Rock's house. Icy Rock was the producer in town and he use to be Tech's producer. Tech had got some deals and went out of town on his own. When he came back to Kansas City going to work with Icy Rock again I was Icy Rock's protégé, and he was like, "Man you should put Krizz on something!" So I paid Tech to get on the song with me and he was really impressed and started to ask me to help him with his music and we kind of formed Strange Music with Travis at that time. I helped Tech with a couple of songs and it was inevitable that I become part of the camp at that time.

You go back to the beginning of Strange Music?

Yeah, Tech was already out at that time but this was the beginning of Strange Music. At that point and over the years I kind of became the glue of Strange Music. If you would ask, "What is your position at Strange Music?" of course I would say "artist" because that is the obvious answer, but what I really am is the glue at Strange Music, musically the glue. There is not a Strange Music album that comes out without me on several songs. I am responsible for writing for several artists too. They do hooks without me, but I am really responsible for coming up with the bulk of the hooks and especially the hits that are on everybody's album. That's what I like to do. I am like, "Hey man, if you are gonna have me on five songs on your album then give me the ones that you want to be the hits." That is what I do. That is what I mean by when I say the glue. Travis holds the business together, Tech is the blueprint for artists on the label, and musically I feel like the glue because you can't put all of these different pieces together without the glue.

How much input does Tech have with all the Strange Music artists behind the scenes?

He knows that every artist is different and he will say, "I don't want Scooby to sound like me, or I don't want Krizz to sound like me." He knows what kind of artists they are and what they do. He use to be involved with a lot of the writing on the other artists albums, and I mean besides his own verses. But now he trusts the artists so much that he lets you do your own verses, and he might come in at the end and say, "Man you should add this!" and change stuff. He usually comes in and tries to put some butter on it. The influence that he has is that you have to be elite and murdering them on every song. We got a friendly competition here. We all push each other; it's friendly competition because we push each other to be the best.

A lot of people in Kansas City grew up listening to Bay Area Rap, and the Kansas sound is very influenced by the Bay. It's good music, but I feel Kansas City needs its own sound.

I think that is what separates us. I don't think you can classify my music as just Kansas City. One thing I learned from Tech when I started was: Make your music to travel! Kansas City is gonna love you too, but make your music to travel around the world. And that is what I do.

That is one of the reasons I like Tech and

> "IT JUST MADE ME REALIZE, MAN, EVERYBODY AIN'T GON LIKE YOU, REGARDLESS OF HOW MUCH YOU DO, HOW MUCH MONEY YOU SPEND, WHATEVER. WE ALWAYS GOT SOMEBODY WHO AIN'T GON LIKE YOU. IF YOU A STAR AND ALL THAT, YOU GOTTA MAKE IT SO PEOPLE CAN'T GET TO YOU THAT EASY."

the whole Strange Music camp. So many artists that I've heard out of Kansas City have had that Bay influence and that's cool, but we have heard that forever. Let me hear something from Kansas that is different. Tech really brought that; I think Strange Music really put Kansas on the map.

Really it is because of that philosophy, because we make our music for the world including Kansas City, including California, Brazil, France and whatever. We make our music for the world and I think that is why the world is paying attention.

I know a lot of people who just love Strange Music. Then you have these Juggalo types who are just mad about Strange Music. I was at the Gathering of the Juggalos, and people were paying $25 for Murder Dog posters of Tech N9ne. Everybody loves us, from the Juggalos to the Punk rockers to regular Rap fans. Everybody loves us and that is our advantage. I target everybody.

It is not one dimensional. You can do the biggest show at the Gathering and then do Rock the Bells and get that Rock crowd.

It is so exciting to be accepted everywhere. I saw this Visa commercial where they said MasterCard was not accepted and this was not accepted but Visa…Everywhere you want to be. I was like "That's our philosophy too, that's crazy!" I never thought about it until I saw that commercial. MasterCard is not accepted everywhere. There is something that is attached to them where retailers are not going to let you use that card there. That limits them! We need to be Visa!

This year all I hear anybody talk about is Strange Music. Where do you see this all heading? Do you think about it?

We see it! We planned for this! I saw an interview with Jim Carey several years ago where they asked him, "You are getting 7 million dollars a movie; are you surprised?" He said, "No, I was just wondering what day this was going to happen on!" That is the same philosophy that we have. We meant to be the biggest label in the world. We are the biggest independent label in the world and becoming the biggest label in the world. I want to be the biggest artist in the world. I say that with a little bit if hesitation because I see how Michael Jackson lived his life. I want to be the biggest artist in the world. I love Jay-Z, Lil Wayne, Alicia Keys and I am not taking anything away from them, but I don't think that there is anything better than us. I don't think there is nobody better than us. We are operating on the same playing field as any elite artist that you love.

Jay-Z is a major Pop artist but he doesn't have that underground feel, that "starting from nothing" feel. It is a whole different feeling.

You can't put it in a box! You can categorize a lot of rappers but you cannot categorize us. I call my stuff "Hip Pop". I mean the most popular Hip Hop there could be.

When you start doing your disco routine and getting naked on stage it's over. I will come to see every Strange Music show.

Naw hell naw dog!! I might take my shirt off. I have to look like 50 Cent before I take my shirt off though. I dropped like 80 lbs and I need to drop another 60. I need that X-Factor.

When I saw you at the Gathering of the Juggalos you looked a lot thinner.

You probably never seen me in person before, plus I dropped like 80 lbs since the last photo shoot we did.

How did you lose all that weight?
I don't eat beef or pork and I work out like 5 days a week. I want to enjoy life. I am raising a son and I want to be able to enjoy life with him. I want him to be able to play sports with me. That is probably the most important factor. I don't want any road blocks. I want my stage show to be elite too.

I feel like the whole Strange Music camp really cares about the fans. When you go to see a Strange Music concert you know you will be entertained for real.
That is another reason why I wanted to work out. When I was 350 lbs we were still giving them a show, but I was super tired and was falling to the ground when we got off stage and I was sick. Now when I get off stage I feel like I can do that again. It takes some people several work hours to come up with enough money to be able to pay for a ticket at our show and I'm not about to be up there just slacking. I want you to feel like you got your money's worth because you paid to come see me. I wanted to work out so I could be on top of my game, so I am not slacking. Even if we are doing 50 shows in a row I want the 48th night to be just as hype as the first night.

I hope that one day Tech N9ne and the whole Strange Music camp will do experimental new styles of Rap, even if you use different names, just break all the rules. That would show everybody how talented all of the artists in Strange Music are.
We do talk about that. That is one of the things that we do where we push our talent even further. I will talk to Tech and we will be like, "Let's do this, or let's try to do a whole Rock album!" Believe me we have already talked about it, and those plans are already in the works.

It would be amazing if you and Tech would work with people like DJ Diplo out of Philadelphia. He did music with M.I.A. and remixed Gucci Mane's album. The clubs would go crazy for that.
Hook me up with him! I'm ready. You need to plug me in with anybody who you think is elite. We need to be like the Super Friends. Strange Music has got the crossover crowd, the Rock crowd, the Rap crowd, and I am just hoping you can get the club crowd.
I don't want to stop until I got the world. I feel like I can get down with the Techno folks just like I can get down with the Juggalos, just like I can get down with the Metal-heads and just like I can get down with the Hip Hop heads and the R & B'er.

A lot of rappers shy away from anything tribal like face paint or tribal clothing, even dancing. All of those elements are in our roots in every race and culture. I wish African American people could be more comfortable with their roots.
That's where Tech even got all of this from, from tribal people. When he paints his face he calls it "the war paint", and when we go on stage it's time to "go to war". It's time to be fearless. He talks about it in his songs, "My face paint is tribal." It doesn't represent a certain tribe, but it represents that whole feeling, cause that is our roots. But your typical Rap crowd is used to seeing the same looking people, the same dudes with the name brands on. We like all that too, but we want to show you something different in addition to that. We all got diamonds, we all got gold chains, watches, cars, all of that, but we don't push that forward. When you see us on stage we got on work clothes. We got on scrubs. On the new tour we've got Dickies on with embroidered name patches like we work in a factory or something. We're the hard blue collar workers of the Rap industry. We don't come out on stage with chains and jewelry on. We have no jewelry when we hit that stage. We come on stage with face paint and with kick-ass mentality.

Jewelry and cars are cool, we know you have it, but show us something different.
The typical Rap fan expects that, and they're measuring and prejudging the rapper off of the size of his chain. With us, once you've heard

one song in our show you forget all about that stuff. We just did a show in Vegas with a bunch of superstar rappers, and I know we shined. I know we stood out from everybody else there because of our performance.

That's what I've loved about Tech N9ne from the beginning. He's in touch with the tribal roots. That's his power. We all need to make that connection with our tribal roots, and Tech N9ne is the only rapper I see doing that.
Maybe the rest of the Rap community doesn't think that's important. But even if it's not important to you when you see our show you're gonna love it. No matter what your objective is when you go to a Strange Music show, we're gonna entertain you and you're gonna enjoy it.

Tech N9ne has a dark feel to his music. Does your music also have that kind of darkness?
The darkness in my music—I reflect on the mental balance that I've had throughout my life. When I have a song called "Bi-Polar", I've been diagnosed as bi-polar and I'm gonna tell you what I experienced. There's a way that I can tell you the story in song form. I have a song called "Anxiety" and guess what that song makes you feel when it comes on? It makes you anxious. Everybody turns up when I do that song in concert. Music is my therapy. I've been to psychologists and I've been on medication. I'm supposed to be on medication now, but I'm not as bad on tour. You know why I'm not as bad on tour? Because I have that outlet on stage where I can get out all the kicking and screaming that I need to do. I can do it on stage! That's therapeutic to me. When I'm at home I don't have that outlet and I usually need some help.

Better that you don't take that medication. They can call you bi-polar or whatever; they call anything that's not normal a sickness. What you have is powerful emotions and wild energy. You need to celebrate those qualities, not try to kill them and numb yourself with drugs.
I've never heard it put like that. That's beautifully put, Black Dog! Now that I think about it, I only thought I was crazy because I was different from the norm. The way I think and act is not the regular way of thinking or being. When something's not normal, when you can't generalize something they say that's crazy. They told me I was bi-polar, but once I started going to my group meetings with my psychologist, like group sessions, everybody in there that was supposedly "crazy" were all super creative people. Once we got to talking we figured out that all of us were artists of some type. Some of us painted, some of us wrote songs, some did crafty things. All of these creative people were considered crazy by society.

Creative people are wild and free thinking. Their minds haven't been programmed to work in the system. People like that don't work good with the system; they can't be controlled or domesticated.
I tell my wife all the time, I hate to be away from my wife—she's sitting right here next to me while I do this interview—I tell her all the time that I can't work a 9 to 5. I used to work for what is now T Mobile for 5 years. I was going literally insane sitting in that cubical. Every morning hittin that alarm, I was going crazy dong that job. I did not fit there. Even though I did a good job and I made it to manager, but I never fit in there. That's why I'm so happy I can live based on my creativity, cause I can never work another 9 to 5. I don't blend in—I don't look like I blend in and I don't act like I blend in with anybody.

That medication they give is made to control you. It will suck all your creativity out of you. The drugs are made to normalize you so that you can do a 9 to 5.
I used to take a drug called Theraquil and it would make me mentally a zombie. I couldn't even think of writing lyrics when I was on it. It zapped my personality. My personality does have its shortcoming. The flipside of my being creative is I'm really anxious and I react quickly. That's how my mind works. I would have to sacrifice being creative in order to be normal in other ways.

It's good to talk to you. You're at a point where you're taking off as a solo artist and stepping out of Tech N9ne's shadow. Tech is probably really proud of you, to have a strong artist like you signed to Strange Music.
Yes sir. I'm not separating from Tech. I will always be a part of Tech Nn9ne. This is just the proverbial cutting of the umbilical cord. This is what he wanted. It's almost like a father to child. You want to keep your child right there with you, but you also want him to grow up and be successful. That's how Tech feels about me. He raised me in this music thing to be as big as him.

It's what is best for Strange Music also. It's not a strong label if one artist has to carry it all. It's good when all of the artists are strong and carrying the label. I'm excited to hear your record when it comes out.
The record is super party time. If I had to describe the record quickly I'd say it's really a good party record. You can play it from beginning to end. Every album that I do you can play it from one end to the next. This album is pretty sexual. If I had to describe this record in one sentence I'd say: it's a damn good thang!

Who is doing the production? At Strange Music do you have a in-house producers you work with?
We have generally about 4 or 5 producers, the producers who've done the music on all of our albums. With me personally, I co-produce a lot of songs on my album. A lot of the songs on my album, the beats are mine. You see where it says, "produced by Krizz Kaliko and Michael 'Seven' Summers". Seven is a dude that produces on all of our albums, but with my album he didn't just give me beats, we created them from the ground up. I came up with a beat idea, I'd call up Seven here's the melody, the bassline, here's the snares, I want it to sound like this. He creates the beat within an hour or so, gives it back to me and I write the song and record it the next day. That's mostly the process on my album. I want to get to the point where I can work with Seven and produce every song from scratch. Any time I have singles those are generally songs that Seven and I produced together. My first album I had "Do It Like I Do It". We produced that together. My second album I had "Misunderstood"; we did that one together. This album I've got "Elevator"; we did that together. Usually the biggest songs from my album we did from scratch. That's the difference. But the producers on my album, you'll see them on all the Strange releases. Young Fire is pretty much exclusively T-Pain's producer but he started out with us and we still do stuff with him. Another guy named Matic Lee, and there's another producer he's bringing out named OG. I work with a guy from Track Boys named Jay White. And I used a kid named Nardo. We all work with them dudes and another dude named MAD. We use all of them, cause they're all diverse so we can get all different sounding beats from them.

Do you record in your own studio there at Strange Music?
We record at one studio. It's not ours. It's called Chapman Recording, owned by Chuck Chapman. That's where we do it. •

MASTAMIND

BY DAVID FRIEDMAM • PHOTO BY MARCUS HANSCHEN
(FREELANCE MUSIC WRITER, COLUMNIST FOR THE NEWS-TIMES IN DANBURY, CN, AND DIEHARD DETROIT RAP FAN)

What can people expect when they get their hands on themindzi?
The real Mastamind. For real. I ain't saying that I ain't been down with this shit 100 percent as far as Natas goes, because that's me. I represent Natas till I die, but themindzi, it's on some ol' other shit, for real. It's gangsta wicked. That's how I feel about it. And it's just real talkin' about my point of view of the streets. There's straight representation throughout the whole record, just straight representation of Detroit.

What made you pick "Forever" as the first single?
I didn't. I ain't picked that shit. You know, it bumps and I love it, but I was feeling like I wanted to come with something else. "Forever," I look at that as, hey, this is how long we've been in this damn rap game. That's how I feel. It's 1990 — it was the start of a new form of rap music called acid rap. And it's never gonna die. I don't care if Esham, Mastamind and TNT disappear off the face of this earth right now. The wicket shit is never gonna die because somebody, somebody is representing it out there and is gonna carry this legacy on. But as far as "Forever" goes, it's just "One to the two a-three a-four-ever." We ain't gonna stop it, flat out.

Your label, Overcore/Gothom, is probably looking to market that song. How do you feel about radio and MTV?
I look at it like this — it's media. We never gave a fuck about radio. We never have. But it's 2000 and that's the way you sell records, really. TV and radio. And as much as we are underground — we are the most underground group in the world — but it's time for people to see it. We've got to get those fans. Because Eminem's fans are our fans, straight up. Kid Rock's fans, half of them are our fans. ICP fans — those are our fans. These people are not seeing us, though, because those same cats act like Esham and Natas don't exist. They done got a lot of shit from us. So we need to get out there, be on TV, be on the radio getting heard — so we can just open somebody's eyes. Some people can't go underground on their own; they gotta be led underground.

Does it bother you that the very groups that call you their greatest influences beat you into the mainstream?
You know what? It really don't bother me as far as someone getting on with their talents.

Just represent where you came from the right way and know who your influences are and don't be afraid to let somebody know. But, really, nobody has to give me credit 'cause Mastamind's in this forever. There's no way that I'm gonna let some of these wack cats out here come out, go double platinum and look at it like, 'Why ain't I there, why ain't I in that position?' I can't look at it like that because I would have blew my fuckin' brains out, seriously. So I just roll with the punches. We started off like 'Fuck the radio. We don't never want to get on the radio.' But we can do this all underground. That's the way we started out and that's the way we can keep it going — with the same attitude.

What part of Detroit did you grow up in and what was it like?

Man, I grew up all over Detroit. The west and the east side, mainly the east side as far as me being a teen-ager growing up and getting into this rap game. Detroit is like every other ghetto. There's stress every day. There's 'where's your next dollar coming from.' As far as the rap game goes, so many cats. When I started, when I first took a demo tape to Esham in high school, it was so many cats trying to get at Esham. And that's how it is in Detroit. Everybody wants to rap, everybody wants to come out with something. I gotta do my thing because the next man is hungrier than me, maybe. I just had to go for what I know. You gotta sound sweet, too. You gotta sound good in Detroit. It's so critical here. That's why a lot of people in the D are scared of us — because they're so critical. They actually think that we worship the fuckin' devil. It's like, 'What?' Detroit is hardcore and that's where the raps come from.

How old were the members of Natas when you all met and how did that meeting come about?

Man, we was all in Osborne High School — ninth grade, freshmen. Esham and T, they was hanging before me. They was the shit in high school. Esham had Homey Don't Play out. He brought out Homey Don't Play, ninth grade in high school. Man, everybody just thought he was the devil. All the women on him and everything. It was crazy in high school. Esham was the star of ninth grade. So imagine him through four years of high school at the same high school. I came around in the 10th grade. I was just the little cat out there doing my thing, rapping. I brought him a little demo tape with three songs on it, gave it to him. The next day he called me and said, 'Let's make a record.' He got me over to the crib and talked about the Natas thing, and I was with it. It just happened like that.

How did you guys come up with the name Natas?

Esham came up with it. Frankly, you know, we were real young. So we were saying a lot of shit. We said some crazy shit on the records. I'm not blaming it on being young, but we was just hyped. We were just mad at the world, really. Officially mad. So it's like, Natas — Esham flipped the 'satan' word backwards and he saw it different. Flat out, I ain't gonna lie. And as time went on, we defined the name Natas, basically saying 'We're just ahead of our time, ahead of the game.' Because we should have been platinum out here but we just sat down one day and said, 'We a Nation Ahead of Time And Space.' We just looked at the letters and did it. And that's how it came.

Even before you joined Overture Music, you had your albums in some national chain record stores. How did you manage to do that?

James Smith, Esham's brother. He's locked up right now. Oh, man, James had it going on. He had that shit going on. He had record stores opening their arms to us. There were record stores telling us to go shove Kkkill the Fetus up our ass. It was hard to get in the stores. We have been through a war with record stores, and who fought that war was James Smith. He had a vision. James Smith and Esham Smith's vision is going down. Even with themindzi. This is how they wanted it. And I'm glad it came out like that. I don't think a lot of cats have been through the war we've been through trying to get in retail and all this shit. But I guess we were just working real hard and we got into some chain stores and we've been selling every day since 1990. We've done sold a record every day.

Overture seems to have done a good job promoting Esham and Natas further on tours with ICP and Tattoo the Earth. How did you end up joining Overture, and who is Santos?

Santos is my man, for real. Him and Esham produced the record and I'm loving it. Santos is a real down to earth cat who knows about us. For him to come fuck with us, he would really have to know our passion and what we done been through in this game. And he does. He understands and he loves that shit. At one point in time, somebody broke in our studio. We were in downtown Detroit. It was around when we were making Multikillionaire or Bruce Wayne or something. Man, we were just hanging around too many of the wrong cats. Somebody broke into the studio, stole everything — even the microphone up in that motherfucker. And that shut us down. So we were looking for another studio and came across Santos. And low and behold, he's got this record company and he knows what he's doing. He knows how to get connects.

It just all worked out, and bless the mic for Santos. If it wasn't for him, I don't know where Esham and I would be. We'd probably be on tour killin' rap cats or something. I don't know. Because we were mad at the world for a minute, getting ready to go and do some dirt. But, hey, we found Santos and Overture. They're representing us across the world. We're lovin' it.

Are you going to be touring any time soon?

Oh, hell yeah. We'll kick it off in Detroit. We're gonna do the State Theater in Detroit, and we're gonna do a lot of cities around Michigan. We're gonna do Flint and Toledo. It's about to start. Definitely next year around February or March, we're going to be touring the world with this Mastamind shit.

It's impressive that Natas has remained together for more than a decade. What do you make of that?

It's fate, destiny. It's just something that we all believe so dearly in. It's gonna take us three to do it. It's gonna take our three minds to do it. We just represent it so well — that's why we've stuck together so long. Because we represent a new type of rap. We feel like our music is nothing like DMX and Mystical and LL Cool J. It's nothing like this other rap music out there. We've got our own style and we represent it.

Why has the mainstream embraced DMX and LL Cool J, and not Natas?

Hey, it goes along with the music business. It's like who you know. As far as the mainstream goes, if we go platinum — let's say themindzi goes platinum — there's still gonna be two million motherfuckers out there saying, 'They worship the devil.' No matter how high you get, there's always gonna be the same amount of people hatin' you. This is our music, we ain't about to change it for nobody. That's what it's about. It's about sticking to what you do and letting people come to you. It just hasn't come to us yet. We've got the streets on lock, though. But the mainstream — all Eminem's fans ain't came and bought our record. But it's going down with themindzi, for real. The mainstream is gonna come to us.

Who are some of your influences as a rapper?

When I started this damn thing, man, all I was listening to was NWA. That's all I was feelin' — NWA, Dr. Dre, Ice Cube, Ren, Eazy-E. But as time goes on, as rap went along, and when I started high school, all I was listening to was Esham. See, I was a fan first. The red tape, Homey Don't Play, Erotic Poetry — that's all we were listening to. And that's my biggest influence — Esham.

Who are some of the other groups you respect from Detroit?
From the D? I've got respect for all these cats out here trying to do
something. I like Royce 5-9. He's doing his thing. I like a group called Rock Bottom. But I'm gonna tell you a thing about Detroit cats — man, ain't nobody representin' like we doin'. Rappers from the D, they're on some other shit. They're jealous of Esham and Natas. It's like everybody's trying to get to that spot we're at. I ain't even gonna name no cats. Cause cats ain't even coming to us real, like 'Oh, y'all doing this damn thing. We all respect y'all for putting Detroit on the map.' Nobody's coming to us like that. Everybody's trying to 'bling-bling' and be like the Cash Money boys. It just don't sound like Detroit rap. Everytime I hear someone from Detroit, they're talking about they're wearing Gators and all this shit. Come on, dog. Be real. Let Jay-Z talk about diamonds and shit. It's something else about Detroit that you've gotta come with and it's all on themindzi. Whoever's on themindzi, that's a Detroit nigga right there. These cats from Detroit, they get my respect. But I ain't feelin' too many of them. Until they come to me with some respect, dog, I ain't got no words.

When people listen to themindzi, is there a message you want them to take from it?
There could be a few messages. The biggest message is flat out good music. I don't care if you don't listen to rap. There's gonna be a song on there that you like and you might even relate to. As far as someone picking up themindzi and all five of the Natas records, I just want them to know Mastamind is down for this shit. All these years, E's been telling me, 'Yo, you're gonna be the main voice in Natas. I'm gonna produce this damn thing, and you and TNT gonna be the voice.' But as time went on, you can look at all the Natas records and they're Mastamind records really. I ain't trippin' but it's just featuring me. And I want them to walk away like, 'Damn, them boys know how to do that shit. I don't give a fuck if it's the rap or the beat. They know what they're doing. And I'm gonna get my money's worth.' Hey, themindzi, they're gonna get their money's worth. We usually put 20 songs on a record; there's only 13 here. So that means they're all bumpin' like somethin' — for real.

Does Natas like meeting fans after shows?
I'm gonna tell you the truth. Me, Esham and T — we're three different people. We represent the same shit, but we're three different people. Esham hates meeting and greeting. I ain't even gonna lie. He loves his fans, and there's a time for meeting and greeting. But this guy, Esham, he's one of the maddest cats out here. He don't ever want to meet nobody and sign autographs — but he would. It's like he ain't got to that level yet where he can feel good about meeting and greeting and signing a million autographs. He's mad at the world, trust me. But me, hey, I'm like at a party. Anytime we do a concert, I'm there. I'll shake anybody's hand and kick it with anybody. At a concert — you can ask people — I'm out in the crowd. That's me. And TNT — he's the same way. We don't mind. We love our fans for real because they know what good music is. We love the motherfuckers for real.

Is TNT thinking about doing solo stuff?
Yeah, he's workin on a solo record. He's trying to give a certain direction to it. He's trying to make some different shit. Cause T really has a style of his own. He's just got to mold it. It's going down. I believe he will be finished with it in a couple months. But we ain't worrying about that shit now. We're tired of releasing records now. One of these records has got to go platinum. Fuck this, man. You know?

Do you have a family in Detroit?
All my family is in Detroit and St. Louis.

Do you have a wife and kids?
No. I ain't got a wife, and no kids. I'm just out here. I'm married to this rap game something tough. And all of them Natas records, they're my kids.

What are your other interests? Are you into the sports teams in Detroit?
Oh, yeah. I love my Lions. I hate the Pistons. Hate the streets. I'm sick of the streets. I've been in them for too long. I don't even do shit but write some rhymes, listen to beats.
What's your favorite song on themindzi?
There's a song on there called 'Detroit,' and I just wanted to roll with that all the way to the biz-ank. But, hey, Santos and Esham was feeling it. I was feeling it. I was rolling with 'Detroit.' That's going to be the second single.

How about the song 'Neva Die" — I thought that was great stuff.
You think so? I mentioned it. That's my favorite cut on the record, too. That shit's saying something. I feel that chorus — 'If I ever had to fight with death, I never lost.' The whole record, it's motivation. I talk about getting money, staying in the rap game, being a legend in this. That's where my mind is. I'm all about coming up. And if you listen to the whole record, dog, it's motivation. Every fucking song is a motivational song. There's a track on www.NATAS.com called 'Motivation.' That's where it all started, right there. You check that song out and you'll know what I'm talking about.

What would you like to say to your fans who have collected all your albums over the years?
Hey, them the truest motherfuckers I've ever known. Anybody who's got a whole fucking collection of the Reel Life shit — that's the realest motherfucker on the planet. 'Cause they know that there's people out here who are talking about some real shit. They know we're all about exposing the good and evil in the streets. People who have got all those records, man, do you think those people think we worship the devil? Somebody who's never heard us would say, 'They worship the devil.' But somebody who's got all the records would say, 'No they don't. They're the shit. They're just some wicket-ass niggas. They just make some wicket music.' I'm telling you, all the fans out there who are down like that — stay down, stay true and I'm with it. I'm making this music for them. That's what it's for. And that's the only reason I do this. •

HOOD STARZ

INTERVIEW & PHOTO BY BLACK DOG BONE

I've been hearing a lot about Hood Starz. You had a big hit last year?
Bandaid: "Bay Swang" with Keak Da Sneak, that came out last year. Produced by Sean T. It got a real big buzz in the streets. Everybody wanted to know who the Hood Starz was.
Scoop Dog: Then we started doin shows and let the people know who we was. They see us in the shows getting wild, shakin our dreadlocks and goin dummy!

That song is off an album or it was a single?
Bandaid: It's from our album, Hood Reality that drops January 24 nationwide. We was in the studio with Guce and Keak. We decided that we wanted to make a song representing the Bay cause we wasn't feelin how so many cats been stealin the Bay slanguage and runnin with the Bay music. "Bay Swang" was giving it back to the Bay. Keak came through, blessed us, and it's been grande ever since. We been hittin the streets, we dropped two mix CD's, that's what kept the buzz goin.
Scoop: You can still get them in the stores right now. Lawless Radio Show, that's volume 2. And volume 1 is called Against The Law: Lawless Radio. It's all Hood Star though.

Your new album isn't out yet?
Bandaid: January 24, 2006. That's our first album.
Scoop: We never dropped an album yet. All the buzz is cause we be on the streets hustlin, doin our footwork, tryin to make our name a household word. The Bay Area has been real receptive to us. They're givin us a whole lotta love and showin us a lotta gratitude. We're from East Palo Alto. That's a small city on the peninsula right in between San Francisco and San Jose. Lotta people don't know about us. We rep our city. Me and Bandaid gonna put it on the map. We like old school, we come from the era of Totally Insane and Chunk. That's the only artists besides C-Funk that came outa East Palo Alto. That's pretty much who our influences is. But we lead our own way, we don't follow anybody. If you heard our music you know. We from the Bay Area, we rep the Bay real hard, but our music is distinctly different from any music in the Bay Area.

The whole Hyphy movement is going on? Are you with that?
Scoop: The whole Hyphy movement is cool. We support that Hyphy movement.
Bandaid: We are Hyphy, but our music ain't Hyphy music. It's hood music. But we love the Hyphy movement. We just a little different from everybody else. We don't wanna fit into any category. But at the same time, we shake our dreads to the Hyphy music too. Don't get it twisted.

Scoop: You could say we're on the Hyphy sound, but it's a different type of Hyphy. In East Palo Alto we got a whole different swagger.
Bandaid: We part of the Hyphy thing, but all our songs ain't Hyphy songs. We got different songs. It's versatile. We rep the Bay and the Bay right now reppin the Hyphy Movement. We're part of that. We just got a diverse sound. When you get the album you gonna see that.

What is the definition of Hyphy music?
Scoop: To be Hyphy is to go dumb, go stupid, go retarded. It's super hyper. It's like energy mixed with alcohol. It's energy mixed with your favorite type of drug, your favorite drug could be music. It ain't got to be a narcotic. It's that energy mixed with that drug.
Bandaid: And it ain't just the music. It's a movement!
Scoop: It ain't just the beats that make it Hyphy. You can just be super pumped about your boys just winning a football game. That's that super energy mixed with that football game—the football game is the drug and that's what got you out there. You just wanna jump over the gate, run in the field, tackle one of them linebackers! You're so damn hyphy, you just don't give a fuck! Like right now I'm getting hyphy just talkin to you at this interview! I'm getting pumped, I'm getting juiced! I'm ready to go dumb. That's hyphy. So off top I'm part of the movement without even tryin to be. It's just a Bay thing. You gotta be part of this Bay world to know what that hyphy energy is.

You broke it down real good. It's like when something happens your emotions get triggered. Your spirit comes out.
Scoop: You trigger and you just get hyphy! Then you just wanna do shit that the average person wouldn't do. Make you wanna go jump on your car. Makes you wanna ghost-ride a whip, make you wanna jump our and watch the whip ride by. Make you wanna shake your dread and just go dumb.

It's contagious too. When you were saying that to me, I caught it. Your hyphiness jumped onto me. I'm feeling hyphy now.
Bandaid: That's why at our shows we're retarded. We get on that stage and we ain't gonna just walk around. We gonna do something silly, act like the real gorillaz, cause that's what we is. We gorillaz and we come from the concrete jungle. EPA is a concrete jungle. It's the smallest city in the Bay Area, but we make so much noise. And because we don't get looked at as much, we get even dumber. My little city be feelin like: y'all ain't talkin about us like you talk about other cities; y'all ain't playin our artists or comin to our city. What? Y'all don't think we good enough? I'm speakin for my whole city right now. That's my whole city thinking and speaking like that. So when we have an event my whole city goes. It's like if you keep a little kid in the house all day, then let him out at a toy store. He's gonna go crazy!

It's a double dose of Hyphy.
Bandaid: Exactly. It's a double dose. The Bay Area always get blackballed, cause we thugs out here. The whole Hip Hop industry wanna X us out because we thugs, but they wanna use our slanguage and shit. We already got a blackball against us. So when we go to the big wigs and tell 'em we got a group from the Bay they're like, "Ah the Bay ain't really doin nothing right now." So we don't get no type of shine. Much love to all the cats in the Bay cause before weren't nobody fuckin with us, but now it's hella niggaz is fuckin with us. It's hella niggaz that come out and fuck with us now. The love and energy is back!

Who are some other artists from East Palo Alto that we should look out for?
Scoop: You should look for my boy G Boyee. Another artist is Madam Alizey. She get down too.
Bandaid: We also got Young Bucky. You can catch all of them on the Lawless mixtapes. Them artists is hot.

How did you two come together?
Bandaid: We from the streets!
Scoop: We been on the block forever. I was with a group called Totally Insane and he was with a group called Never Legal. My homeboy Ad Capone, he in the feds right now. Then a couple other dudes went to the pen. We just been in the streets. I was doin some solo music as Scoop Dog. Then after that me and Bandaid got together. He come in the studio and drop some shit on me. We been on the same streets, we done everything since we was kids together.
Bandaid: Everything from lickin shots to robbin niggaz—you name it, we done it. We ain't no rappin niggaz, we some thug street niggaz.

In Oakland they have the Hyphy thing goin on with the sideshows and everything. Is that going on in East Palo Alto?
Bandaid: It's all over the Bay! Richmond, Vallejo, Frisco, everywhere. That shit originated in Oakland though, don't get it twisted. Hyphy, a lotta the Bay swang come from Oakland.
Scoop: That's a Keak Da Sneak word. Off top, lotta this shit come from Keak, come from Oakland.
Bandaid: We 20 minutes away from Oakland. We 20 minutes from Frisco and 20 minutes from San Jose. We the center of the Bay. But right now Keak is on top of the Bay. And a lotta the shit that these niggaz be stealin come from right here. So for him to be on top he can rep the Bay. These other niggaz is using our words but ain't yellin the Bay. Now we got our own nigga up there and muthafuckas in the Bay gonna feel that.

When did Hood Starz get started?
Bandaid: In '99 I got caught up, I went to the pen. 2003 I got released, got back on top of my toes. Released another Never Legal album, didn't really do no promotions on it and it was a flop. Then my nigga Scoop Dog was workin on some solo shit. When I came home I went to the studio to jump on his album and we laid something so clean we decided to make it the single for his album, but it never dropped. So we decided to do this Hood Starz thing. We also got a magazine called Hood Star Magazine that we droppin. Look out for that too. Double market, double promotion. You know how we do it.
2005 was a turning point for the Bay. We got the radio support, the clubs, the streets. Next year is going to be big.

> "THE TITLE "FOLLOW ME HOME" BASICALLY MEANS FOLLOW ME HOME THROUGH MY CITY, THROUGH MY LIFE. I'M GONNA SHOW YOU THE INS AND OUTS THROUGH MY LIFE, THROUGH WATTS, THE TRIALS AND TRIBULATIONS, WHAT GOES ON IN THE HOOD, IN THE GHETTO. THE MIND STATE OF A PERSON LIVING IN SOUTHCENTRAL, IN THE GUTTER. FOLLOW ME HOME AND I'MA SHOW YOU."

Scoop: Something gonna blow next year. Something gonna give. Pressure breaks pipes, you dig? The whole Bay Area is applying pressure. The pipes gonna bust and it's gonna be hot shit just flying everywhere. It's a beautiful thing. All the artists in the Bay Area are coming together and showing love, they're starting to support each other. A lotta people from different cities been supporting the Hood Starz. We ain't got no bad blood with nobody. We gonna make it happen. •

PASTOR TROY
BY BLACK DOG BONE

The first time I heard of you was when you did that song about Master P. What was that about?
We ain't playin down here. He was on something different than what we represent down here in Atlanta. All that material stuff ain't what we about down here.

I don't get it....
You know, P, he rich, man. He does a lotta talkin about that street stuff, when we're the ones down here in the streets.

But you know Master P comes from the streets. I knew Master P a long time ago when he was in Richmond and just starting. Master P was just like you at one time, but he just became very successful. That doesn't make him any less real. What will happen if you make a lot of money as Pastor Troy?
That's what this whole thing is about, sellin

"I WAS TRYIN TO GO TO COLLEGE AND THE WHOLE NINE. BUT THEY DIDN'T WANNA LISTEN TO ME. WHO WANNA LISTEN TO A LITTLE 20 YEAR OLD CAT FROM THE STREETS IN COLLEGE? COLLEGE TEACH YOU HOW TO BE AN EMPLOYEE. DON'T NOBODY TEACH YOU HOW TO BE A BOSS."

records. If you wanna be on top, go at the big dog. So that's what I did.

What made you want to make your name off of dissing Master P?
That was a strong business move. Look how everybody talkin, Who's this dude that dissed Master P? They's callin my name in the same breath as this million dollar man.

Master P's a Black man who came up against all odds in this White dominated society. Why do you want to come up dissing another Black man?
I'm tryin to catch up with P so we can do this together and squash all this.

I don't think Master P had any problem with you. Master P didn't even know you.
He didn't. I just came out the blue.

You're from the South. You know that 35 years ago in Mississippi a Black kid couldn't even go to school. A Black man couldn't walk into a restaurant where White people were eating. You know that? And here you have Master P who millions of Black kids look up to as a role model. I don't know why another Black man would want to diss him and destroy him.
It's like this my man, this thing's way deeper than that. I got a family that I have to feed. It ain't nothing to do with Black. It ain't nothing to do with White. It's about my situation. I have to get to another point in my life. I'm not concerned with Mater P. That's over with. That was the media puttin all that attention on that stuff. I just made a song.

Master P is one of the most respected Black men of this time. He's like a god.
But he's not god.

All humans are god if they do godly things. Malcolm X is a god because he did a godly Martin Luther King is a god, because he did a godly thing.
Yeah well I did do something godly, cause I put P outta the game.

One of the problems we have throughout history is when one Black man gets something going some Uncle Tom comes and tries to destroy him. We need to come up together as a people.
I'm in Atlanta tryin to survive!

You're going to sell out your brother just so you can survive?
This thing's deep than that. You gotta know me better to ask me questions like that. You gotta be in Atlanta. It's a new world order goin on, it's a brand new day. Everything thing here is about that money.

So it's OK to sell another Black man to get your money?
I'm independent Black owned. I'm not dealin with nobody. I'm not sellin nobody out. I don't know Master P. P ain't nothing to talk about.

Why did you write a song about him if you don't know the man?
Cause I can write a song about anything I want to.

Millions of kids look up to Master P...
Millions of kids who used to look up to Master P until I came and dissed him. Now they look up to me. I'm the new hero. This is war man, ain't nothing sacred in war. Ain't no rules.

You think what you did was the right thing?
What I did was the wise thing.

more about selling a black man saying that P bought his contract...

What's that got to do with anything? Master P ain't nothing to me. This is Rap. Rap music. It's about who can rap the best. I feel that I have more abilities than Master P. I rapped against P and I won. My Rap sounds better. I won. I ain't got nothing but love for P. it's all a big game to sell records. Burger King and McDonald's go at it every day. He's got a record label, I got a record label. We're in competition.

about jesus christ

You could have dissed any other rapper, you could've dissed Method Man or Puffy....why Master P?
I dissed all them too. Master P, if I were to meet him today I would apologize to him and we would do a song together.

121

You're coming from Atlanta, but you're not doing music like Goodie Mob or Outkast. You're more Gangsta.
That's the underground Rap in Atlanta. We got gangstas here. We got dope here, we got guns. You name it, it's here--Atlanta. It's boomin down here. So much money. Folks is just migrating to Atlanta.

A lot of people have moved there from New York, so you have that Hip Hop element in Atlanta too.
You gotta check 'em. I'm checkin 'em. They floodin my city with all that stuff.

That's not really Atlanta?
It's not. They're flexing the game. I could take you to deeper burrows and you could see it, sure enough. Atlanta--country, Southern, Gangsta.....

Who else is happening in the Atlanta underground?
Me and Playa Fly got it sewed up Memphis to Georgia. Out of Atlanta there's nobody else doin that Gangsta Rap.

How did you get into doing Gangsta stuff?
I lived it. It's all I knew.

What made you really want to rap?
Me and my potnas got together, we was tired of sellin dope, and we knew how much money we could benefit from this Rap game. So we put the CD together, dropped it independent, went to sell it out the trunk. We put the yayo up and we been doin it ever since.

When did the CD come out? That's the one that has the song dissing Master P?
Yeah, NAME . It came out September of '98. We were down there on the grind. I had a studio set up on top of this store in Augusta. I used to be in there every day writin raps, makin beats. The studio was called The Church, on 9th Street.

What happened after you finished the record?
We pressed it up and we went to boomin. It caught fire. It spread to Tennessee, Florida, South Carolina. It's all up in New York now, it's on.

That album's about a year old...
I'm about to drop a new one now. It's called Pastor Troy, Face Off. It's comin out first of January.

How would you describe your sound?
It's the hardest music ever. Reality Rap, the realest. You can hear in my voice, I'm a drill sergeant. It's a war goin on.

Do you think since you came out that there's a lot of street Rap happening in Atlanta?
Yeah, it's wide open now. There's a dude down here named Drama--#7 on the Billboard charts and he's followin my style. All these people, they followin me.

Everywhere in the South they put out Gangsta Rap, but Atlanta has always been know for Outkast and that kinda sound. Do you think that music represents Atlanta?
They represent they side, they hood. I represent mine. They came up better than I did.

They were probably influenced by New York, don't you think? But then there's people like Big Oomp Records with Sammy Sam, and Ghetto Mafia who do Gangsta shit.
Right, they represent Atlanta underground. Like Goodie Mob and them, they with the majors, there's only so much they can say. And their beats are more Hip Hop. My stuff ain't like that, my stuff bangin, rattlin trunks. One of the problems in Atlanta was that everybody was signin with the majors and when you with those majors, it's only so much you can say, so much you can do. While I could go and make my beats any way I want to, make 'em grimy as I want them to sound.

So you think you changed the situation in Atlanta?
Yeah, it's wide open now. I crunked Atlanta up. I crunked it up. it's so many lives about to be saved with this Rap game.

What's you connection with Three 6 Mafia and Hypnotized Minds?
I just did a song with them. It's gonna be on they new album. it's hard. They lovin me out here right now.

I always here your name. But I always wondered what your problem was with Master P......
Everybody wondering and I can't wait to tell everybody it ain't nothing. Just business. Look how I got my name out there now. It was just a business move to set me up for this new album. This new album gonna tell 'em everything.

What are we going to get on your new album?
Nothing but the Gangsta shit. I'm the baddest rapper. Tupac and Biggie came back in me, I'm the one, I got all of it. Ain't nobody out there now will be able to touch me. I got it.

How made your beats on your first album and on this new one?I did. I produced everything.
How did you learn to do all that?Hands on. I bought the equipment and just put my hands to it. Learned, figured it out. I got a MT3-3000 and the ASRX. Then I got an old keyboard I had and that's it.

You just taught yourself? What motivated you to do it?
Because I knew I could do it. You never know if you can till you try. I tried and it worked. Make it work.

What were you doing before this album?
I was tryin to go to college and the whole nine. But they didn't wanna listen to me. Who wanna listen to a little 20 year old cat from the streets in college? College teach you how to be an employee. Don't nobody teach you how to be a boss. I wanted to be the boss, so I'm the CEO of my own record company NAME. They don't teach you that, they just teach you to work in the system with the rest of society. I need to go to Bill Gates' class.

How did your last album do?
Shit, it sold good. I'm almost gold.

Do you have other artists signed to your label?
Yeah I got a female artist named Rhonda, her album's entitled G.I. Jane. Man, she is raw. She hard like a nigga. She from Augusta. Then I got the Down South Georgia Boys' album. They album gonna turn some heads, nothing but Gangsta shit, from Atlanta. It's time. You bout to be hearin from me for awhile. •

CHUCK BROWN GO-GO IS A DC SOUND

BY GREG "GATE$" DAVENPORT
PHOTO BY MARCUS HANSCHEN

I think one reason that Go-Go has lived on so long is that the people of DC are very proud that DC has its own music.
Go-Go is a DC sound. When you come to DC you're gonna hear Go-Go, I don't care what else you hear. Go-Go is a dominant factor here in Washington DC. Go-Go belongs to DC and we wouldn't care if it didn't go nowhere else but DC. That's the way we feel about it and that's the way Go-Go fans feel about it. If the rest of the country wants to pick it up then good, if they don't we couldn't care less.

It seems like Go-Go is really about performing.
Yeah. One thing I like about Go-Go is it's so consistent. You got the most wonderful people in the world. Washington DC, Maryland, Virginia, they're the most loyal and honest fans in the world. These people are the greatest. Without the fans it wouldn't be no Go-Go. DC would not have their own sound. They love you all day long. Even if they don't love you, they'll show you some appreciation and some encouragement and let you know what you have to do to get better. I love DC fans, they'll never let you down. I've been all over the world and I can't wait to get back home to DC.

Do you think that since you first created Go-Go music it has changed a lot now?
It has changed tremendously. I don't mean to be critical, but I have to say what's true. I have to speak my honest opinion. They need to incorporate more music. Right now they're playin most of the Go-Go grooves and a lot of the music has been taken out. This is what I don't like. I don't like the fact that the music has been taken out. A lotta the younger groups that are comin out now are incorporating more music. I really appreciate that and I'm sure the fans do too. A lot of the Go-Go groups now are just playin the grooves.

You mean the melodies and words are not there? That they're just playin the groove and talking to the audience, but the music is not there?
Yes sir. See, I started all of that. I started talkin to the audience, all that. James Brown is the top man in the world for doin that and I've learned all of that from him. I love James Brown. I give him all the credit in the world for bein such an inspiration to me. Ever since 1958 when I first heard him. He got to my heart. I wasn't even playin music when I first heard James Brown.

It's interesting that you say they're not incorporating the music. The main thing that separates Go-Go from other music right now is that they play live instruments with a whole band. Drums and guitars and rhythms...
And horns. I would love to see these bands add some horns. Trouble Funk had horns, they never got rid of their horns and I love them for that. Rare Essence, I see they got one horn they're startin to use. Donnell is a very talented young man, I think he should add more horns to his horn. I use two or three horns. I never hit the stage without at least one horn. If my horn player was sick or if I fired somebody--cause I fire people if they do wrong, nobody quits this band--I'd find somebody.

I heard that you were originally from Carolina?
I was born in Carolina, but I grew up in DC, all over DC. I was born in North Carolina. My mother brought me away from there when I was 4 or 5 years old. But I've gone back down there plenty of times. When I was a little kid I ran away from home and I used to go back down there and hang out there with some of my relatives and work on the farms. I'd pick cotton, I'd plow a mule, I used to drive a tractor. I also worked at the saw mill. I used to work for 50¢ an hour, 75¢ and hour, which was good money back then for a little kid like me.

Why did you run away from home?
So I could get experience for myself. My mother and father were very poor. They weren't able to take care of me the way kids should be taken care of. I didn't want to be a burden on them, so I left and when they seen me again to come back I got a pocket full of money to give my mother and father. I wanted to make them proud of me. During that time when I ran away from home I got in a lot of trouble. I went in jail a few times. I don't wanna get into that right now, but I'll give you a hint--that's where I found myself. I learned and developed my talent when I was incarcerated.

So you started playing guitar when you were 24? You never had played the guitar before?
No. It was easy for me. I had never been a guitar player. I had experience with guitars, I had stolen a few of 'em when I was a kid. When I needed some money to get something to eat I might steal a guitar and sell it. But I didn't learn how to play it till I got locked up.

What was it that motivated you to play guitar?
When I was locked up I was given the opportunity by the prison authorities to play the keyboard, play organ for the chapel, for the prison choir. That was a good offer, but it did not impress me too much. I could practice two hours a day, but I didn't want to stay in the chapel and practice religious songs two hours a day. So what I did, I ended up getting a guitar. I got one of the inmates to make me a guitar down there. They made me one. And the rest is history. I sat on my bunk and I could practice any time I wanted to. That way I wasn't limited to two hours a day, and I could play all kinds of music. I didn't wanna play in the church. I grew up in the church, I left home and I left the church.

How did you learn to play the chords?
I sat there and learned. It was easy for me. Once you play a keyboard you can play just about any other instrument. See I played piano in church when I was a little boy. I started at seven, eight, nine years old. When I reached the age of thirteen I left home and I didn't play piano no more, cause I was out in the street, I was a little homeless runaway kid. I didn't get interested in music again until I was 24. I learned how to play the guitar at the age of twenty-four.

You had a good ear for music?
I have a great ear. I would say I have a great ear for music, simply because I never learned to read one note. You had two-three other kids out there when I was in prison, I learned just by watching and listening. You had guys in there that had played with Count Basie, Duke Ellington. You had great guitar players down there. I learned a lot from these guys. I thank god the day that I went to that prison. I'm glad that I went there.

I heard you were in a prison called Lauden. Where is that?
Right down here in Virginia. I had been to three or four other penitentiaries before that, but I had never learned anything. Only thing I had learned from the other jails I went to was how not to go back down no more, to that same jail no more. But when I went to Lauden it was like school to me, it was like college. You know what I did? I got my high school diploma in Lauden. I had never finished high school until I went to Lauden. I got my education there. They put my diploma up there in the library on display.

It's amazing. I was reading about you and I was amazed. Your life really inspired me. At twenty-four years old a lot of people are done with life, and you started your life at twenty-four.
I got out of Lorton and I ain't looked back since. I was there 3 years, 9 months. I had eleven years, but I was such a good prisoner, I was a model prisoner. And plus I could box, I been boxing all my life since I was a little kid. I got into jail, I did a lotta work out, taught some younger guys how to box. Some of them came out and turned professional.

Because you got serous about music you put boxing aside?
Yeah, I gave up on that. I was a sparring partner. I never was a contender. I used to pick up a few dollars sparring with guys. Like that.

You've had a lot of experience in different fields.
I've done it all. Plus I'm a professional bricklayer, I'm a stone mason. I did every kind of work. When I got married I used to drive a truck, tractor and trailer. And on the weekends I used to play music any chance I got. In some little nightclub or in somebody's house party or something. I started off playin for barbecue sandwiches, chicken sandwiches, and all the alcohol you could give me. And I will say, I became an alcoholic--not a drug addict, I was a drunk--but that didn't hinder my talent. I would say it helped enhance my talent, it helped develop my talent. When I took a couple of drinks I could sit down and practice for two or three hours. It was just me and my guitar, I didn't have no band. I'd go to somebody's house and play house parties. They'd feed me, they'd give me liquor. The next week somebody'd invite me to their house. I was getting invited to everybody's house. I had a good time. Then I started playin with different bands around town. I got a lotta experience in that. It was 1962, '63, '64. '65 I played with a group called Los Latinos. I love Latin music. I love Blues, Jazz, I love classics, I love Funk, Rap, Country Western. I can play all that kinda stuff. When I played with Los Latinos we played Top-40 with Latin ingredients. I love drums. I love African sounds. I love the sound of African drums, Caribbean drums, I love that. So when I put my whole band together in 1966 I decided to put all those ingredients in my band. That gave me a different sound from everybody.

How old were you when you started playing those house parties?
I was like twenty-six, twenty-seven. I did that up until around 1964, '65. I was close to thirty I guess.

At that time what kind of music was going on in the neighborhoods?
You had James Brown, you had Otis Redding, you had Wilson Pickett, Smokey Robinson and the Miracles. I did all that stuff. Back in those days you had to sound like the record. I did Latin music. I did African music.

You were singing in the Latin group?
I was singing with it. I did the Top-40. Whatever you heard on the radio, I could play it. The band added that Latin flavor. I still got that Latin sound, but now I use it as Funk. I keep my congas, my cow bells, my timbales, by tambourines. I keep that stuff.

I heard that you were also influenced by Disco, how the music would play continuously…..
In Disco you got a hundred beats a minute. I slowed that down to about seventy beats a minute. In those days they had Go-Go girls, Go-Go clubs, Go-Go shows, but they didn't have no Go-Go music. That's how I decided to call this music Go-Go. Smokey Robinson has a tune "Goin to a Go-Go…" that was about going to a Go-Go party. There wasn't any Go-Go music. When I put this music together I called it Go-Go, because it never stops. It just goes and goes and goes, one song into another. When you do Top-40 you gotta make it sound like a radio, you gotta make that stuff sound good, but I had my own ingredients in it. After a while everybody started catching on to it.

How old are you now?
I'll be 67. I'm lucky I still got a voice. Actually my first wife sent for my birth certificate and they put on there Charles Lewis Moody, which was my real father's name. They said I was born August 22 in 1936, which would make me 65. I said, OK you gonna give me a coupla years off for good behavior, I appreciate that.

When did you really get into music?
Like I said, I was playing piano for the church. My mother was a great singer. My mother also played keyboards. I was born with that. I can play any instrument I wanna play. I can pick it up and learn to play within six months. I can do that. My sons, I got kids that are the same way.

How many kids do you have?
Got a lotta kids. I've got five right here in the house. They just play. I've got twelve guitars here. All my talent came from my mother. And my father could sing, my real father.

New Orleans had it's strong music history, Detroit had a lot, but we never hear much about DC. I think Duke Ellington was from DC?
Duke Ellington was from DC.
But he wasn't really doing stuff in DC.

When you think of DC you think of Go-Go and Chuck Brown.
That's right. You can't even talk about Go-Go without mentioning my name. Other people have tried to take credit for what I've done. I just sit back and don't say nothing. Next thing you know it's blastin all over the radio, "Whoever said this…blah blah blah…. Chuck Brown's the man that created Go-Go." I let the people set the record straight. I let the people name me the Godfather. I didn't designate that name for myself, my fans did that. It's what you do. Eventually you will be recognized. Somebody else can come out tellin lies and try to claim that, but you don't have to do nothing. Sit back and let things speak for themselves. I've been out here longer than anybody. The consistency is what counts. I'm the only artist that could play in this town 6-7 nights a week if I want to. Can't nobody else do that.

In your words can you break down the Go-Go sound for us?
You got the basic beat. The way I got the idea, the basic beat came from the church. It was real fast--boom-cha-oom-cha-boom-cha, and everybody's shakin tambourines. Then you had a bass drummer over that like you do in a marching band. Then you had another guy playin the snare drum, 4 or 5 people are playin drums. Then you have people playin the cymbals like in a marching band. That's the way it was in my church. That beat. I hadn't heard that beat again until Grover Washington came out with "Mr. Magic." He had that beat. I played that song, that's one of my theme songs. I been playin it ever since it came out. This is where I got the idea. I said I know that beat, that's an old church beat from when I was a little kid. Grover Washington must've went to the same kinda church I went to. He slowed that beat down and that thing was just unbelievable. This is where the Go-Go beat came from. I took the beat and moved it around and syncopated it. That's where my Go-Go idea beat came from.

You put that basic beat behind most of the music you did?
Right. I mixed the congas and everything with it. Even if I do a top forty tune I put that beat behind it. But it's moved around. It's syncopated and different variations. If you listen to "Bustin Loose" you will hear that same beat with some double kicks in it. I love that man, Grover Washington. I never would've thought about bringin that beat, I might've found another beat. But that beat has got a spiritual vibe to it.

I heard that Chuck Brown has really inspired and really helped the young groups out. Often the big name artist doesn't do that, but you are a true Godfather.
I love to help. I love to see young groups get known. I'm takin 911 to New York with me Saturday. Get them some exposure. I'm very interested in helpin these young groups. I even go down to the schools and try to give people the inspiration to do Go-Go. This music has been isolated here in this city for so many years. Trouble Funk helped out a lot in keepin that Go-Go music going. Another group out there that I love so much is called The Backyard Band. Backyard, great group. The lead rapper for the group, a great distinguished voice. Different from anybody else out there. They've been around for a long time and I think they should go much further. You got Northeast Groovers. You got the Junkyard Band, little boys came out beatin on buckets. They didn't have no instrument, but they had the groovingest sound you ever heard. And they get better as the years go on. Now you got a new group out called 911. The group is new, but the musicians have been around for a while. Godfather Mark with that group, he plays the keyboard, he plays with me too.

What I've noticed about your music is you don't use too much words in your songs, which I really like. Sometimes you don't need so many words to get it across.
"Money money money, I need money. Money money money…" I wrote that in 20 minutes. Could you imagine how I wrote that song so fast? I was broke! In order to write I have to

> "YOU CAN'T EVEN TALK ABOUT GO-GO WITHOUT MENTIONING MY NAME. OTHER PEOPLE HAVE TRIED TO TAKE CREDIT FOR WHAT I'VE DONE. I JUST SIT BACK AND DON'T SAY NOTHING. NEXT THING YOU KNOW IT'S BLASTIN ALL OVER THE RADIO…"

be inspired. It's easy to write a song about needing some money. You wanna go right to the point. That's the way I write. I'm good at puttin all that music together. When I do write lyrics it has to mean something. You can't just sit down and write. I wrote that song in 20 minutes cause I was broke. And I ain't need no money since.

I heard that "Bustin Loose" was a song that you played for a long time before you recorded it.
Two years. I just wanted to do it. I had about a hundred lines of lyrics to that song. But I used the two that were the most effective. The reason I played it for two years, so I could get it tight. If you listen to that song it's tight as skin. I had to fire 3 or 4 musicians to get them to play it the way I wanted it. I had to fire 2 drummers. One drummer said, I don't wanna play no stupid beats, that's an old fashioned beat. I said that old fashioned beat's gonna be a new fashioned beat. What you're tellin me is that you're old fashioned, so you about to go up outta here. You're fired. I know where I'm headed, I know exactly where I'm gonna go. Lotta them don't know that, I know me. You gotta have confidence in yourself. How you expect anybody to have confidence in you if you don't believe in yourself? That's what came first with me, I believed in me. That's how I got those guys to cooperate with me. Now you see the results. The results are very positive.

Which of your albums are your favorites?
That's hard to say. But my two favorite live albums are Your Game and Go-Go Swings. They're the two best live albums out there.

How many albums do you have out?
I got stuff that ain't never been out. I got stuff that I recorded 30 years ago, never been out. I got stuff that been on the wrong record company where they never gave me a dime. I don't wanna get into that, cause I'll get upset. I got stuff that ain't comin out unless they turn it over to me. They're waiting till I die to put 'em out, the bastards.

When you were in prison playing guitar did you think anything like this could happen?
No. I wanted to play for my enjoyment and I like to see people happy. My intention was to keep a day job and play music part-time. But it turned around. Next thing you know I didn't have time to go on a day job period. I never dreamed I'd be in the Hall of Fame. All I ever wanted when I first started this business, I said Well, I'd appreciate it if I can work my full-time job and play part-time on the weekends. That's all I looked forward to. But as things got better- I could play full time and work part time. I was grateful for all that. You have to be grateful, then all the good things will come to you. Whatever you do, big or small, do it well or don't do it at all. When I realized I could play without even workin a day job, that really thrilled me. I ain't had a day job for 35 years man! I had no idea that I would get this far.

What would you consider to be the big break in your music career?
I was playin at the Washington Hilton in front of 3,000 people. I opened up the show for a top notch House band called Bobby Felder and the Blue Notes. Carla Thomas was on the show, she was a big star, and we were proud to be playin on the same stage as a big star. That was the first big gig I had. That was in 1966, when I first put my group together. Then I played in the clubs for a year and a half for $10 a night, beer and barbecue. Then I asked for a raise, club got so packed, they had lines outside. It only cost 75¢ to get in. The place got so packed it went up to a dollar and a quarter. That's when I asked for a raise, "Can we get another 5$?" "Yeah, we'll give you $15 a night, but that means no free beer." "No problem, thank you sir!" We started getting such a big crowd, people started comin out, wantin to book us, "We wanna take you uptown and give you $17." Everything started opening up for me.

After all you've been through, you look great for your age. You really look young and healthy.
I thank you sir. You've made my day. But you know I do exercise. I don't lift weights or nothing, but I do exercise. I do 12 or 15,000 push-ups in one week. When I was in the Marines, I did a lot of Marine push ups. I come out of the Marines, I went to jail. I was in jail even before I went to the Marines. I put my age up. I used my real father's last name with is Moody. Charles Moody. I wanted to go to the Marine Corp, cause I'd been goin to the jail since1946. I was always athletic. I played football in high school. And my wife was a nurse, a certified nurse, and my wife was also a pharmacist. She graduated from pharmacy school. She knows every kind of medicine there is. And that helps keep me healthy. And I stopped drinkin. My wife stopped me from drinkin. I haven't had a drop of alcohol in almost 4 years.

You probably eat good too?
Oh yeah. I eat good. But I don't eat correctly, my wife tries to get me to eat correctly. I like a lot of Soul food. I'm a country boy. I like to eat fat back and collard greens and cornbread and biscuits and ham hocks, stuff like that. And when my wife ain't lookin I'll go somewhere and get that.

Are you still living in DC?
I'm down in St. Charles County. I'm in the country, in the suburbs now. I don't live right in the city, I got a nice place in the country. But I've lived all over DC and all over Maryland.

Have things changed a lot in DC since the time you were growing up?
Of course it changed tremendously. When I was growin up we fought in the streets with our fists. Get up and shake hands and we're buddies again. But now young punks out here got guns. They can't fight with their hands. I hate that. And it makes me scared to carry my shit, cause I'd be scared to use my shit. I grew up usin my hands, knockin suckas out and bustin 'em in the mouth. That's how I grew up. But now you can't do that. You hit somebody with your fists now, son of a bitch will come back and shoot you. That's the difference.

Rap is the biggest music in the country right now, but it seems like it never took off in DC. Why didn't Rap hit DC? I never hear Rap coming from DC.
DC's not a Rap city. They like Rap, but Go-Go is our music. My daughter is a rapper, she's rappin with me. She mixes Go-Go with Rap and it sounds great. Wait till you hear the record I'm gonna put out on her. Her name is KK and she's a great rapper. I also got a little 11 years old son who raps with me. All of my sons rap, all of 'em. I got one son, 40 years old, who's got his own band. He's older than my second wife. My oldest daughter is 51 years old. She's down in Richmond Virginia, and she says Y'all got that from me. And all my kids can sing.

I think the new music of America will be a mixture of Rap with Go-Go. I think what you're doing is changing history. Like you were talking about Jill Scott.
She's giving you a hint. It will happen. Rap will mix with Go-Go, Go-Go will mix with Rap. Even Kurtis Blow. Snoop Dogg, all of 'em listen to me. And I put Rap in my Go-Go. I be rappin in my Go-Go. I love Rap music. I can rap New York Rap, I can do California Rap, I do Snoop Doggy Dogg, LL Cool J, I do all that stuff. But I do it on a Go-Go groove. I slow it down and I do it my way. •

TRAP OR DIE YOUNG JEEZY

BY GREG "GATE$" DAVENPORT • PHOTO BY ERIC JOHNSON

You're so hot in Atlanta right now, they're bootlegging your shit because they can't get enough mixtapes.

> "I DIDN'T REALLY UNDERSTAND THE BUSINESS. WE WENT FROM THAT AND WE HAD A GROUP CALLED THE BIG BOYS ON YOUNG GUNS ENTERTAINMENT. WE DROPPED THAT, IT REALLY DIDN'T DO NOTHING. NIGGAS GOT FUCKED UP, LOCKED UP. A LOT OF NIGGAS GOT MURDER CASES. A LOT OF NIGGAS WENT TO THE FEDS. AFTER THAT, IT WAS KIND OF FUCKED UP BECAUSE WE HAD INVESTED A LOT OF BREAD, SO MY MAN WAS LIKE, "WE GOT TO PULL THIS SHIT OFF." BY THIS TIME, I HAD LOST ABOUT THREE OR FOUR OF MY POTNAS, LIKE MY EVERYDAY NIGGAS. I STARTED OFF DOING THAT SHIT TO KILL TIME."

That's why I just did the other one. It's crazy because right now I'm on the road at least four to five days out the week. I'm getting what niggas get for shows with gold albums. All this off a mixtape. Like I said, it means something. Niggas do mixtapes and you know that shit cool, but niggas don't make that big of an impact. It's like the streets feel a nigga. I don't give a fuck about the radio shit. The radio banning me and they ain't playing my shit now. You know, they playing the shit with Puff and the shit like that but they won't play my shit, but we got these streets baby and that's all that matters. At the end of the day I'd rather go in Magic City and hear my shit anyway, because I know niggas in their gonna appreciate my shit in there -- they gonna fuck with me.

All that payola in the radio, you aren't getting in that. You might as well go on and break your bread over at Strokers and get your shit played up over there.

I tell niggas, I be in the club a lot, I see niggas come through there, ask any of them from Strokers to Magic City to wherever, Pinups, wherever. Them girls respect a nigga because I been doing this shit since I was 16. When my peoples used to own it I went in there when I was 14 and I been the same way ever since I been in. Like, being on the streets period. Everything I say somebody can stand by it. Them girls tell me all the time when I come through, "You the only nigga we knew period that done did anything with hisself and still come through and show love. You was just the same nigga you was two years ago." And niggas speak on that shit, about what they got in they rhymes to the point I don't even really say that shit no more. I'm tired of showing these niggas. Niggas is two years behind me, I'll run circles around these square-ass niggas. For real, these niggas got the game fucked up. They thinking because you on now and you get some shit you on. Nigga, I had all that shit before I got on. You get a coupe, I got a coupe. How you want to play it? You want to go to Walter's? What's up? For real, everybody can vouch for me from Walter's … anywhere I fuckin' step my foot in, anywhere I eat at. I don't give a fuck if it's the local KFC or the Popeye's, they know I come in deep and we eating good.

When did your first mixtape come out?

The first group I had was in '95, when I had got out. We did that mixtape called "Hell In ATL." We did that, dropped it through Ichiban in Atlanta. That did pretty cool. That was like back in the day. Back then a nigga was just putting money into shit. I didn't really understand the business. We went from that and we had a group called The Big Boys on Young Guns Entertainment. We dropped that, it really didn't do nothing. Niggas got fucked up, locked up. A lot of niggas got murder cases. A lot of niggas went to the feds. After that, it was kind of fucked up because we had invested a lot of bread, so my man was like, "We got to pull this shit off." By this time, I had lost about three or four of my potnas, like my everyday niggas. I started off doing that shit to kill time. Going in the studio and whatever and I did a song and my man was like, "Shit nigga, fuck it, you do it." My nigga Kinky B. I just started rapping. It was crazy because I was doing the shit, but niggas was acting like they was liking it. But I'm thinking it was because I'm so cool. I did it. I put out my first album.

That's "Come Shop With Me?"

Nah, I put out an album before that. It was called "Thuggin' Under the Influence." I did about a couple of thousand units. Ten, 15 maybe. Nigga really wasn't checking that bread because it was other things. A nigga went from there to like, just other shit and it was a long time span. So when I came back to it I did "Come Shop With Me." I was going around paying niggas, doing the dumb shit. I ain't know the business so I'm in studios getting full-day blocks. Spending all types of unnecessary money. Giving niggas five, and six, and seven, and $8,000 a track for shit I should've been paying three or $400 for. Going to all these big studios. I used to fuck around at Dallas Austin's studio. That's when niggas started knowing me on the scene, because we was the only young niggas shining. You know, with diamonds on and the jewels and the cars and still doing music in the big boy spots because street niggas wasn't fucking around. Niggas was buying they own little studios.

When did "Come Shop With Me" come out?

I did that shit in 2001-02 and I think we put it the end of '02. It did maybe 80-70,000 (units sold). But like I said again, a nigga wasn't checking that bread, because niggas was thinking with a whole different mind frame. So when I did "The Streets Iz Watching," the whole time I been begging DJ Drama like, "Man, put some of my shit on a mix CD, put some of my shit on a mix CD." He wouldn't never do it, so I was like, "Fuck it, Ima buy my own mix CD." So, I got with him, got my bread up and at the time I put out the little single with Bun B and that shit was killing the club so when I put it on the mixtape and got 'em out, niggas was like, "Damn, this the same nigga." Niggas got a hold of the shit dog and the shit started spreading like wildfire. It's like I'm damn near a celebrity or some shit. I be in the club doing my normal shit, poppin' the Crissies and having fun, and a niggas walk up to me like, "Nigga I love yo shit," and I'm like, "What?!" I couldn't even be in the club now. Everybody run up to a nigga. Like I told 'em in my rhyme dog, "Two record deals and 270,000 mixtapes later. From the streets of the Chatt to the hoods of Decatur."

How did the Def Jam and Bad Boy deals come about?

The Bad Boy shit came about…I was fucking with my man Des working on my album. This was right before I got to Def Jam…

So are you signed through Jazze Pha?
Naw, naw, I ain't signed to Jazze in no way, shape, form or fashion.

Just Boyz N Da Hood are signed to Jazze?
They're actually signed to Bad Boy.

How does Jazze come into play, you were always talking about chopping it up with Jazze Pha.
Don't get me wrong, I chopped up with Jazze from a whole different point. Jazze respected me as a man. He used to see me out riding and shit and always asked me, "Damn nigga, what the fuck you doing? How you get this car?" It was that type of shit. That was the person that kind of got me in some doors that niggas wouldn't let me in. You would be surprised what I've been through. Radio won't play me. They was banning me out of clubs. Then I couldn't come to clubs because of the company I kept. It was like a whole bunch of shit. Niggas couldn't say my name and such. Through Jazze niggas was seeing that I could really rap. He was taking my shit to niggas who wouldn't fuck with me because they was scared of me or scared of my company. Puff (P. Diddy) knew me from the streets. Puff saw a nigga out doing his thug theezy all the time. Puff knew me, my niggas and everything -- the whole nine. Jazze was fucking with Boyz N Da Hood at first, but then my man Blok took them to Puff. I wasn't even in the group. I did a song and when Puff heard the song he was like, "Well, why don't we get all of them?" They was like, "The nigga Jeezy over there. They trying to get him at Def Jam." He was like, "Jeezy? Jeezy, Jeezy?" When the name met the face I was his mans. On some cool shit with Puff I was like, "I'll do one album. Really, just pay me for my vocals." Because I had a lot of shit on my plate at the time and if I couldn't give him 100 percent I didn't want to give him none at all. I was like, "I know we can do this one because we here and you know we can always renegotiate for another one." But at the time I had my Def Jam deal on the table and that meant more to me than getting into a group. You know I fuck with Big Gee, Big Duke -- I love them niggas, but at the time I had my own agenda.

It's hard to split the profits with a group…
Yeah, and I got my group, USDA. We was doing our thang. We was warming up the streets. We had the streets already warm. Then I thought about it, "If I fuck with Puff, they got to let me in the industry. How you gonna tell this man you not going to play my record because I'm a street nigga or you heard I hang around street niggas?" You can't tell him that. He's not gonna go When I got my Def Jam deal I first fucked with Kevin Liles. Him and LA Reid signed me. But it was crazy because as soon as I got signed Kevin left. Now it's me and LA, but LA fuck with me. When I took them the video they loved, they kept it. It's like '05 gonna be my muthafuckin' year, for real. I can't accept no for an answer. I ain't even knocking, I'm kicking the muthafuckin' door in. I peep it. These industry niggas don't want to let a street nigga in, because if you let street niggas in it's gonna be a whole other industry.

Hell yeah, it's going to be a whole bunch of street shit.
It's so political. The DJ knows, "He can't fuck me up because he needs me to play his record. He ain't gonna punch me in my shit."

The music industry is so corrupt. These niggas on some 7th grade shit.
That's why they won't let niggas in. As for me, I've been fighting all my muthafuckin' life. I ain't got shit to go back to. All I know is I was spared a lot of muthafuckin' times and I'm here and I ain't fucking this shit up for nobody or nothing. I want that 50 Cent muthafuckin' paper and I will not stop until I get it. For real. I ain't impressed by these niggas' cars, they watches, they bitches -- none of that shit. I got that shit. I want a spot in this shit, man. No disrespect at all my nigga, but it is what it is. Ima get me a spot in this shit. I live by what I call "My Theory". It's sad to say, I used to tell myself, "Ima sell a whole bunch of records or do a whole lot of time, but I'm cool with that shit." But I was blessed, and I got a chance to

> "THAT'S WHY I JUST DID THE OTHER ONE. IT'S CRAZY BECAUSE RIGHT NOW I'M ON THE ROAD AT LEAST FOUR TO FIVE DAYS OUT THE WEEK. I'M GETTING WHAT NIGGAS GET FOR SHOWS WITH GOLD ALBUMS. ALL THIS OFF A MIXTAPE. LIKE I SAID, IT MEANS SOMETHING. NIGGAS DO MIXTAPES AND YOU KNOW THAT SHIT COOL, BUT NIGGAS DON'T MAKE THAT BIG OF AN IMPACT. IT'S LIKE THE STREETS FEEL A NIGGA. I DON'T GIVE A FUCK ABOUT THE RADIO SHIT. THE RADIO BANNING ME AND THEY AIN'T PLAYING MY SHIT NOW."

sell a whole bunch of records instead of do a whole lot of time. So with that said, I feel like it's like the streets, a nigga in the way of my bread, it's on and poppin' man. Let's get it.

Are you afraid that now that you're famous, people are going to test your gangsta?
If a nigga was on some rap shit it would be different, but this is who I am. I'm a real nigga and niggas know me for being a real nigga. But if a nigga try to take it, I got something for him. This music shit is new to me, but a nigga's making his way. But I ain't had no problems with nothing thus far. I go and I do my shows and niggas love me, just like I love them because we cut from the same cloth. Real recognize real. Real niggas do real things, that's why we fuck with each other. That's why all the niggas who come to my shows come to get that thug motivation shit on -- hear about this money so they can go back out there and get it.

What's CTE and what's USDA?
CTE is my record label, Corporate Thugs Entertainment. Me and my nigga Kinky B own that. We're managed by Coach K. USDA is my group. My nigga Slick Pulla, and my nigga Fi Chief, and my nigga Big Dank and myself, that make up USDA -- United Streets Dopeboys of America. I'm about to drop a street album with the fam. We got a couple little singles off that. When we do our shows niggas love it.

Where are you originally from?
Georgia dog, because what it is, my family in southern Georgia and I was between ATL and there. I'm from GA. I've been in South Georgia and ATL all my life, back and forth. I think I left ATL came back and came back again. I wouldn't say one without the other. Niggas know I'm from the ATL and then niggas know me from being down that way.

What was it like growing up for you? When I hear your music you started hustling at an early, early age.
I mean, know what I'm sayin', basic shit. Pops gone. A nigga fucked up. Me, moms and little sister in like a one-bedroom, so a nigga made shit better for the family and did what he had

to do.

Where were you at in Atlanta?
Like my niggas, my older cousins was the first generation of niggas around here getting money. My cousin Jo Jo, Lil' Dave, so it was like I was with them. That's where I lived, me, my mom, my aunt and all us. We stayed in Mechanicsville, Decatur, it's just so many places. That's why I know all the niggas in the city and they know me. My family was like the niggas who was on, getting the money and shit. It was like everybody knew them so I was always known as lil' cuz. We was living with them so every time so we had to actually up and move too. I was all over. That's why I know niggas from the East Side, West Side, South Side. I really know every nigga around this muthafucka just on the strength of that. I think that's got a lot to do with why my shit is catching like it is because a lot of niggas know me and can vouch for me.

nigga with the new coupe. The young nigga with the new J's. The young nigga with the up-to-date watches. Seeing that, and putting money into other niggas and the shit not working and me knowing that we all real…we just need somebody to let them know where we coming from. I just took what was in my heart and all the shit that I been through and all the fucked up things that happened and transformed that shit. Ever since then, I just started taking it serious. It's like I don't feel like I rap. It ain't my intention to get on there and rhyme or make words to go together. It's something I feel. I just get on that muthafucka, it's whatever. It's just like I said, it comes from the heart. I live it. It's nothing to really just talk about Friday, ya feel me?

How would you describe your transition into the rap game?
Ima be real my nigga. I just hope nothing I say don't comeback and bite me in my ass.

or looking in my rearview mirror or sleeping in my bed wondering if the doorbell gonna ring. Real talk, it's like a lot of niggas talk about this shit, it's me for real. You just got off the phone with DJ Cube, a nigga I know of, just ask the nigga how I got down. Everybody know me like that. It was a risk, because it was like if it flop, you know how that go.

That is scary, especially if you've been on the block and that's all you know. You ain't got no basic life skills. You can't balance no checkbook.
I couldn't even tell you. Like I said, we can go back to question 1 or 2, it's a lot of my niggas fucked up, locked with some double digits for real, behind some other shit we believed in. I hear it in they letters and I hear it in they phone conversations, how bad they want a nigga to just make it. It's crazy. When this is all you know and you step away from one and you enter into a whole other realm and it's nothing

> **I JUST TOOK WHAT WAS IN MY HEART AND ALL THE SHIT THAT I BEEN THROUGH AND ALL THE FUCKED UP THINGS THAT HAPPENED AND TRANSFORMED THAT SHIT. EVER SINCE THEN, I JUST STARTED TAKING IT SERIOUS. IT'S LIKE I DON'T FEEL LIKE I RAP. IT AIN'T MY INTENTION TO GET ON THERE AND RHYME OR MAKE WORDS TO GO TOGETHER. IT'S SOMETHING I FEEL. I JUST GET ON THAT MUTHAFUCKA, IT'S WHATEVER. IT'S JUST LIKE I SAID, IT COMES FROM THE HEART. I LIVE IT. IT'S NOTHING TO REALLY JUST TALK ABOUT FRIDAY, YA FEEL ME?**

It ain't like none of that studio gangsta shit.
I know enough people that they can ask to find out if there's anything they want to know. A lot of niggas asked me that before though. I'm proud to say that. I got down with the best of them. I been all over this muthafucka really.

Did you get arrested at any time? Any run-ins with the law?
Nothing to brag about, because that ain't what real niggas do. I had my close calls. I had my times. I been on a couple of cases and shit where I ain't know whether it was gonna go good or bad. Nothing really crazy. A nigga been in some scary situations where I been fucked up, apprehended, snatched up on some other nigga's shit. I was blessed to get out of a lot of situations, but a lot of niggas that was with me didn't get out of those same situations. Real niggas do real things and I'm here, and I'm here for a reason.

How did you start rapping?
I don't even consider myself a rapper, to be honest with you. I ain't the type of nigga that's gonna sit around and rap all day. I'm the young

Everything ain't everything. It's crazy my nigga, but Ima just say like the hardest part of my transition was leaving everything I know. It was a risk because I was already that cool nigga in the club. I was always the nigga that came in the club with the new whip. Hitting Magic City up, making it rain in that muthafucka. Hitting 112 up and killing the parking lot in the new Modena Ferrari. It was a risk because the whole time I was doing it niggas didn't know. The DJ might play my shit in the strip club while I'm in there, but niggas wasn't knowing it was me. Niggas who knew me knew, but none of the bitches in there working or none of the people. I was that cool nigga. It was like a risk. My mans and them heard the shit. A lot of niggas I kick it with it in the street them niggas was going crazy, but I'm thinking like, "This my nigga, he like it or my shit tight because I'm his partner." But as time start going on I just started seeing muthafuckas in the club moving and getting into it and reciting a nigga words. It was like damn! It's such a good thing because it gave me an opportunity to be the same nigga that I am; fly, be a gangsta about it, because ain't no bitches over here, all that shit. I still can walk around without looking behind my back

but fuck-niggas and bitch-niggas. These niggas is hoes dog, these niggas is bitches dog. It's kind of crazy to me because I get the little funny questions – where you from? You know I don't really got to get into all that. Niggas know I'm from GA. Niggas know I rep the A. Niggas know I been here. I ain't got to get into that because I don't know what this shit gonna be like two years from now. I don't know if this shit gonna pop off to where I can do some Jay Z shit or I got to do some other shit like other niggas do, get an album and get on and the shit don't work and they got to get back on the block and do what they do. Mind ya business nigga. I don't want you all in mine, because I don't know how this gonna end for me. Like I was saying, these niggas is bitches. It's hard to deal with fuck-niggas because, like in my world I can fuck a nigga up. A nigga get wrong, we going to his mom house, we shooting up everything we see moving. A nigga get wrong in the club, we smashin 'em. Niggas know my family, how we get down. It's straight gangsta shit. In this world, niggas talk shit from a distance and sneak diss…

Or call this nigga and ask about you like a bitch.

And my job ain't to prove to no nigga that I'm real, because I know I'm real and I know what I've done. I know what I did before rap. I came into this rap game with everything every nigga in the game rapping for now. Jay Z didn't come into the game with a fucking Franck Muller and Jacobs and shit like that. This shit I'm already up on, so when I'm out, I'm blending in with the nigga. Niggas out with they minks, so I got my mink on. Nigga out with new coupe, I'm in the new coupe. Nigga out with shines on, the shines on. Nigga with the bad bitches, I'm with badder hoes. Niggas go to the club and want to party and make it rain in strip clubs, Ima make it thunderstorm. That's just me. That's besides rap though. And that's just the person who I am, so I don't feel like I should have to prove nothing to niggas. But most of these niggas so fake they want you to prove them that you real, so they can feel like they real.

They're caught up in the image and that's something you are trying to leave behind.

It's hard though because when I'm out the only thing that makes a difference and keeps me going, on some real shit, is when I'm out and I do shows and niggas recite my words like they feel where I'm coming from. I know everything I said was the truth and it came from my heart. It make a nigga feel like he done something at the end of the day and it means something. Even when I was a street nigga on some street nigga shit, niggas see me out or whatever, niggas dap me up, but it ain't like now. I'm out now niggas really speak to me. I see it in they eyes. They tell me, "I love what the fuck you doing." And I can see the respect and it's not intimidation. It don't feel like they got to pose the image like, "Fuck that nigga." It ain't like that, it's love, like, "Hey man, when yo next shit drop? I'm at ya next show. " And all this shit is off of mixtapes and that's what's big to me.

When I listen to your music, me being from Florida, I feel like you're talking to me. When you were like, "You were short anyway bring a stack," that's real shit.

The only reason they play that shit on the radio because it's a language we speak. Like street niggas speak a language. You can tell by a nigga's swag and his movements and how he carry himself if he's the nigga he proclaiming to be. So when you talk like that and radio see … they playing it because they don't know. They think that shit is like getting crunk. "Oh, it's getting crunk. Oh, it sounds good. It sounds cool." But only street niggas can read the lingo. They can only understand it. They can speak it. You know that, you know what the fuck I'm saying, "Bring a stack." It's a language. I got 24 years of this shit in me. Like from day one, just doing me. It's like, just being a gangsta. This shit real to me now because it's like, I can't let niggas down. Niggas really depending on a nigga to make some shit happen. And what's crazy is when you in the club and you see niggas who don't have an idea about what they saying, but they kind of just know, that let a nigga know it's power in words. It's like a secret code. You might say it to another nigga and it's only between you and him because ya'll cut from the same cloth. So to say that shit to the public and they get it the same way, that's what a nigga wanted to say but was scared to say it.

A lot of people are scared to say some shit like that.

Man, fuck it dog. I've been risking it this long.

It's like you risked your life for some other shit, so you're going to be scared of some words?

That's why I goddamn Tupac 'em man. I'm in the studio everyday, my nigga. To me, it wasn't never about going platinum. It wasn't never about selling no million records. It wasn't never about fucking no million bitches. It wasn't never about none of that shit. I just wanted to be heard, because I knew when niggas heard what I had to say they was gonna feel me -- and that happened. I told my man Coach K, I said, "When this 'Streets Iz Watching' hit the streets, everything's gonna change." It changed everything.

What's 2005 hold for you?

Trap or muthafuckin' Die. January 25. "Trap or Die" is about to be the biggest muthafuckin' mixtape ever dropped around this city. Like I said, my other one did 200 numbers, I'm trying to do crazy shit with this one. It's got the DVD, the video trailer, a day in the life, kicking it with a nigga, fucking off, everyday shit, a lot of shows and performances, a lot niggas interviewed speaking on a nigga and shit, asking muthafuckas in my environment what they think about a nigga. It's big, I got some cuts on there. I got a single for the mixtape. A lot of niggas don't do that, but I always do that. I got a single called "Trap or Die". You got to look for it. I know it's niggas sitting back there going, "Is this nigga real or is he fake?" Or "Maybe he just got lucky and put out a mixtape and got hot, but can a nigga really rap?" Tell 'em when "Trap or Die" comes out, all of their questions will be answered. •

TURF TALK

BY SCOTT BEJDA • PHOTOS BY MARCUS HANSCHEN

What is behind the title of your new album "The West Coast Vaccine"?
I chose to call it "The West Coast Vaccine" because I feel that what the West Coast is missing is a new face. I feel that the cure to the Coast is that we need some new faces out there, and I felt like I'm one of those new faces that could represent the Coast to the fullest.

There is a lot of attention on the Bay right now. Why do you think there wasn't as much attention on the Bay a few years ago like it is now?
I don't know! Maybe the music got better, but I can't call it. I just know that they are listening now and we got to take full advantage of this situation that we got right here. I don't know why they weren't checking for us and I can't call it, but I just know ever since Turf Talk been in the game they have been checking for it!

You have built yourself up a nice fan base already! How does that make you feel, being that you have only released a couple projects?
It makes me feel hella good; it makes me feel like my work is hella appreciated. From day one I watched my cousin E-40 and them when I was growing up. I seen how they was hustling and I looked up to them a lot. A lot of kids grow up and want to be an astronaut and shit like that, but I wanted to be an MC. That was really my career choice—I wanted to be one of the dopest rappers on the planet. So it really makes me feel good when I see that there is a lot of other people out there who believe in me just like how I believe in myself.

Once you get that fan base established they will ride with you until you put out your last album.
Fa' Sho! I'm hoping to get more and more fans in the near future.

You have something that a lot of rappers don't have and that's the ability to reach the average everyday muthafucka. You can really communicate with people through your music. Have you always been like that?
I think it has to do with my lifestyle and what I went through, because I was born in the Bay Area and then I moved to Southern California and then later moved back to the Bay. I was raised in Southern California and then came back to the Bay in 1999. So being that I lived the gang bang life and I hopped into the D-boy lifestyle too, I think my music comes across to all different people. There is people all over the world who have been through the same kind of shit that Turf Talk has been through. And as long as your music comes from your soul then you will be able to reach the soul, and what comes from the heart will be able to reach the heart. I think that is the key right there because everything that I write is something that I have been through and there is no made-up shit.

When you were doing the D-boy thing, did you ever get popped by the law?
I got two or three dope cases, man. Not to glorify it or nothing, but that was the thing that made me transfer and put all of my focus into this music. I was catching cases and shit so I wasn't too good at selling drugs.

How would you get caught, snitches?
Naw. You might grab your pack and switch it to another spot and when you are on your way to switch it the police might hit the block right there. All kinds of shit happens in the hood. I never sold to no decoys or shit like that, but it happens out there in the hood. If you are gonna be out there in the hood it's a part of the game. You are gonna do some time and you are gonna see some walls. One day sooner or later you will see sometime! It's just the wrong place and the wrong time, baby!

What advice would you have for these younger cats who are thinking about slangin' right now? What would you tell them?
I don't know their situations in life and what they are going through, but I know that I hated selling drugs because I felt like I was hurting my people, but at the time nobody could tell me nothing because of the situation I was in in my life. Get your money, man, but when you find an avenue get out and do something positive with your life.

What was it like for you growing up?
It was hard but I had Mom and Pops in the house. My house was cool but I was just a victim of my environment. It was nothing but gang bangin going on and I was caught up in that. I got kicked out of every school district that I attempted to go to. That's how it was growing up in Southern California for people out there who was active like that.

Back in those days when you were doing some grimy shit, did you ever have any older cats try to reach out to you to try to get you to change?
Not really, because I wasn't looking for that and if you're not looking for change then you not really even trippin'. I was really just having fun, because when you grow up with your homeboys since kindergarten you are just trying to have fun. I wasn't trying to do anything positive at the time because I was in the mind frame of just living that life.

All the experiences you had, do you think that makes you a better storyteller with your rhymes and what you spit?
I think it does, being able to go through that shit and seeing other people go through that shit. I have seen some real sick shit and only a real nigga can feel it if they hear it in the Rap. I think that everything that I have been through in my life makes my style.

How does your family feel to see how you have changed? Are they happy for you?
They are happy for me because I was getting into a lot of trouble. Back then—I ain't even gonna lie, and this is another thing you can tell the youngsters coming up—I would have my note pad and my pen and I would be writing raps, and even sometimes my family members would look at me like I was dumb and say, "What the hell are you doing? You need to be into your books." Now I can see it in their faces that they are proud of me though.

> "FROM DAY ONE I WATCHED MY COUSIN E-40 AND THEM WHEN I WAS GROWING UP. I SEEN HOW THEY WAS HUSTLING AND I LOOKED UP TO THEM A LOT. A LOT OF KIDS GROW UP AND WANT TO BE AN ASTRONAUT AND SHIT LIKE THAT, BUT I WANTED TO BE AN MC. THAT WAS REALLY MY CAREER CHOICE—I WANTED TO BE ONE OF THE DOPEST RAPPERS ON THE PLANET. SO IT REALLY MAKES ME FEEL GOOD WHEN I SEE THAT THERE IS A LOT OF OTHER PEOPLE OUT THERE WHO BELIEVE IN ME JUST LIKE HOW I BELIEVE IN MYSELF."

What some thought was a waste of time back then is what probably saved your life!
Fa sho, and it's probably gonna damn near take care of them, this pen and pad!

Do you think the new album will open up some more doors for you?
I think the doors will be wide open on this one. I put a lot of hard work into this project just to show the versatility of an artist on this album. On some songs and some hooks you wouldn't think it was me. I tried to do a lot on this album different to show these A & R's and these labels that Turf Talk got the whole package and we can put him on a song with this person, this person, and this person and he will show up. On this album I really wanted to showcase my skills and show people that I am not just a one-dimensional rapper. You can't just say that I am just Hyphy or you cant say that I am just Gangsta, because I want them to say that this muthafucka is an MC.

What made you do the independent thing when you probably could get a deal anywhere?
Really what it is, man, is I am a team player. When my first album came out I wasn't ready for the majors, and I wasn't ready to go major then. It is called artist development and Forty developed me to get ready for what is coming right now. I feel that the independent route is really what is best for me right now. I am getting a lot of experience and I am learning a lot about the business.

When Scotty Pippen came into the game he had Michael Jordan to learn from. How important of a role is E-40 playing in your career?
Forty and Mugzi is the root of my career. They really taught me how to not only be an MC but how to conduct myself and be a man and how to talk to people! A lot of cats don't have that kind of guidance, so that's a blessing. E-40 is one of the dons in the Rap game, so all I do is sit back and soak everything up because I would be a fool if I didn't.

You could probably write a book about everything you've seen!
I can. Just of me coming to Sick Wid It and seeing all the shit I have seen, and being up under Forty and going around the world with him, I can write a muthafuckin' book.

Mugzi seems to be staying mainly behind the scenes. What is Mugzi's position in Sick Wid It?
Mugzi is Forty's right hand! Forty is still fulfilling his career as an MC and he is also a CEO. Forty has help from Mugzi because Mugzi is about his business. Mugzi plays the background, but he is really a crucial piece of the puzzle. He makes the machine move and go around. While Forty is out doing the groundwork Mugzi is at home handling the corporate side of things.

It sounds like a very stable corporate entity, plus it is all family orientated.
Right, I was really trippin' how The Click was really a family group. That's a tight organization!

You are still in the early stages of your career. Where do you want to see yourself five years from now?
In the next five years I want to put out artists, because I was talking to my dude Laroo, who is an artist on label Sick Wid It Records. He really laced me on some shit! The Sick Wid It deal is really good for Turf Talk, but it might not be good for my homies, so I got to make an avenue for them. Right now me and Forty is talking about setting up some distribution through Sick Wid It slash whatever. I'm gonna launch my shit called Hood Thang Entertainment. I'm gonna put artists out

> "I GOT TWO OR THREE DOPE CASES, MAN. NOT TO GLORIFY IT OR NOTHING, BUT THAT WAS THE THING THAT MADE ME TRANSFER AND PUT ALL OF MY FOCUS INTO THIS MUSIC. I WAS CATCHING CASES AND SHIT SO I WASN'T TOO GOOD AT SELLING DRUGS."

through Hood Thang and then I'm gonna stick with Sick Wid It. I want to establish myself as a dope ass artist first before I start doing a bunch of other shit. I want to get my feet planted in this Rap game and represent this Coast to the fullest first. Once I get my respect and get people behind me then I will start making the big moves.

Do you have your own family?
I got two beautiful Daughters and two step-sons and I love them to death. That is who I am rapping for. To tell you the truth, I am cool right now because I got a couple cars, and a house so I'm straight and I am happy with life right now. But if Turf dies today then what about my kids? That's how I feel! I'm really rapping for my family so when I am gone they are papered up.

You are creating the foundation.
That is what Forty is doing. That's our tree right there! We always talk about this: Forty was put here to do a job because he does so much for our family and friends. That's how I want to be, because if I am in a position to help that is a beautiful thing.

What do you do in your off time?
I live three lives, dog! I am still tied in the hood with my niggaz forever, but we are turning everything positive to give something back to the hood. I play that role, then I play the rap role and then on my off time I am the father and the husband. I am juggling three lives. I try to keep everything cool so on my off days I'm at home with the family chilling staying out the way.

Back to the album, what is gonna be the first single?
The first single is "I Got Chips" featuring E-40 and produced by Rick Rock. It is something to warm cats up for the album to let you know it's coming. It is us talking about the money we are spending and just having fun.

Will there be a video?
We are going to do a video to a song I got called "Dough Boy" featuring E-40 and B-Legit. It's produced by Droop-E. We're gonna really try to push this album independently. This is an independent album but it will be pushed like a major.

What has been the overall response from people when they hear your music?
They dig my style because I don't sound like anyone else. I guess what people say mostly is that I got a different style. They say I got a weird style!

You are an original. How did you develop your style?
I got it from where I stay because there are some things in my raps that a Northern California person might not understand but a Southern California person will understand and vice versa. I just mix it all up with my lifestyle and I use different words from different parts of California. I am giving you my secret, but it's all good. I mix it all together and that is how I do my style.

You can get The Bay and L.A. to get behind you like that.
I got to because I feel like the only person that could bring California together as a whole is a person that has lived on both sides and has had respect on both sides. Right now L.A. and The Bay are working together a lot more than in the past. I don't single myself out like, "This is Crip or this is Blood." I'm just a hustler! I'm doing this music and I am speaking for every nigga on the corner that has been through something in life. I don't single myself out because I am speaking for everybody all over the fuckin' world!

A lot of people tell me Cali has some bomb-ass weed. Who do you think has the best trees?
California has the best weed, and I have been everywhere and I ain't found no weed better than the weed in the Bay Area, man. We smoke all kinds of weed out here! We're gourmet about our shit!

So there ain't no drought season out there then?
No, there ain't no drought out here baby! If there was a drought season in the Bay on weed there would be a million murders around this muthafucka!

Does it enhance your creativity when you are in the booth?
I think all it does is relax me. I come to the studio and sometimes there might be fifteen niggaz in there and I smoke a little and pour me a little drank and it relaxes me to where I can focus on my music a little more. But it don't help the lyrics or no shit like that. If people really know how I write my raps I just sit down and whatever the fuck pops in my head I just write it down.

Can you be anywhere and get a thought and stop what you are doing to write it down?
I could be anywhere! I turn on my Nextel and record! I can just pull out my phone and have about twenty metaphors ready to go.

Do you work fast when you're in the studio?
Once I got the lyrics the recording process is no longer than about five minutes at the most on a verse. The only thing that takes time is to write the verse.

On the new album did you rap fast on some tracks?
I did a little bit of everything on this album! I did some fast shit, some slow shit and everything else. I did it all on this album! People will see a well-rounded album with many styles mixed together. Like I said, I wanted to showcase what I can do on this one right here.

When you make your music do you go in there with the intention to make it for everybody?
No. I just go in there and do whatever I feel. I vibe off the beat and whatever the music is saying, that is what I go on. It's all about whatever the music is saying!

Besides Forty and B-Legit do you have any other features on "West Coast Vaccine"?
I got Freeway on there from Philadelphia and I got the big homie Too Short on there who is my folks, and basically I got the camp on there. I wanted to show my skills and not have a gang of people on here.

With the album as a whole are you happy with the finished product?
I am happy with it, but with anything you do you feel like you could do better. But overall I am very happy with it. I feel like it is dope. With Forty I don't talk about me and him in the same category but I don't feel nobody put nothing out in The Bay doper than it though. I buy everybody's shit so that is why I speak on it like that.

Are you doing anything with film?
We are filming "Turf Television" right now. Everywhere I go I got the cameras following me working on this "Turf Television" little DVD. I want to show people what level I'm on because we are independent but we live like stars out here in The Bay.

been taught and that's gettin' that bread!

Back when everyone first started gankin the lingo and the slang from the Bay ya'll could have been viscous about it. How do you guys feel about it now when people take the slang?
With me I see it as a whole different way because I actually lived out on Southern Cali. I would hear what the Southern Cali niggaz would be saying about the Northern Cali niggaz and then I would hear what the Bay would be saying about Southern Cali. I just learned to back up off of that because we are all one as a whole and we are all California. Who said because I am from the Bay I can't wear Chuck Taylors? I look at it like "Fuck it, we are all Cali." If they want to pop they collar then they can pop they collar too, and if I want to throw on my chucks then I will. It's a Cali thing, man! •

I have always been a fan of Yukmouth, C-Bo, Spice-1, and E-40, and I think you are right up there with all of them. Did you think it would move so fast for you?
I didn't it would move this fast, I just knew I was hungry and would take advantage of any opportunity that I got and I was gonna make myself one of the dopest muthafuckaz and not let nobody hold up on me. People might be like, "Forty is his cousin and that's how he got on." That's cool if you say that on the first album, but you can't say that on the second and third album. You can lead someone to the water but they have to drink. Forty brought me up to the plate, but I had to hit the ball because if I hadn't hit the ball I wouldn't have been shit. I came in and hit that muthafucka!

There are so many different towns in the Bay, but it seems like everybody is working together without boundaries. When did it really become that way?
I give the credit to the radio stations because they got behind us and really started supporting us out here. We started having a gang of shows out here too! Promoters started doing a gang of shows with different artists and that started bringing us together. You might have a show with three other artists that has a song on the radio and that just brings us together tight. Me and Mistah FAB went to Europe together and kicked it out there for a month and that made us cool. That made us all kind of humble and that is the key. That's what Forty taught us from day one is to be humble.

The Bay and LA are by no means places that you can take lightly. How do you stay humble in such an area where violence can erupt at any time?
I think because The Bay has always been about getting money. When the Rap wasn't hot we had the pimps out here and the dope game was big. It has always been about money out here, so when we see we got a chance to make some money we put all the bullshit aside. The Bay has always been about money, so we are just doing what we have

> "I AM A TEAM PLAYER. WHEN MY FIRST ALBUM CAME OUT I WASN'T READY FOR THE MAJORS, AND I WASN'T READY TO GO MAJOR THEN. IT IS CALLED ARTIST DEVELOPMENT AND FORTY DEVELOPED ME TO GET READY FOR WHAT IS COMING RIGHT NOW. I FEEL THAT THE INDEPENDENT ROUTE IS REALLY WHAT IS BEST FOR ME RIGHT NOW. I AM GETTING A LOT OF EXPERIENCE AND I AM LEARNING A LOT ABOUT THE BUSINESS."

TWIZTID

BY GREG "GATE$" DAVENPORT • PHOTO BY JOHNNY BUZZERIO

Do you have other releases than Mostastless out as Twiztid?
We did an album for Psychopathic that was like and underground style one, then we re-released it on Island/Def Jam with 6 new tracks. It's the same album with some new tracks on there so it'd be fresh for anyone who bought the underground one. We were getting like 200 to 300 e-mails every 2 days of people sayin that they couldn't find the record, no one stocked enough of it. So when we got with Island/Def Jam they had the power to get it in every store.

Twiztid used to be in part of a group called House of Krazees who were legends in Detroit. Can you talk a little about how that group got started?
In about 92 me and Monoxide, who at the time was EXP and my name was Mr. Bones, we were starting a group called House Of Krazees. And ROC who is now called Sol, he had more experience with music. We had never done a record before, so we asked him to do some tracks for our album House of Krazees, Home Sweet Home. He was straight. At the time he was in another band with his cousin. Then we were like, why don't you be in our band and it'll be a lot easier. Before you knew it there was a whole album recorded with all three of us on it, that was the beginning of House of Krazees.

How did the name come about?
Probably because we were all a little bit strange. We were on some ol' weirdo type shit. It's the same typa shit we're into now. We tried to take it into a perspective where like the world is a house that encaged and entrapped all the crazy people.

People like Esham and ICP and House Of Krazees had developed a unique style of music in Detroit. It's surprising that the media never recognized what was going on in Detroit.
It was definitely overlooked. It's always been like that, and in a sense, it's still like that now. It's like the stuff that we do is so underground. If you're not Back Street Boys or Limp Bizkit no one cares to pay attention to what you're doing.

House of Krazees had a lot of albums out. What happened?
We had somewhere from four to six albums. The idea was there, but there was no motivation. It was so bootleg. The shit wouldn't even come out on CD, it'd just come out on cassette. There was no heart in it. It had a lot to do with the label. Walt didn't know the first thing about music. That's a lost cause right there.

Does Twiztid sound similar to House of Krazees, or is it different?
It's a different sound. When we did the House of Krazees shit it was kinda like a basement bootleg type thing where it was more or less like a job. Beats were provided, we would write lyrics and we'd just record 'em. With Twiztid it gave me and Monoxide a chance to get in the studio and actually have 100% creative control over our entire project. It unleashed a whole new side of us, which is now Twiztid.

> "PROBABLY BECAUSE WE WERE ALL A LITTLE BIT STRANGE. WE WERE ON SOME OL' WEIRDO TYPE SHIT. IT'S THE SAME TYPA SHIT WE'RE INTO NOW. WE TRIED TO TAKE IT INTO A PERSPECTIVE WHERE LIKE THE WORLD IS A HOUSE THAT ENCAGED AND ENTRAPPED ALL THE CRAZY PEOPLE."

How did you come up with the name Twiztid?
One of the reasons is because we're always gettin twisted, gettin high, smokin weed. We all sat down--Shaggy, Violent J, me and Monoxide--we talked it over and decided that would be a perfect name for us.

When did House of Krazees break up and you come together as Twiztid?
About '96. And the first Twiztid record, the national one, was released June 22 of this year. In between there was like a 2 year break when we were recording stuff and trying to get on our feet.

Were you using a lot of Rock guitar in your music with House of Krazees?
Since the beginning with House of Krazees we were using shit like that. Monoxide is more the Rap side of it, and I like a lotta Rock music. So we twist both sides together.

What music do you listen to?
Anything from Godsmack, Black Sabbath, old school Motley Crew, Kiss.

Punk Rock never influenced you?
Yeah, in a sense. One thing about Punk Rock, it's all about individuality. It's not what everyone else thinks is cool, it's what you think is cool.

Did any particular Punk groups influence you?
Probably like the Sex Pistols. It wasn't a major influence. But they created a movement where you don't have to have the hundred dollar sunglasses to be cool. Just who you are makes you cool. Not so much the music as the genre. It's what Punk Rockers did that helped us out a lot.

If you had to describe the Twiztid sound to someone who had never heard you before, what would you say?
I would say it's Alternative Rap. It's not Rock, it's not Rap, it's like a mixture between them. We'll go into some stores and our music will be in the Heavy Metal section. We'll go into another store and we'll be in the Alternative part or in the Rap/R & B category. No one knows how to describe what we do. I'd say it's Alternative Rap. It has a very wicked feel. It's not your average "a bottle of water and a towel on stage" Rap. It's none of that.

You rap in your music. And the beats are Hip Hop beats or Rock beats?
The beats are a mixture of Hip Hop and Rock type beats. On a couple tracks we got guitar rifts.

Who does your production?
On our album it's like a 60/40 breakdown. Mike Clark did some of the production, and me and Monoxide did the rest of it. On some of the tracks Mike Clark, us and ICP, we all sat down in the studio and banged out the tracks.

How would you compare Twiztid to ICP?
There are some differences, but nothing major. We're all part of the dark carnival. I'd say they're more comedic than we are. There's more of a comedy aspect with ICP than us. We're more on a serious level.

Do you mean lyrically or on stage?
Lyrically. They'll make you laugh. You can listen to an ICP record and crack up. You'll be laughing by the second song. With our stuff you'll nod your head and say, Damn they said some shit that really hit home with me. That would be the main difference to me.

What made you go into that direction, focusing on the darker side of life.
What we do is try to show the dark side. It's reality, it's all reality, and in our opinion reality really sucks. Every day you can look out the window to see reality, but you won't pay $7 to go to the movies and see reality. You wanna be entertained. We try to keep it entertaining, keep it dark, make sure that it'll take you to another world. You can go to the store right now and buy eight Rap albums that are pretty much the same. People talkin about how much dope they sell, what kinda clothes they wear, and shit like that. We're not interested in that. We wanna scare you, we want you to be afraid when you turn off the lights at night. We make music that we like to hear and if everyone else likes it, then it works.

I think people who listen to Brotha Lynch Hung or C-Bo would like your shit, but the Rap audience isn't really aware of what you're doing.
With both us and ICP the label Island/Def Jam pushes us like a Korn or Limp Bizkit, like an Alternative Rock band. That's why a lot of the Rap consumers overlook us like it isn't even Rap, when actually it is. It just has a hint of Rock & Roll mixed into it.

You paint your faces white and black like ICP does. With House of Krazees you used to wear masks?
Mystery always makes people wonder. Who's behind that mask or paint. With House of Krazees it was a pumpkin mask. Now with Twiztid we're like dead souls, we're phantoms that walk the earth. So we don't look like everybody else, we have black circles around our eyes and white faces.

What influenced you and your partner to write about the subjects you write about?
We don't like to take all the good parts of reality, we take the bad aspects. Like shit you see on the news at night before you go to bed. Like 6 or 7 kids got killed in a drive-by shooting or some little girl got kidnapped. That typa shit that everybody wants to turn their heads away from, to not acknowledge it. That's what we use as fuel to write our lyrics. We wanna make music that bothers people. We use that aspect of reality. The rest of it is just stuff that we like to hear. We like horror movies so we wanna make horror movies.

What side do you take in this, do you take the side of the psychopathic killer? Is it a positive thing?
We take the side of the psychopathic. That's who we roll with. I don't see it as positive or negative. That's part of Twiztid. We're either or, we're both and none. That's why we're Twiztid. There is not middle ground, we are the middle ground. With Twiztid we don't have to have a reason. We do it cause we want to. We do what we want cause we want, we don't have to have a reason. We're not the white or the black, we're the gray. We're not the wrong or right, we're in the middle. We take both good and bad, wrap it up and that's Twiztid. It's our opportunity to talk about anything that we want.

Do you feel hateful toward people?
It's not so much hatred toward people, but more hatred toward people without open minds. If you can't listen to it with an open mind then we have hatred for you. We always have love for the Jugalos cause they got love for us. That's how it goes.

It's not like you're totally disgusted with society?
We are. That's totally true. But if like there's a person that disagrees with what we say, but listens to it with an open mind then we got love for that person. But if someone looks at us and say, I don't wanna hear that shit, that's bullshit, they're just talkin shit--then we don't have any love for them.

It's serious stuff you're talking about and there's a lot of anger too.
Oh yeah, there's definite anger. Sometimes you gotta scream for people to listen to you too.

I heard your record has been selling good.
Yeah, it's only been out for 6 months and it's already to 150,000 records. We're really impressed with how it's doing. And this is just the beginning.

Who did the artwork for your CD? It really sets the atmosphere.
That's Chaos Comics. They're doing a comic book for ICP. I used to collect comics ever since I was little, and they drew a character called Lady Death in Evil Ernie. I used to collect all their comics and they were like one of my favorite comics. When I found out they were doing the ICP comic books, we thought maybe they should draw our cover. They were down to do it and it came out beautiful. It was an honor, because they created one of my favorite comic characters.

You were really into comics as a kid?
Hell yeah. Anything to escape the boring reality that we live in--horror movies, comic books, all that shit.

How was it for you growing up?
It wasn't bad. We grew up in the hood. Now when we go back to the hood it's totally different. You got these little baby gangsters lookin at us like Who the hell are you? Hey man, we founded this muthafucka.

What part of Detroit did you grow up in?
East Side.

That's where Esham and Sol and a lot of people grew up?
Oh yeah, it was jumpin over there. Eminem used to be out there too. I don't know if he grew up there, but he used to come by Monoxide's house and kick it.

You still live there?
No. It's gotten so crazy down there. It's like if your face isn't on the scene every day you're pretty much an enemy, so we had to get the fuck out.

Monoxide, why do you think people have been so slow to wake up to Detroit? There's so much amazing music coming from there?
Because everybody's scared of it. They don't know what to make of it. It's a different sense of reality. It's not drive by shootin or sellin a half pound of weed. It's more like, I'll cut your head off and kidnap both your kids. People are scared of it. They don't know what the fuck's goin on.

How did you get into that type of stuff?
We heard what Esham was doin and just added to it. We took it to our next level.

Esham influenced you?
We all grew up together. It was always in our face. I guess you could say we were influenced.

Detroit is the only place coming with all that wicked shit and using the rock guitars.
It's starting to go over. New York tried it. They had their Gravediggaz and Flatlanders, whatever, and they fuckin bombed. They couldn't do it right.

What are you listening to now?
A lotta the South, a lotta Southern Rap. Some West Coast stuff like Korrupt, Dogg Pound.

What you're doing is really Rap, more than groups like Limp Bizkit or Korn.
Big time.

What do you think about groups like Kottonmouth Kingz?
Kottonmouth is good. They're my friends. They're doin their thing.

Do you think they were influenced by you and ICP?
Could be. You can see the similarities. Granted we're 10 times darker.

About your lyrics...
It's what you're about, it's what you got inside of you. Everybody's probably got it, just some people can't find it. The deeper and darker you look the deeper and darker it becomes.

Do you look at it as a positive thing or a negative thing?
Positive in a negative way. Like everything we say sound negative, but if you listen to it everything's got a point, a purpose.

Do you listen to a lot of Rock too?
I listen to Rock. Like Godsmack, Rage Against The Machine, shit like that.

When you were with House of Krazees you were using Rock rifts?
It was in there, but not enough. That's probably one of the main reasons we split, cause of the direction we were going. The direction in that band was not right, like goin in circles. •

INTERWIEW WITH AL KAPONE

BY GREG "GATE$" DAVENPORT • PHOTO BY MARCUS HANSCHEN

You've been workin on it for about six months now.
Yeah, we've been puttin it down. It's 16 songs on the album. Straight real nigga shit. Everything's comin from a real nigga perspective. Even when I do a shoot-em-up-bang-bang song I'm not sayin I'm just shootin niggaz for the hell of it. If a nigga put my life in danger then I automatically think I better get them before they get me. Ain't no love, no remorse, it's do or die. I got songs like that on there. I got some freaky kinda songs, freaky women. I got shit about gettin money--all the different kinda ways you can hustle to make money from pimpin to rappin to sellin dope. I got the real buck wild shit on there. I got a couple of smoked out kinda songs. I got a nice lil' shake-that-ass song for the women that like to shake it a little bit.

When we first went to make this album what was in your mind?
When I first got to makin this album it all reflected on the title. The title basically says it all, Goin All Out. I wanted to make that kinda statement, let everybody know I'm puttin everything into this. For everybody that tried to deny me. For everybody that know the struggle that I been through. I got the opportunity now, I got a major force behind me. I got E-40, I got Sick Wid' It/Jive behind me. With this album I wanted to make a statement more than anything. No matter what kinda song, each song had to be done to the point that when you hear it you know that I'm dead serious. It's do or die. I'm finna show everybody. No matter how long it takes a nigga can make it happen as long as they stay true to themselves and don't let nobody else hold you down. You can do this, but once you get the opportunity you can't sleep on it, you can't take it for granted, you can't slack in no kinda way. You gotta be on point about everything.

You built the whole album around the title?
In a lotta a ways everything in the album did revolve around that title. Even if the subject of a particular song don't seem to have anything to do with the title, I'm still goin all out on it, you'll feel it.

You were one of the pioneers of Memphis Rap. How long have you been doing it?
Man, it's been ten years in this game. When it first started there wasn't many people in the Memphis Rap scene. Gangsta Pat, Al Kapone, Eightball & MJG, Pretty Tony. Then Skinny Pimp, Three 6 Mafia, Playa Fly, everybody else really came after. We really paved the way for the scene. But since we was like the first a lot of us got caught up and didn't know what to do. Eightball & MJG survived because they got with somebody that had the money and the vision and pulled them out of a bad situation. They were gettin hell at one point in time, and when Tony Draper came and took 'em away to Houston. The rest of us were goin through struggles. We had the fame first, but we didn't know how to elevate the fame and use it and make it grow. A lotta the other artists really learned from our mistakes, and they came up off of it.

Also, back ten years ago Rap was all about the East and the West. Nobody was talkin about the South. You probably had a hard time just to be rapping in the South.
At that time as far as the South goes, Rap-A-Lot and Geto Boys paved the way for the South artists. Before Master P, Cash Money or anyone, it was Rap-A-Lot. That's who we looked up to, along with the popular West Coast artists--everybody was big on the West Coast. But Memphis always had its own sound that I hear now in a lot of other people's music. Like Missy Elliot's got a song called "Hot Boys". That's a Memphis track. Tupac did "I Cannot Break The Pain" on his All Eyes On Me album--that's a Memphis track. We were doing that kinda stuff way back, but people in Memphis felt that was just a local sound. They figured that for us to break in at that time we needed to do what was popular everywhere else. That mentality played a part in leading the early artists in Memphis astray from what we had goin. What Three 6 did was they capitalized off of what we shoulda been doin all a long--doing the Memphis sound strictly. Three 6 Mafia just kept doin the Memphis sound and they kept feedin the Memphis sound to the public. They came up off of something that was already paved. It's all good though, cause people like Three 6 and Skinny Pimp, they really kept it alive.

Other than the local stuff, most people in Memphis were listening to West Coast Rap?
At that time mostly it was NWA. We were

> "THE TITLE BASICALLY SAYS IT ALL, GOIN ALL OUT. I WANTED TO MAKE THAT KINDA STATEMENT, LET EVERYBODY KNOW I'M PUTTIN EVERYTHING INTO THIS. FOR EVERYBODY THAT TRIED TO DENY ME. FOR EVERYBODY THAT KNOW THE STRUGGLE THAT I BEEN THROUGH. I GOT THE OPPORTUNITY NOW, I GOT A MAJOR FORCE BEHIND ME. I GOT E-40, I GOT SICK WID' IT/JIVE BEHIND ME. WITH THIS ALBUM I WANTED TO MAKE A STATEMENT MORE THAN ANYTHING. NO MATTER WHAT KINDA SONG, EACH SONG HAD TO BE DONE TO THE POINT THAT WHEN YOU HEAR IT YOU KNOW THAT I'M DEAD SERIOUS. IT'S DO OR DIE. I'M FINNA SHOW EVERYBODY. NO MATTER HOW LONG IT TAKES A NIGGA CAN MAKE IT HAPPEN AS LONG AS THEY STAY TRUE TO THEMSELVES AND DON'T LET NOBODY ELSE HOLD YOU DOWN. YOU CAN DO THIS, BUT ONCE YOU GET THE OPPORTUNITY YOU CAN'T SLEEP ON IT, YOU CAN'T TAKE IT FOR GRANTED, YOU CAN'T SLACK IN NO KINDA WAY. YOU GOTTA BE ON POINT ABOUT EVERYTHING."

really into that Gangsta shit. With a name with Al Kapone--it was ironic that my grandmama and mama used to call me Al Kapone ever since I was real little. But it was definitely the West Coast Gangsta shit that was goin on at that time. Before that it was the East Coast stuff--the Run DMC and LL's--I was influenced by all that, used to buy it and listen to it. But by the time I got in the game it was NWA and Ice T, Too Short, that typa stuff.

What motivated you to start doing Rap at a time when nobody was doing it Down South?
I loved it so much, I just loved Rap music. I was one of the first people in the town that was hip to all the Rap slang and shit. It made me stand out, made me different from everyone else. People'd be lookin at me, What the hell's wrong with dude? I was into it deeply. I was scratching at that time, I was break dancing, learning everybody's raps. Then I started writin verses. But what really made me think I could be a rapper was listening to Ice T. He was the first dude I heard that was talkin about shit that I saw was goin on. I was growin up in the projects, and he was talkin about street shit. "You mean I can talk about what's goin on around this muthafucka and make records?" Goddamn! That really motivated me. I started doin the shit. Then what really set me off again was Gangsta Pat. Gangsta Pat was the first Memphis rapper to really blow up. I really just got off my ass and went after it whole heartedly. And shit blew up before I knew it. The lil' songs and shit I did became popular. I was makin songs for me to listen to. I'd give a DJ a copy here and there, they ended up puttin it on mix tapes and playin it in the clubs. Shit blew up. Then it came down to me not knowin what to do with that situation and not havin the right people, not bein able to grow off it.

What was the first songs you put out there?
Everybody in this area know me from "Lyrical Drive By". They gonna talk about that forever. They still play that on the radio today. That was the hit. Everybody probably could tell you what they was doin around that time. They could probably tell you about fights that broke out in the clubs when they played that song. It was an exciting time. The get buck wild energy that we had when we did the Gangsta Walk, I feel like I brought that to the stage and to the music. I feel like I brought that get buck energy to the music. It came from the clubs and doing the Gangsta Walk.

Did you put that song out as a single?
It started out being on mixtapes. It was on everybody's mixtape, every DJ in Memphis had that song on their mixtapes. They put it on there cause they knew people was gonna buy it for that song. I remember one time, I had never met DJ Paul, and people kept sayin there was this new dude who put my song on his mixtape without even askin. I met Paul one day and he was like, I heard you was hot at me about puttin the song on the tape and I want to know is it cool. I was like, Just do what you gotta do to get your ass in. I ain't trippin, cause everybody else used the muthafucka anyway. If you ever get a chance to show me some love one day, show me some love one day. I ain't never in my life woulda known that he would be part of a group that would blow up. Goddamn it nigga, if you're readin this nigga, you need to show some love like I told you back then.

Where did you meet him?
He came up to the studio where I was recording.

You're about the same age?
No, he's younger than me. I was doin shows in '91 at high schools and shit. I remember doin one at the high school Paul was goin to, Hillcrest. They was gettin my autograph and shit. I feel like I did my part in settin up some shit for Memphis.

The first rapper from Memphis I ever heard was Al Kapone. One of the first CD's Murder Dog ever got was Al Kapone, Name of CD. That's when we started opening our doors to the South. You lead Murder Dog to the South.
I'm proud that I played my little part in makin it happen.

You were going by Al Kapone then, and then you started calling yourself Ska-Face Al Kapone....
But anything I do now is gonna be under the name Al Kapone. This is how the whole situation started. When I first came out I was Ska-Face Al Kapone, that was back in '90. I released a coupla underground tapes with that name. At that time Geto Boys was the leaders in the South. I was always a big Geto Boys fan, I was buyin their first album, Makin Trouble. At first Scarface was DJ Action. But I think on their third album they were introducing each member of the group and they said he was Scarface. I was like, Damn! But he was in a group, so I felt I could still go by Ska-Face Al Kapone. Next thing I know he dropped a solo album, Mr. Scarface Is Back. He done blew up with it first. Then he said the line, "There's a lotta wannabe Scarfaces, I heard the name in '89 different places...." Ah maan! I couldn't use the name no more. Fucked up. I was already known by that name. I was with a company at that time and they was concerned about it. That's when I started goin strictly under Al Kapone. After doin a few records under local companies, I got through with all my contracts and started my own label, Alkatraz. At that time I had been through so much turmoil with goin through different companies and my career not bein handled right, I felt like even my name had been fucked up. I felt like, Fuck it I'm gonna go back to Ska-Face Al Kapone like I first did. Fuck it! So I started releasing records, compilations, everything under Ska-Face Al Kapone. But every time I used Ska-Face Al Kapone muthafuckas would start comin up to me, "What happened with Bushwick Bill?" or "Was that 2 Pac in your video?" and shit like that. I was still concerned about havin Ska-Face in my name. When I got the deal with E-40 we talked a lot about it. We even talked to Mean Green about it in Houston. We decided to take Ska-Face off my name. I want people when they hear my name, they know it's me. I don't want them to think I'm somebody else.

How did the deal come together with Sick Wid' It?
It started with the South West Ryders compilation E-40 put out. Only E-40 could answer why he even called me in the first place. He said he had been readin up on me in some magazines and stuff. He finally got in touch with me and asked me to be part of the South West compilation. After that the hype that I got off of bein on that compilation elevated me more. I ended up doin more compilations with other people, and I did my own compilation, Memphis To Tha Bombed Out Bay. I hit the road with it and I went out to the Bay and ran into E-40 again. He was doin a picnic for the kids--he was signin autographs and shit. So I took my posters and my shit I had and I was out there signin autographs too. He musta seen me out there all the way from the fuckin South, got a line of people at his event and I'm signing autographs. We talked for a minute, he was like, Get at me later on. I got with him a little later, went out to the crib, he fixed me a nice big cup of gorilla milk. Just so happened he was workin on a track called "Gorilla Milk". He asked me, Think you could write something? So I wrote me a verse right on the spot. It was just that energy. About a month later he called me up, You ready to do this? That's how it all started. We got all the paperwork together and it was on ever since.

When did you actually sign with him?
It was February of '99. I started recording in May. I recorded a string of songs. I came off for a minute, vibed off what I had, took out what I didn't like. Came back, did a few more, got some different producers to work with me. I wanted to really make sure I did an Al Kapone record, the kinda record that I know niggaz love me for.

How many songs did you finish?
I did 22 songs, but I'm only using 16 of them. It's all done now. I got them in order,

everything. Ready to roll. It's one of the best records I ever recorded. I got with people, real hardcore critics. I got a lotta constructive criticism. Not only in Memphis, in the Bay, in different parts of the South. Every place I go I'm, Don't bullshit, fuck how I feel, tell me what you think on the real.

> "IF THEY GO AND BUY A RECORD THAT GOT A LITTLE BIT OF EVERYTHING ON IT, MAN I DIDN'T BUY THIS NIGGA FOR THAT MAN. YOU CAN'T JUST BE MIXIN THAT SHIT. IT'S LIKE A MUTHAFUCKA PUT FROSTED FLAKES AND SUGAR SMACKS AND LUCKY CHARMS AND FRUITY PEBBLES ALL TOGETHER IN THE SAME BOX. AIN'T NOBODY GONNA WANNA EAT THAT. WHAT THE FUCK? IF I WANT SOME FRUITY PEBBLES THAT'S WHAT I'M GONNA BUY. WHEN I WANT FROSTED FLAKES I'LL BUY A BOX OF THAT. I DON'T WANT THIS SHIT. THAT'S HOW THE BUYIN PUBLIC FEELS. YOU GOTTA KNOW YOUR AUDIENCE."

What are we going to hear?
You're gonna hear Al Kapone at his finest. You're gonna hear the Memphis flavor. You're gonna hear the crunk shit, the buck shit. Al Kapone was always a mixture of Down South/Memphis shit and the West Coast flavor. I was so influenced by the West Coast, it's always gonna be a part of me. It's a mixture of both. But I gotta get on stage and act a damn fool. I gotta have them kinda songs that when I hit the stage I'm gonna act a goddamn fool. Niggaz is gonna be like, That nigga's crazy as fuck. That's the typa song I really concentrated on. I feel like that's what really made my career in the beginning, I was able to go to different places and perform and people could feel me off the performance. I did songs that I could hit the stage with.

Can you name some of the song titles off your album?
"Now I Gotta Get Ya", that's one they've been playin on the radio in Memphis. They got a sneak peak in Memphis and it got hot. It's a get-wild-ass song. Then "Super Crunk", that's another get-wild-ass song. It's a duet me and E-40 did. I know niggaz is gonna feel that shit. "The Pimpin In Me", that's a song me and MJG did. For real pimp shit.

Where did you do that song with MJG?
We recorded pretty much everything here in Memphis at a studio called The House Of Blues. One song was done in the Bay. It was a track that Mike Mosley produced, the "Gorilla Milk" song with me, E-40 and Eightball. I know people gonna feel that one. Then I got "Make Me Rich"--I redid the old Too Short song, "Cuss Words". I kept that hardcore vibe that it always had and just refined it a little bit and made that shit bumpin as a muthafucka once again. Wasn't a whole lot to do cause the shit is the shit regardless. I can't wait to perform in the Bay with that muthafucka. Then "Bootleggers Beatdown"--we're talkin about beatin the shit out these bootleggin muthafuckas. Takin money outta our goddamn pockets. Got a little something for the women to shake some ass off of. Then me and Shuga T got a little freaky song on there, kinda like Too Short and Lil' Kim typa shit. You might hear it and get hot, wanna bone some. I guarantee when niggaz pick up my shit they're gonna feel it.

When is the CD going to drop?
We're lookin at a March release. Once thing I wanna say to everybody that know me personally. When you see me don't ask me to give you no free tape or nothing. Go out and buy it. Y'all supposed to support me before anybody else. Buy my shit, man. Don't be waitin on me to give it for free. You'll run out and buy the next muthafucka's shit, but you waitin on me to give you mine. Support me! Show me some love!

Who did your production on this album?
For production I worked with a dude named SMK. He was the producer that worked with me on the "Lyrical Drive By" song. We got a chemistry when we work together. When we do stuff we come up with that vibe that niggaz love me for. He's got a unique sound, and I know a lotta people kinda bit his sound and came up off of it. We ended up gettin back together and doin a few songs. Then I got a dude named Neil Jones. He's a real talented cat. He can play all kinda instruments, he can program drum machines, he can play drums, he can run the SL board, he's real talented and he did some stuff with me. DJ Squeeky did a coupla things for me. Me and Squeeky go way back. He always comes with that Memphis sound. Then, like I said, Mike Mosley did one. I always heard a lot about Mike Mosley and I was honored to be able to do that on a Mike Mosley track, as well as other Bay Area producers. Then of course we got Alkatraz Productions with J-Dogg playin the keyboards. J-Dogg did a lot of keyboard lines in there. Alkatraz Productions, that's my production company, so I played a major role in getting the sound I wanted. I played an instrumental role in choosing the right producers and getting the right sounds that I need to be getting. I didn't let no people tell me what I should be doing.

People were trying to tell you to do something different?
Some people might feel like East Coast tracks are better, they might try to push a lotta East Coast tracks on me. That ain't the vibe I do. My audience ain't gonna accept that from me. I wanna make sure I feed my core audience, cause over the years I done built up a core audience. And they been buyin a lot of my independent records, and I wanna make sure they get just what they love and be able to spread it to the next muthafucka.

Look at Cash Money they just kept coming with their own sound. Either you love it or you don't. They didn't change for anybody. A lot of people try to please too many markets at once and they come weak in end.
A lotta times a rapper feels like they could rap over anything. And 9 times outta 10 they could rap over anything. But when it comes to sellin records--say there's a dude that's really into East Coast flavor. If he wanna get East Coast flavor he's gonna buy the record from the artist that's gonna give him that flavor. Now the same buyer might be lookin for some Down South shit or Midwest shit. When they go buy your shit that's what they wanna hear. If they go and buy a record that goat a little bit of everything on it, Man I didn't buy this nigga for that man. You can't just be mixin that shit. It's like a muthafucka put Frosted Flakes and Sugar Smacks and Lucky Charms and Fruity Pebbles all together in the same box. Ain't nobody gonna wanna eat that. What the fuck? If I want some Fruity Pebbles that's what I'm gonna buy. When I want Frosted Flakes I'll buy a box of that. I don't want this shit. That's how the buyin public feels. You gotta know your audience. That's what E-40 told me. You gotta make sure you feed your hardcore

audience. If you got a hardcore audience--doesn't matter if it's only 500 people--feed those niggaz what they want. A lotta niggaz buy your shit if you get popular because it's the hype at the time. They're not just true fans that'll buy your shit regardless. Like Jay-Z's the shit, so all the niggaz go out and buy Jay-Z. But soon as the album come out and niggaz say that shit ain't tight, then only the hardcore fans are gonna buy the next album. The so-called fans that bought the last one are on to the next hype thing. You have to stick with your audience. And if you get hot you ain't gotta change, just sell the shit out your shit while you're hot. That's the way Master P did with No Limit. While they were hot they sold the shit out those muthafuckas. No if P hot now or not, don't even matter. When he was hot he made sure you spent every dime on his shit. He got his.

You know how in the Appalachian Mountains the people intermarried too much and their kids start coming out retarded and blind and stuff. Do you think that's happening with Rap? That Rap music isn't branching out enough or growing?
I think where Rap is today. People are lookin at Rap as a way out now. So everybody wanna put out a record. There was a time where niggaz put out Rap records cause that's what they felt. I just loved to rap. I loved listening to Rap music and it's what I love to do. Now a lotta people put out Rap records because they think they're gonna be the next Master P. It's a way to get out of sellin dope, it's a way to make money. I feel that cause niggaz is strugglin. You're always lookin for a way to come up. I just feel like the game is over saturated because everybody thinks they can put out a Rap record and come up. It don't work like that. It's a hard game.

Then there's no creativity in it. When you listen to music from another period each artist sounds different from each the other. Like Marvin Gaye sounds very different from Willie Hutch. With Rap it anybody can get a sample, put a couple of beats, put the keys and you have a song.
What's goin on is just what you said. A lotta people are just puttin songs together real fast and puttin it out. What they're missin is when you go and record, you're recording a vibe and a feel. You ain't just throwin something out there. That's why when you buy a Marvin Gaye album you buy it cause you like his feel, you like his vibe. The kinda Rap that's always gonna elevate is the kinda shit that you

> "I WANTED TO REALLY MAKE SURE I DID AN AL KAPONE RECORD, THE KINDA RECORD THAT I KNOW NIGGAZ LOVE ME FOR."

can feel. That's why Cash Money's so hot, because they got their own vibe. No Limit had their own vibe. Suave had their own vibe. Rap-A-Lot had they own vibe. That's what the public's gonna grab hold of. If they can feel that vibe and if it's the kinda vibe that they like, that's what they're gonna pick up on. That's why right now the radio stations and the major labels are back in control. There was a time when you could go buy independent shit and be proud to have something that other niggaz weren't up on. But now you got so much independent shit out there the average consumer's like, Shit I ain't even heard of this shit. So they're lookin to buy what they heard on the radio or what they're seein on video. That's why the power's shifted back to the radio and major labels. That's what's killin Rap. What always kept Rap alive was the fact that--no matter if a major label wanted to fuck with it or not--the streets was gonna keep it alive.

If there hadn't been any independent movement E-40 wouldn't be doin it. Three 6 Mafia wouldn't be here. Cash Money wouldn't be here. No one would have signed any of them except for the fact that they were selling major units on the streets.

I feel like radio and all the commercialism is killing the real interesting Rap.
You said it right. It's hard for an artist to keep their identity, the Rap aritsts end up tryin to make more commercial Rap. The public's done got brainwashed to buy whatever's bein pumped up the hardest on the video and the radio.

It's like McDonald's Rap. Everything is streamlined, packaged and here you got it. When you got to eat at McDonald's you know what you're going to get. But when you go to some independent little burger joint, you just don't know until you try it.
And the question is, what's gonna happen to preserve a healthy Rap movement. Cause the consumer doesn't want to take a chance on a lot of independent shit anymore. There's too much independent shit.

There's too much out in the market and people don't have time or money to try everything.
It's got to the point now that muthafuckas don't wanna buy shit comin from outside of their own home town. It got real regional right now. Muthafuckas buy what's in their hometown. If the shit don't sound like what's out of their hometown, they ain't gonna fuck with it. A true Rap fan is gonna appreciate all the different flavors. They'll be like, I wanna hear some South shit. I like that East Coast shit too, or I like that West Coast shit too. But a lotta Rap fans have got to the point where if it don't sound strictly South--it could be doper than a muthafucka but they won't touch it cause it don't sound like South shit. And a West Coast nigga would be like, I don't wanna hear none of that East Coast shit, I only like West Coast shit. Muthafuckas ain't even Rap fans no more, they only wanna buy shit from their own spot.

What happens when the power shifts back to the major labels and radio is it's gonna be hard for independent niggaz, especially niggaz that are not located where the major labels have got their headquarters. The people that are at those headquarters are gonna focus on the people that are right underneath their nose. It's hard for a nigga from Texas or Florida or Chicago, Seattle, it's hard for them to get a deal with a major. Number one, they're too far away. For someone that's right there, they can just drive up the street and go holler at the label and get a deal. That don't mean that those people are any more talented than the ones in other areas. Then it's hard as hell for a nigga to come up. That's how it was and it will go back to that if we let the power shift to the majors. And it's becasue of the market bein oversaturated. The buyers ain't goin by word of mouth no more, theyr'e goin by what they hear the most on the radio and video. It's gonna be hard for us unless we find some kinda way to straghten the situation out in some way, to keep that street credibility strong. And also to keep niggaz from gettin so locked into only buyin shit from just their area, blockin out Rap coming from other places. If it's good it's good, no matter where it came from.

You see it all the time how any New York rapper gets major media support. Not because they're so talented, but because they're from New York.
I feel rappers from the East Coast, really they got it better than everybody else for the simple fact that no matter what city you're in you hear East Cost shit get played than niggaz in their own town. The biggest hero in your area still can't get love like a nigga from the East Coast.

MESSY MARV

BY BLACK DOG BONE • PHOTO BY MARCUS HANSCHEN

A lot of people have been saying the Bay is back. What do you say?
It's not that we're back. We've been here. I feel that we've been standing here all along. They've been runnin off with our game and stealin our words and becoming millionaires off of our style. We always been here. We just been overlooked. It's a blessing that E-40 got the deal with BME and Lil Jon. Now we have the focus on us again.

Why have they been overlooking us?
We're an industry within ourselves, that's why. We come from the independent hustle. The industry really is made up of puppets and people who control the puppets. And we're them dudes who say, "Fuck y'all we gonna do what we wanna do anyway." When they see that they don't wanna deal with us. They just wanna deal with people they can control. That's why we've been overlooked for so long.

Bay Area artists are standing their ground and demanding deals that work for them. For that reason a lot of them are not signed to majors.
Right. And they can suck my dick. I've turned down 4 or 5 deals, $700,000, 1.2 mil, $500,000. That ain't no money to me. You do the math. I can sell 50,000 units and get $6 a CD. That's damn near a million dollars a year. If ya'll wanna fuck with me, you know what to do. Come correct. If not, I'll see you on top. We always be where it's crackin at anyway. We at the BET's, we at the Soul Trains, we at the Miami's, we at yo' mama's house. We everywhere.

If someone offers you a lot of money would you sign?
I'm in a litigation right now with a few companies. I'm not gonna say who it is, but there's some possibilities. I was in New York for 30 days hooked up with boy from the Brooklyn. My boy Rich the Factor put me on it. I stayed out there, it was real good energy. I got like 6 deals on the table. Created a bidding war. Russell Simmons Music Group, TVT, Irv Gotti, Jim Jones and the Dipset over there. Stern it up, waken asses up.

You haven't made any decisions yet?
I'm not saying anything until I get my muthafuckin money! It's lookin real good. If you all know Messy Marv, you know I set a standard for this Bay Area. I am a trendsetter. Click Clack Gang, we are trendsetters. We push a movement. It's real.

You've been around a lot longer than Hyphy, but you are still an important factor in this whole Hyphy movement.
I might have played a major role in it, but Mac Dre is the source behind that whole Hyphy

movement. We lost a good man.

Why do you think Mac Dre was responsible for the whole movement?
When Dre got out he got focused and he jumped on what was hot. It was time for something new. Mac Dre was like, "Fuck it, we done did the Gangsta shit. Now it's time to have fun." And that's what he did. It's been developing ever since. Then Thizz signed Mistah FAB. He got the whole retarded Yellow Bus thing going and we been moving forward ever since. Me, I support the Hyphy movement, the high energy dancing and all that, but I don't do that. I'm about the streets. We are the streets.

Except for you and Guce, San Francisco Rap has never been real hardcore Gangsta. A lot of San Francisco Rap has had an Hip Hop element in it.
It go way further than me. We can't just talk about me right now. It go back to Cougnut. It go back to Huey MC. It go back to Rappin 4-Tay. We been sayin and portrayin this Gangsta shit. Runnin the murder rate. That ain't nothing to celebrate or nothing—my folks is killin my folks—but go back to the old days and you'll know Frisco ain't never been soft. Cougnut, Huey MC, Rappin 4-Tay, them is the people I was influenced by. When you say Frisco you got to say all

> **"YOU DO THE MATH. I CAN SELL 50,000 UNITS AND GET $6 A CD. THAT'S DAMN NEAR A MILLION DOLLARS A YEAR. IF YA'LL WANNA FUCK WITH ME, YOU KNOW WHAT TO DO. COME CORRECT. IF NOT, I'LL SEE YOU ON TOP. WE ALWAYS BE WHERE IT'S CRACKIN AT ANYWAY. WE AT THE BET'S, WE AT THE SOUL TRAINS, WE AT THE MIAMI'S, WE AT YO' MAMA'S HOUSE. WE EVERYWHERE."**

of that—RBL Posse, Cellski, San Quinn, JT the Bigga Figga. It's not just me and Guce.

Frisco always had that fast tempo music. TC, RBL, they had faster beats than the rest of the Bay. Where do you fit in with that sound?
I don't fit in that sound. You know what sound I fit into? I just got that real street shit. It ain't no sound with me.

One thing I've noticed with you, you never work with just one or two producers. You always work with different producers.
With Scalene and with our whole movement we're paying. We're goin to the see the Lil Flip's. We're goin to see the Lil Jon's. We goin to see the David Banner's. We're payin for what we want. We're not accepting no handouts. We don't want no handouts. Our whole thing is quality. When you get a Messy Marv CD or when you get a Click Clack CD, you know if you put that muthafucka on your pipe and you take one pull it's gonna be crank. You're goin right back to the store to pick that shit up. We got candy for your ear. That's what I bring, ear candy. Whether you street, whether you Hip Hop, whether you R & B, it's gonna be candy for your ear.

How do you pick your beats out? What makes it a Messy Marv beat?
Ask Loot.

Do you look for beats that have that Gangsta element?
It ain't the beat, man. We can get any beat and make it Gangsta. It's just the realness. I can take any beat and put the Messy Marv stamp on it and it's gonna be street.

What is the Messy Marv stamp?
Black Star quality, that's my stamp. Quality.

Throughout your career you never joined with any other crew. You've always been doing it on your own.
That's how I was raised. You stick with your own. You ride with your own. You stand up on truth. You stand up on principal. And you don't jump ship. Whether it's good right now or it's bad right now, you stay with the family and what you know. That's how I made it so far. For me to go with another situation and be up under another muthafucka? That ain't never been me. I got too much money and too much heart for that. If it ain't crackin for Messy Marv and Click Clack right now, we sit down and wait. It's gonna crack, cause we push a hard line.

What's Click Clack? Is that your crew?
Click Clack Gang: Young Boo, Skrill, Looch and Home Wrecker, Jessica Rabbit. That's the group. Click Clack been around forever. We get the name from jumpin out at muthafuckas and cockin that thang back. This ain't no shit we done made up. Eddy Street 2007 is on some Click Clack shit. Whether we sell a million, whether we don't, whether we eat, whether we don't, we gonna jump out and cock that thang back. Click Clack's been around a long time. Even in the 70's they was jumpin out and cockin that thang back. Like Huey P. Newton, Matulu Shakur, on some real political Black shit. Standin up on truth, standin up on principal. We jumpin out and cockin that shit.

Right now what are you workin on?
My new album is done, "Draped Up And Chipped Out 2". The Click Clack album is done. We're also workin on a couple of DVD's, "The Diary 2", "Wake Your Game Up" the movie and soundtrack, "Mess" the movie and soundtrack. I also did a video/musical "Tycoon", kinda like the Jay Z "Streets Is Watchin" shit, same hype. That's what we're workin on. With Victor Jones, the R & B sensation. Real shit, we're workin on the real.

Who did you work with on this new album?
It's beautiful! Juvenile is on my new album. 112's on my new album. Mike Jones is on the new album. B-Legit is on the new album. PSD and Hoodstarz on the new album. Sean Paul of Youngbloodz is on the new album. The new album!

Is it very different from your earlier works?
I would say the last album I did showed maturity. The "Disobayish" album showed the hungriness, the smash. This album right here, this is to set the record straight that we're not starving. Whether we get a deal or not, this is us, this is what it is. What you know about me? I was ballin before I had a deal.

Of all your albums, which one got the best response?
I sold about 40 of "Disobayish". I sold damn near 30, went to jail and came back with no promotions, on "Bandannas". This new one, I'm gonna give it to 'em. As far as the marketing and promotions, I'm out and I'm really focused. I'm tryin to turn my negative situation into something positive. I think this album right here is gonna set the standard, set the trends for the Bay in 2007.

You represent the Bay, but you also rep Frisco. What's the difference between the Oakland sound, the Frisco sound, the Vallejo sound, the Richmond sound?
It's nothing different. Richmond, Vallejo, Oakland, San Francisco, San Jose, Berkeley, we all the same. We're all out here tryin to eat with this heat. It's nothing different. It's all the same. It might be a different way that a

muthafucka's sayin it. It might be comin out the speakers into your ear with a different sound, but it's the same shit. It's Bay Area. It's jump out, cock that thang back, nigga what you got, give me that! If not, be cool, I'mma see you in the club, we gonna pop these bottles. That's what it is. I love my niggaz.

You said you've been reading up on Black power. What brought this on?
I know. Because I went to jail and when I went to jail I really seen how fresh my people's skin was and how intelligently they was talkin. Bein behind bars for so many years just woke my game up on a whole 'nother hype. This Blackness, they're scared of us. They lock us up for years and years because they're scared of us. That's why I'm speakin on this shit because when I went to jail this last time it woke me up. But I've always been about my Blackness. You can ask Dead Prez, you can ask Kweli. I always pop this Blackness wherever I'm at. Yeah, there's this Gangsta side of me. But hell, I'm a product of this society. This is where they put me. This is what I do! This is where y'all put me. I got to eat! You muthafuckas ain't gonna feed me, right? You ain't gonna give me no money or no opportunities, so don't talk about what we doin out here. We doin this shit to eat. We snatchin the purse, not because we want to snatch that bitch's purse. It's cause we hungry, homeboy. Don't give us that title, like we just doin wrong. All of this shit is about Blackness. Whether y'all like it or not, y'all muthafuckas ain't gonna give me no choice. You ain't gonna feed my son. So if this is how I live then this is how I'm gonna get it. Show me some respect

It seems like being in prison woke you up to another side of life. You met some people in prison that brought some understanding into you?
Naw. I'm a man. I don't get it from other people. I sat on my bunk every fuckin night, read my bible and thought about direction for when I touch down. That's all I did. As far as me writin raps, I didn't do none of that shit. I'm not a rapper. I am a chemist. I am a street nigga. I am me. This is what I am.

But when you were in prison, you started seeing things differently.
That's right. But I can only say so much. You can't really put no bad name on me. I live how I live. I get it how I get it. I'm a product of society. This is where y'all put me. This is where I am and this is how I got to get it. We ain't never had no time to go to school. We all dropped out early. I can only speak for me, I dropped out early. I ain't had no time to do that shit. I had to put some food in the fridgerator. I like new things. I like them nice things. I like bad bitches. So I had to get out and make my money. So don't say no punk-ass shit about, "Them niggaz is this and them niggaz is that." Cause truly, what is you niggaz doin for the community? We givin away bikes on Christmas. We're

> "IT GO BACK TO COUGNUT. IT GO BACK TO HUEY MC. IT GO BACK TO RAPPIN 4-TAY. WE BEEN SAYIN AND PORTRAYIN THIS GANGSTA SHIT. RUNNIN THE MURDER RATE. THAT AIN'T NOTHING TO CELEBRATE OR NOTHING—MY FOLKS IS KILLIN MY FOLKS—BUT GO BACK TO THE OLD DAYS AND YOU'LL KNOW FRISCO AIN'T NEVER BEEN SOFT."

givin away turkeys on Thanksgiving. We out fuckin with and interacting with our people. Nigga, we doin way more than they doin for the community. So leave that shit where it is. If y'all wanna come fuck with us come fuck with us. If not, we'll see you on top.

You say you're not a rapper, but you're something else….
I'm a prophet. I'm a prophet from the street. I'm just giving you my story. This is me.
You're using Rap as a vehicle for that?
Not necessarily Rap. I'm using pimpin as a vehicle to get this shit out. Bitch, when you're out there on the track tell everybody out there, "Mess is sending me for a good cause!!" I'm using all this shit for an outlet. When I'm out there on the radio, all this shit. We're using this shit to better our situation.

You say you're not a rapper, but no matter what you have a talent with music. You've got the lyrics and you've got the flow. That's why we're here talking today.
No. It's not because of that. It's because you understand my story and you might have listened to a few of my songs and said, "Man I went through that. That's real" or "I might go through that." That's the reason why. Not because I'm a rapper, but because you understand my story, Black Dog Bone.
But I know you take your music seriously.
Right. That's why you don't hear Messy Marv on 10 or 20 or 30 album features. Because that shit is bullshit. If you want Mess, come spend them chips ASAP. If you want a concert, come spend them chips ASAP. Other than that we don't fuck with you. If you ain't family we don't fuck with you and we don't need to fuck with you, man. We got our own problems. We got our own situation and we gonna push a hard line. This is what we do. Whether you wanna fuck with us or not, y'all gonna have to deal with us.

You're considered one of the top rappers in the Bay. I think you take that serious.
I take all of this serious. Life is serious. Don't get me fucked up when I say I'm not a rapper. I'm just sayin that people understand my story. I take all of this shit serious because I eat off of this shit. You got to separate the real shit from the fake shit. That's what I do. •

SHAWTY LO

BY SCOTT BEJDA • PHOTO BY WORD INK

Your song "Dey Know" is a huge hit already. What is the concept behind that track?
"Dey Know" is real up tempo, catchy, and it makes people move. I didn't intend for it to be like that, but people really liked it. It really put me out there as a solo artist and let people know that I'm here. It's still heating up and BDS is still going up weekly. Everything is looking real good!

How do you feel about your recent solo success?
I really feel blessed and it's unbelievable. It was very unexpected because I wasn't trying to be a rapper, but people thought I was when they heard a couple of my songs. I haven't been rappin' very long at all. The people let me know that I was good enough to do this.

When did you start rappin?
I started rappin' two years ago when I came home from prison.

How long were you in there for?
I did a year. I was facing twenty to forty years. I got a year for three different cases and they ran all concurrent into one year.

Before your solo success you had a huge group success with D4L. What is the main difference between being a group member and a solo artist?
When I'm with the guys they handle shit and when it's time for me to put my little thing down I do. I wasn't trying to be no rapper so there wasn't as much involved. As a solo artist I give them me and my story. Of course there's a lot more involved but it comes with the game.

When did D4L first come together?
I started the group in 2003, but at that time I wasn't trying to be a rapper. I was just trying to be the man behind the scenes just getting money, but when I came home from prison I did a song.

> ""DEY KNOW" IS REAL UP TEMPO, CATCHY, AND IT MAKES PEOPLE MOVE. I DIDN'T INTEND FOR IT TO BE LIKE THAT, BUT PEOPLE REALLY LIKED IT. IT REALLY PUT ME OUT THERE AS A SOLO ARTIST AND LET PEOPLE KNOW THAT I'M HERE. IT'S STILL HEATING UP AND BDS IS STILL GOING UP WEEKLY. EVERYTHING IS LOOKING REAL GOOD!"

Why did you start rappin'?
People had made me mad, and I made the song "I'm The Man". That song was the first solo song that I made by myself. When that got out in the streets people said, "That's the type of music we want to hear from you because we know you're from Bankhead for real!"

At that point did you know you had the goods?
No, I still didn't know. I take that back, because after that song I was getting acknowledged and that let me know I had what it took. Once I got the feedback from the people it inspired me to keep going, so I would say yes, it did let me know I was ready for this.

Are you doing a lot of traveling and touring right now?
I'm on the road right now, and I have about one day at home a week. I never have any home time. I go to Rap City tomorrow, and I go to MTV on Wednesday. I just aired at number 10 on BET last Thursday on 106th & Park.

What is the title of the album and who did you work with on it?
The album was produced by mostly in-house production. The album is called "Units In The City", and it drops February 25th. I got D4L, Gucci Mane, Jeezy, Ludacris, Twista, and Plies featured on there.

That's a lot of big names. How does it feel to work with so may talented artists?
It's a good experience. I've been blessed to be able to have worked with several big artists. We just try to give the fans what they want.

Does the album compare in anyway to the D4L stuff, or is it something that is totally different?
It's totally different. The D4L album had a lot of feel good music. This album does too, but this time it's just me. When we put out the D4L album the world accepted it and they had fun with it. On this album you will dance and have a good time, but you will also get my real story. It's based on me. It's my life story and my adventures and everything that I have been through. It represents me to the fullest. People want to hear the true story. The real Bankhead story!

Do you think the album will be a success like the single?
I hope so, but I'mma let it do what it do. I'm just going to stay focused and keep promoting and hitting the road. I got these mix CDs in the street and they are feeling that too. I got "I'm Da Man 1", and "I'm Da Man 2", and they are loving that too. It's crazy right now. •

JAYO FELONY

BY BOODAHMAN • PHOTO COURTESY DEF JAM

How does In The Trenches measure up to your earlier albums?
I had a lot of fun releasing all of my shit, but the bottom line is I just got a team behind me having my back which I really never had in my career. The label that I'm at now, we're in it through the thick and thin and that is the difference now.

How does it make you feel to see the West come back?
I have been representing Diego since day one and LA. When I got started I was on the run. That was where me and Jay met out here in LA. I'm happy to be a part of what is going on and everybody finally being together and putting all this beef aside and moving forward to make the West Coast stronger. It's a blessing and I'm happy to be here still standing strong.

Were you at the West Coast conference?
Definitely! I popped up, made my appearance. It was real cool with everyone coming together trying to move forward bringing the Coast tighter making music like we use to do. Back in the day that was what it was! Everybody was dealing with everybody and we were on each other's projects all the time doing shows, tours and the whole nine.

What can you tell me about In The Trenches the album?
In The Trenches is off the meat rack! I finally made an album where I had fun with it and the label let me be creative and do what I wanted to do. I made a good album and it's not an album that I made out of frustration, but an album I made for everybody to get into and see what I'm really made of. I know this is gonna be one of the tightest albums coming out of the West Coast this year and not only the West Coast, but out of the industry as a whole. It's gonna be real big and we're gonna have a lot of fun with it.

What's behind the song "100 Bars"?
I just released some anger on there and show the world that the West Coast does have some lyrics. However they wanna label it, but as an MC I feel that I am one of the best out there. I'm not just talking about it, but proving it. There are not a lot of MC that can hold 100 bar songs and not get boring. It is catchy all the way through and it's off the meat rack. When you hear that you are gonna be like "Ahhh man!" It ain't for play I'm here to stay. I'm a true MC and regardless of me not putting out an album in a couple years. My skills have sharpened up even more and a lot of people are gonna be in trouble if they don't know how to rap. Cats will lose their jobs. With everybody coming together, and with me, Snoop, Xzibit and Game all these doors are back open. People will see I'm out here to have fun and make money. At the end of the day I was one of the only West Coast rappers that was on everyone albums like a Snoop. I was on Ja Rule, LL, Scarface, Xzibit, Kurupt, E-40 and it is about to be on again. Blow niggaz out on their own songs so you better come to the table!

Who did the beats for the album?
I got some off the meat rack shit with my boy Jelly Roll, who did something with Snoop, Jadakiss and Method Man. He definitely blessed the album and we did four or five tracks on the album. I got my boy Black who laced me with the title track "In the Trenches". I got Havoc from Mob Deep; he did the "Rifleman" song we got on there with me, Mob Deep and Kurupt. We got that group called The Riflemen! Then we got Scott Storch and we are about to do it big with him and one of those records is gonna feature Snoop and The Game. Then I got DJ Silk, who has been working with me for years. He did the one "I'm So Into You" featuring Sleepy Brown. That track was for the females and I ain't just coming back trying to kill up everybody. I got a song called "Can't Sit All The Way Down On It" because I really gave it up all the way for all of the females. When I play that record they don't give a shit what I'm saying because they just wait for that hook to come in "Betcha can't wait to get down on it." That's the business man! I had a lot of fun with this record man and my record label really had my back.

Aren't you doing something with the movies too?
It is off the hook! It is called "Eyes Of Darkness" and it's like a comedy/horror flick. I play an artist that is shooting a video which isn't that hard and on the set something happened that where this crazy clown gets killed by the video girls. This muthafucka ends up killing every muthafucka on the set. My boy Del directed it! I got my song called "1,2,3" which is actually the song I'm doing in the movie. It's going to work out real cool.

The Riflemen, is that your group?
That is gonna be real bi! Mr. Kurupt and Tha Dogg Pound are about to do this little tour and get it crackin'. We put all that bullshit behind us and now it is about to be real big. The group is Havoc and Prodigy of Mob Deep, 40 Glocc, Kurupt and myself. When we ride together there ain't too many cats that can fuck wit it. Everybody is calling us the super group! We ain't never said that before, but that is how people are putting it. They know me and Kurupt ain't to be fucked with on the West and we got one of the East Coast's crews that have been holding it down since day one and that is Mobb Deep.

Is the group working on an album?
We got a lot of songs done already and some mixtape records done, but we are about to really put it down and handle our business and get the deal done and it is really gonna be big. Now that Kurupt's business is straight it's a lot of doors being open for that project. We are shopping it right now and have a couple offers on the table. It's about to be big! Tell my boys they better bring their lunch on that Riflemen record because I ain't playin'.

You were once signed to JMJ, did you know him good?
That was my dog! I basically used to live with Jam Master Jay. He is the one that got me in the game and helped me become who I am. Much love and respect to him for even believing in me way back then. He put up with all the crazy shit of my childhood when I was raw fresh out the hood, not really giving a fuck. He dealt with everything that another muthafucka wouldn'ta dealt with. He stuck with me until I did get on point. Even after I left the label he was still doing things to help me out and get me further out in my career like getting me on Scarface's album and stuff like that. He was still helping out! Me and dude was real close! That was my dog! He taught me a lot, and the first album I came out with he produced a lot of the shit on there.

How did all that fame feel?
It was all just a blessing. Jam Master Jay did put me in the game and when I was at Def Jam Jay had all of the juice up there. He got me rappin' on shit like Jason's Lyric soundtrack and The Show soundtrack and it was crazy to me. They took me fresh out of the hood homey! I'm watching Def Jam Comedy and seeing my shit playing on there. I got a good start just from being with Jay.

Did you drop any underground shit in San Diego before you got with Jam Master Jay?
I dropped something called Give It Up For The Hood where I was dissing my enemies. That was what basically got me my deal. That was the product that I put in the stores on my own on consignment. I was on the run from YA, which is Youth Authority. I was on parole and they were looking for a muthafucka so I just left town. I ended up taking one of the tapes to Jam Master Jay's mothers house and then dude came looking for me in LA and we hooked up and it was over.

Why were you on the run?
It was like one of those situations where I was violating parole and once I turned I was off parole and they couldn't do nothing to me no more. I just had to stay out of their state until I turned a certain age. That was the California Youth Authority and that's where all the hard heads go before the penitentiary. If you hurt somebody or murder somebody

or whatever they keep you up until you are 25 and then they make you an M number and send you to the pen. I was on the run from that shit when I came to New York. I went into Virginia and my brother picked me up and took me out of town.

How did you get the contact on Jam Master Jay?
I ran into a manager that was from New York and he took me out to Jam Master Jay's mom's house and that was when we left the tape up there and he came looking for me. That's what started it all right there. The tape helped me get the deal and just grinding on my own. I put a tape together with just two songs on it and that led to me getting the deal.

Were you in the studio together with Scarface when you did the song for his album?
Actually on the song that we did for The Last Of A Dying Breed album. It was me, Kurupt and Daz on that record. We were all in the studio together knocking it out. At the time we were all young and it was a blessing for us to even be in there with Face making a record. Me, Kurupt and Daz were real happy about being on that project.

It sounds like you have real good chemistry with Tha Dogg Pound?
It is pretty good! Not tooting my own horn, but it says a lot for me not being from LA, Death Row, or Dogg Pound, but I was in the middle of all that shit. A nigga can rap my ass off man! I had fun with them because the chemistry was there and they know what the fuck they are doing on the mic. Before all the bullshit went down we were all together. Even though I wasn't from that camp we all made a lot of hit records together. It was all like a team! Everybody is back together and now we're about to do a tour with me and Tha Dogg Pound. At the end of the day all that beef was a bunch of drama and bullshit that we could've gone to the table and put behind us so we can move forward and get this money, because that is what it is about. From myself, if I never have another problem with another West Coast artist I'm not going public or saying shit about them in a magazine or nothing. I'm gonna tell 'em "Look, let's go to the back and beat each other up and make a song together afterwards." If it ain't serious enough to take a muthafucka's life, then it ain't serious

> "I POPPED UP, MADE MY APPEARANCE. IT WAS REAL COOL WITH EVERYONE COMING TOGETHER TRYING TO MOVE FORWARD BRINGING THE COAST TIGHTER MAKING MUSIC LIKE WE USE TO DO. BACK IN THE DAY THAT WAS WHAT IT WAS! EVERYBODY WAS DEALING WITH EVERYBODY AND WE WERE ON EACH OTHER'S PROJECTS ALL THE TIME DOING SHOWS, TOURS AND THE WHOLE NINE."

enough to hurt a muthafucka's pockets.

What will we hear on the new album?
They're gonna see the anger and the happiness and everything that an album is supposed to be. It's a well rounded album! You have a lot of artists out here today who'll make one or two good records and put those records out as singles to sell their record, but then you go buy their records and it is a piece of shit. From dealing with Jam Master Jay and studying the Ice Cube's and the NWA's, I know how to put albums together if nothing else. If I never came out with a video and people just knew my album in the store it would sell because people know I won't make two hot songs with the rest of it being bullshit. I can't do it! I put my effort into everything that I do. This is an album that everybody can get into whether you are a Crip, Blood, females, East Coast, West Coast, or Down South. There is something on there for everybody. I'm not finished with my collaborations; I got a couple more sledgehammers. What I learned from Def Jam was to kill a fly with a sledgehammer.

Who is on In The Trenches so far?
I got Kurupt, Mob Deep, Sleepy Brown and I'm about to do the song with Game and Snoop this weekend. Then I'm about to do one with Yo-Yo as well! I got one more record we are trying to put together with me, T.I., and Juvenile from the South. My album is all done as far as my solo songs and everything is arranged and ready to go and we are knocking out these last couple of records. I just got about 3 more records to do! I'm happy to be back and all of the doors are open for me. I don't have no beef with nobody or no gripes. One thing that me and Kurupt knew by that West Coast conference going down was me and Kurupt is gonna benefit a whole lot from that.

Why?
We were the main two artists that were getting cut out of our fuckin money because we were household names that people love to hear. Now that the bullshit is out of the way, The Snoop Dogg's, The Game's and everybody wants to work with us because we love what we do.

You were more angry on Crip Hop, but it sounds like you won't be as angry on this one?
Exactly, you hit it right on the nose. Crip Hop was an album where I was going through a whole lot, but at the same time don't act like it was all my muthafuckin' fault. These rappers were doing sneaky little shit to me because I wasn't signing to their labels. I don't want to go into it and bring up old news, but at the same time muthafuckaz was trying to sign me to their labels and I wouldn't sign to their labels and they did little subliminal shit to diss me indirectly. The past is the past and it is time to make money and move on. I'm willing to shut those doors and move forward with my life and career. •

TELA

**BY MATT SONZALA
PHOTO BY RICK MAPES**

Who were some of the artists you were listening to coming up?
Shit a lot of shit. Black Sabbath, AC/DC. Around that MTV era, Def Leppard. Cuz that was the only stuff we really would see on MTV so I got turned on to that. Before that it was like the Temptations, Marvin Gaye, all of them. Anything that's out there I done heard. I done went through all phases. Even at one point in time, country. Oak Ridge Boys and all that shit.

Did your family listen to different types of music too?
My family was more into Gospel. I'm talking about the old hymn gospel. And that Motown era. I'm the one that really came into the house with a variety of shit. When hip hop came along it got down here a little bit later than it did in other places so it was hard for us to get to it. But we managed to get it. I got down with a partner who was a DJ and we'd be on a lot of tapes—Hilltop Hustlers, Steady B, Marvalous Marv, Cash Money, all of that. Even before then, ones that started this off like Kurtis Blow and all them. I think the two hip hop records that really had an impact on my life was Raising Hell from Run DMC and No One Could Do It Better from The D.O.C. I was down for it when Run and them did their thing, but then when D.O.C. dropped that I was like yeah! I officially want to be a part of it. I got game from everybody. Face and the Geto Boys, they really gave the hope that you could come out of the South and do this shit. You ain't gotta be corny with it. You can express your true feelings. So I believe they really started that for everybody out of the South. I know they did with me. And I think sometimes people forget that they the ones to jump this thing off, and what J did in bringing them together.

You have a long history as a rapper.
I been through my ups and downs in this business. Shit is very vicious. It's very vicious game, but at the same time too it's a lovely game, a beautiful thing to be a part of. Nowadays I'm trying to get more into the music instead of just constantly thinking about business. For the past three years my mind has just been on the business of it—that can kind of rob you of what you really in it for at times. I'm not saying that I don't want the bread, because I definitely want the dough, but at the same time I want to do what I've been selected to do. Sincerely. And sometimes shit like money and bitches can kind of cloud that up. I say bitches, not just females, but you know the business can be a bitch at times, or

even niggaz. So I'm trying to get back to loving the art of it and expressing myself truthfully for what I want to do. I just want to do my thing and I want people to appreciate my records and pick them up as a Tela record. Instead of putting labels on it like this record ain't street enough or not this enough, just pick it up and listen to it from a musical standpoint. This is my creation.

Were you doing any other type of music before you started rapping?
I was in the jazz band, I was in the marching band. I played percussion in the church band also. So a motherfucker who just really judge me on maybe some shit that they hearing they have no idea about the background cause I'll jump on the set and I'll lean on the best of 'em.

When did you start getting off into production? Did you do any production on your first album?
I always sat in with the producer. I always been a producer. There's no way that I could do a song without giving some input on it. I'ma do something and that's been since day one. Really that's how I got my record deal.

Did you know 8Ball and MJG before signing to Suave House?
Yeah, we came up back when there was this record label in the Mound. Ball, I first met him at a talent show and he won the talent show and the label was a couple of streets down from where Ball and G lived. It was real good. They always involved me and I was with a couple of more cats. We used to get in there and it's just like it is now, niggaz just being there and helping out the best way they can. As a matter of fact Ball was the one that told Tony Draper about me. They reached out and asked if I had a demo together and I said yeah, but I didn't have a demo together. So I went and worked on some shit for three or four days and they was fucking with it. And there you have it. I went down to Houston and got turned on to niggaz Screwing it up. Muthafuckas being leaned up. A whole different scene coming from Memphis.

How did you end up leaving Suave and going to Rap-A-Lot?
Shit well I wanted to get paid man. I wanted my money. I wanted my just due. I finally got a chance to meet J and we kicked shit around. It was just time to move on to bigger and better things. Suave definitely jumped the career off but it's just like in any relationship, if it's going bad it's time to move on. If you ain't growing from it, it's time to move on.

What's the title of your new album?
It's called Double Dose. It's not a double album but you getting a double when you listen to shit off of it. It's a double shot. It's the best of Tela for sure. That's what we felt listening to the record. It's a double dose. That playa, that realism, that pimpin. Whatever you want, it's there. I'm giving the truth. We got a song on there called "Double Dose" and anybody with a playa bone in they body can listen to it and get something out of it. This what this record is about. So I'm trying to give the game on these songs. When you make a purchase I feel that you should purchase something of substance. I got "25 Hoes," that's a real good song. It's back with Ball and G and Jazze Pha. It's "Sho Nuff" all over but it's 2003. It's killing em. It's a song that when you hear it you'll never forget it. I'm proud of that. It was great to be back in the lab with them and that lifts up my spirits. I got one called "Tennessee Titans," and that's a line up of cats from Tennessee that's putting it down. We got Gangsta Boo, Yo Gotti, Haystak, Criminal Mane, Maru and Me. And this is a line up of muthafuckas that's really holding it down. You hear this song and you ain't from Tennessee you gonna want to be. It's like what DJ Quik did with Compton. Me and Devin on a song called "Down for Me." I need a hoe that's down for me… Sli$ce T produced that one.

I always thought that you and Devin worked real well together.
Me and Devin hopefully one day, we might just fuck around and do an album. Take it back and spin off of "Sex Faces," something on that vibe, some real freaky shit. I also got a cut with Bun B called "Dreams." It's just about when niggaz in the game trying to flip, do they thing, hustling the best way they can. But folks they throw a lot of obstacles in your way to destroy your dreams. So that's with Bun B and Game—a little cat out of Compton, he real raw. Really the whole collaboration, I didn't really go too far outside what I been doing. Me and LoKey we back at it on a track called "Tear It Up." It's some party/club shit. It's a real good album. It's a strong record. •

LORD INFAMOUS

BY SCOTT BEJDA • PHOTO BY ARICK ELION

Your new album "The Man, The Myth, The Legacy" is one of the best albums I have heard in awhile! Where have you been the last few years?
Thank you for the compliment. I have had some issues for awhile and I had to do a stint of time. Me and my kinfolk Paul got love for each other, but I was just ready to venture out on my own and try some different things. Things are going good now, and I came out with a pretty good album. This time I was able to use all of my own ideas as opposed to a lot of Three 6 Mafia songs with Paul and Juicy. I finally got a chance to do my own thing.

It's good to see you doing the sniper flow again. I have always loved your style.
I had to go back to that. People love the lil' uzi spit I do and I had to go back and mix it with the dark satanic Gangsta shit that everybody used to hear from Lord Infamous. I went back to my original style. I didn't like that style that I was using at the end of my time with Three 6. Three 6 was getting a little too commercial for my taste. We were doing just as well and making just as much money sticking to the old formulas. I wanted to go back to the old dark Three 6 Mafia that the people fell in love with at the first place.

I always wondered by you switched up your style on Tear Da Club Up Thugz?
I switched up the style because Paul use to always tell me, "You need to simplify your style because some brothers don't read the stuff you read, and they are not into the dark arts like you are." I tried to simplify, but it wasn't my fault that people weren't educated or into the things that I was into. I was diluting my own style and I had to stop doing that. I felt that unless you put them up on some knowledge then they won't be on no knowledge. I'm not going to short work myself because some people are ignorant to the things that I'm talking about. They might want to go and learn some things if they hear me spit it.

Your style is what makes you unique! That is why people buy Brotha Lynch, or Tech N9ne because they are unique in their own way!
I love cats like Spice 1, MC Eiht, WC, and DOC. They got that sick flow. I also like the dark rappers like Ganksta Nip, Point Blank, and K-Rino. I have always been on the wicked side of things. I call it the dark art.

That's the real because if you look at the way the world is there ain't nothing nice out here.
You're right! We live in a world of turmoil. This is Satan's realm. This is not God's realm at all. I try not to love things of this world because if you're a worldly man then you're not a godly man. That is why I don't glamorize the bling. I only have one song about that and it's a mockery of ice. I'm talking about robbing the rappers who support that shit. I'm making fun of bling. Everybody has to have big ass rims or chains to sell records. They know they can't get no fans unless they got all this fuckin' jewelry. Plus on top of that, a lot of them don't even know that they got fake ass diamonds on. The people they are buying it from get fake shit. These fools never seen the color spectrum of a real diamond. They don't even know where they are buying it from. How many niggaz do you know have a license as a professional jeweler? A lot of cats don't know. They are getting these diamonds from killing our brothers from across seas. Rap is a fashion show. It's not about if you're bumping. When I was coming up it was about what you were coming with. I'm getting away from that shit because I am sick of it.

Do you think there is no such thing as talent anymore?
There isn't. It's 90% business and only 10% talent. Back in the day when Rakim and KRS-One was putting it down there was a whole different game. Now there is a lot of bullshit ass niggaz in the game. I talk about dope because I grew up around dope. I'm not talking about moving 1,000 kilos, because if you're moving that much dope then you're not even in a studio at all—you're hustling. Some of these rappers are talking about how much dope they are hauling but you ain't no real gangsta. Real gangsta's laugh at rappers because they make real money. Some of these niggaz ain't never did no real time. They got locked up for a couple of DUI's and now they think they are gangsta. Some of them get a little battery on their girl friend and they think they are gangsters. These niggaz ain't never shot shit! That's why I don't deal with these cats and have a whole lot of features.

I agree. There's way too much bullshit in Rap these days! That's why I'm giving you a raw interview right now because I have been with you from the get go. Murder Dog is not a commercial ass magazine. To us it has always been about the music first.
Right, but these niggaz are getting away from the music. Nowadays it's fuckin' model shows and faggots coming out with fragrance. I'm looking at Puffy going to model shows and Pharell putting out a fuckin' fragrance. What the fuck? These niggaz on some gay shit! That ain't hip hop. Hip hop is a culture and they're getting away from the culture. Everybody wants to be a rock star these days, they don't give a fuck about the music. Everybody is trying to be actors and shit too. I did few cameos in a few movies with Paul and them. I respect that but that not me. I can't do that; I'm an MC and that's what I do. I ain't never tried to get filthy rich off of it, I'm just trying to survive. I don't know how to do nothing else and rap is how I live. I do work with my grandfather who's name is Willie Beauregard. That's the only man I respect as far as working with and doing manual labor. Other than that I have always been a writer.

When and how did you start writing?
I started off writing songs but I couldn't sing so I started MCing. I grew up around pimps, drug dealers and gang bangers. That is what I was raised around. I was cutting school going to the studio. I did the gang thing and you're always down but I'm not part of that world no more. I'm just affiliated. I can't tell you what gang but I am forever that. The ones that know me know what it is with Lord Infamous. If you look at my jail record you will see my track record. There ain't nothing fake about it.

The best thing is to be honest with your music. That's what fans want to hear.
I'm not one of them cats who will just hop on a record and wear all this jewelry because I don't do that. I don't drive no big fancy-ass car. I roll with my girl because they took my license a long time ago, and I don't drive Bentleys either!

The money that is spent on a Bentley can feed many children. What would you spend 100-$200 grand on?
When I get a check like that I give some of it to my mom. I might take my girl out, pay bills, and I just try to survive. Also I got habits and I support them too. I'm trying to chill out on that though because that's the reason why I got in so much trouble. I still pop my pill, sip some syrup, and treat my nose every once and again but that is just the way I do.

You don't want that kind of stuff to take over your life. Did you always know your limits?
Not like I do now and I'm trying to maintain and get a grip on it.

To survive in the world that we are living in right now your mind has to be as sharp as nails.
Right, right! I'm just thankful that I still can think straight. I have got my priorities straight now.

Do you think you will ever be in Three 6 Mafia again?
I'm always Three 6 Mafia. I am one of the founders of the group. I am the one that came up with the name "Triple Six Mafia"; a lot of people may not know that. I created that name. Me and Paul grew together and one of the first places we ever did a song was in church. A lot of people might not believe that either.

How old were you? Were you nervous?
I was only like ten years old. We was nervous as hell. We did "Amazing Grace". Paul was on the keyboard and I sung. That is insane because later in life we ended up calling ourselves "Triple Six." You got the exclusive on that!

Did you used to listen to Esham? I see some similarities in your subject matter.
Me and Paul were both big fans of Esham. I remember back when all of them fires were hitting Detroit. Esham was into the dark art. I wonder what happened to that cat?

Esham is about to release a new album called "Sacrificial Lambs."
Esham has been putting it down for a long ass time. I was a real big Ganksta Nip fan too. When we started we were called The Serial Killers and we did a show with Ganksta Nip in Club Obsession. We were still in high school.

That's crazy. What else was going on in Memphis at that time?
After I got kicked out of high school I was hanging out in North Memphis and I started hearing about this cat. I had a girlfriend at that time and she lived in Hertz Village and she would always tell me about these cats named Skinny Pimp And 211. One day I was playing basketball with 211 and I didn't even know he was 211. One day I was riding the bus and I met Crunchy Black and that was before I knew he was Crunchy Black. I didn't know he was this cat that everybody was talking about at the skating rink. He was juking his ass off and everybody knew about it. I sat behind him on the bus and we got to talking. We were both in blue dickies and chuck tailors because back then we were into the LA culture. I told him I got a brother named DJ Paul and he was making these mixtapes. Crunchy had already met Paul one time and we didn't even know it. That's how we hooked up with him. I met Skinny in North Memphis and Skinny hooked us up with Juicy J. Then Paul met Juicy and he started coming out to the house.

How did you meet Koopsta Knicca?
Koop is from Texas. He came out here after his mother and father passed away. He was an orphan. Crunchy was an orphan too but he would stay with his auntie and in and out of detention homes.

How did Gangsta Boo get into the picture?
Paul met Boo from high school. Everyone was telling us about this girl who could rap real well. Boo was like a tomboy back then. That is how all of us came together.

When did Scan Man and MC Mack join up?
Scan Man was Koopsta's friend and so was MC Mack. Project Pat was in prison at that time and his first time was a robbery charge. When he got out he started rapping with us. Pat started jumping on Juicy J's mixtapes, and then he brought out "Murderers, Robbers". He recorded some of those songs at my house in South Memphis. That was back in 1991-92

Just like I say about the Hot Boys, I would love to see all of you get back together and do something again. It that possible?
That would be so difficult for that to happen. We have all grown so far apart over the years.

You're giving us a good history lesson today! What were some of the first tapes that you put out way back in the day?
I did "Come with Me To Hell Part One and Two" with DJ Paul back in 1991. I also had the Lord Infamous solo album where I had the song called "Licking My Nuts". On that album I also had the song called "South Memphis" and it was a big underground hit. I did another album called "Portrait Of A Serial Killer"; that was our very first DJ Paul and Lord Infamous album. Then we did another Serial Killer tape. All of the OG Three 6 fans will know it by the picture that we took in front of this red 6-4. When we got all the way up to volume sixteen we were ready to do "Mystic Stylez". We knew it was a good record but it took way off and sold 100,000 in the first month. That was when all of us were together. It had Gangsta Blac, Skinny, Killa Klan Kaze, K-Rock, Project Pat, and all of us. We recorded the album in like two months. It just took off. By now "Mystic Stylez" should be like a platinum record because we re-released it and we did a Screw version. After that we did the EP "Live By Yo Rep" and then came "The End Chapter One" and "Chapter Two: World Domination".

How does it feel to have your own solo album out after all of these years?
It feels real good. A lot of people have been waiting on this. People can't believe that it turned out so well because I have been gone for so long. I'm real proud of this. Believe it or not it has been about three or four years since I touched a pen. I didn't write anything until I started working on the album. I picked the pen up and everything flowed! I just wanted to give my fans that old Lord Infamous.

My favorite tracks are "You Don't Want None", and "I'm Wit It". You had some excellent production on there too.
I did some composing this time. A lot of times I would help Paul and J compose tracks. The album was produced by Enigma, D.J. Sounds, St. Kittz, Jae Bino, and Quota. This album has worldwide potential. This album lit a fire for me because I had a point to prove. A lot of people thought that I couldn't do it without Paul and J and Three 6. I had to show them that I am Three 6.

You had one line where you said "Even though I'm not with the Six talking bad on my brother will get you impaled." Tell me about that!
I was talking about that Kia Shine kid. I heard he was talking shit about my brother. He said some shit about shooting a machinegun, but Paul don't need to shoot a machine gun because we got niggaz that shoot it for us. To tell you the truth, I don't like Kia. I think he is sweet and has some feminine ways. He probably gets fucked in the ass!

Are you pretty happy with the album?
I'm happy with it and I can't complain. I had something to prove to myself. Me and my little brother talked a lot and he told me I'm good at it and I shouldn't stop doing it. Everybody always said that I shouldn't let my talent go to waste. The truth is things were really messed up for me. I was suicidal and I tried killing myself. I was depressed and I didn't know where my life was going.

You tried to kill yourself?
I tried to cut my wrists.

How did you get out of that dark place in your life?
My girlfriend helped me out a lot. I guess that is what I needed in my life. I was at Logan's Restaurant and she was a waitress over there. We talked a lot and got a lot of shit off of our chests to each other and she told me I should go back out there and do it. A lot of the fans helped me too. I needed somebody in my life at that time. I was by myself going through depression. I suffer from depression and I wasn't taking no medication or nothing. Actually I tried to commit suicide two or three times. I cut my wrists twice and I over dosed a couple of times too.

Was it with cocaine or what?
It was cane and taking a lot of pills too. I don't mind you putting this in the interview because people need to know about addiction and suicide. If I had killed myself I would've never put out this album. I'm back on my feet now and this is something people need to know.

I know it would be hard to get the old Three 6 back together, but do you think you will ever be in the group again?
I think it could happen but people would have to bring some egos down. I think there is a possibility that me, Paul, and Juicy could work it out. I think Boo has burnt a lot of bridges with Juicy and them, and Koop has been out for so long. I like Koop and me and him have always been cool. Koop is my nigga! I don't know about Crunchy because lately he has been ego trippin. At one point I went to his house but he wasn't being real hospitable with me. I guess since he just came off of a double platinum album he thought he was the shit or something. We were gonna do an album called "The Other Half Of The Six" and we were gonna get Boo and Koop on it but Crunchy was on some big head shit. I just said "Fuck it, I'm gonna do my own shit!" I would still like to get Crunchy, Boo, Koop, and Chat together and do an album though.

www.officialblackrainent.com

A lot of this shit I really haven't thought about in years. This is some good shit you need to put down in the interview. •

YG INTERVIEW

BY BLACK DOG BONE • PHOTO BY JOHN RICARD

There have been a lot of rappers coming out of LA since NWA, but when I heard you I knew you were going to be a star. You've got it!
I'm on my way, bro. I'm on my way!

You're not on your way, you're there. Everyone is talking about YG right now.
Maan, I don't know! Shit, I don't know what's goin on.

I feel like your new album is going to be one of those landmark albums that really brings the West Coast back.
The album is coming out for 2014, "My Krazy Life". And I feel like it's going to be one of them landmark albums that puts the West Coast back to where we were a few years ago. Cause the music on the album is real cultural. It's real Hip Hop, real Rap, that I'm giving you. A lotta rappers out right now is not giving you the real culture of where they're from. What people think of the West Coast, what people think is from the West Coast, that's what I'm giving you. I'm giving you the culture of the streets where we come from, where the majority of the people like me come from.

That's what I like about you; it's that Compton culture. It's that real LA Gangsta music. That's what NWA, Eazy E and Ice Cube represented. When I hear your music I really feel Compton. Did this come naturally out of you or did you have to think about it?
This shit was natural. This shit came upon just me doing me, me doing what I do. That's how I do everything, I just do me. And Mustard played a big role in it too, because he produced the music. Before Mustard wasn't making beats. Around that time I didn't have no good beats to record on, and around that time Mustard started making beats. Then we was just goin in the studio and he would hear a hook I made for another song and he'd take the vocals and make a beat to the shit. He was makin the music off of stuff I was rappin about. He's from LA too, from the other side, but we all from the same environment, from the streets. We all live our lives the same in some type of way. He took the way my raps sound and made the music to that, and that's what we got today.

Mustard took samples from your vocals and made beats?
He didn't really take samples. I was recording all my music in my room on Protools myself. So he'd just upload Protools and listen to songs that I had already recorded to beats that wasn't good beats. Then he made beats to the acapella's. He'd play the acapella and make the music to that. And it's all blowin up.

How did you meet Mustard?
I met Mustard like the end of 2008. He did my first mixtape I ever put out; it's called "4Fingaz". I met him through a mutual friend. The friend who connected us was my street manager at the time. He connected me with Ty Dolla $ign and he connected me with Mustard. Mustard was deejayin in the local clubs all around LA, so I knew of him already, but I didn't know him. Then I was performing at all the clubs, so we both was knowing of each other, but we didn't know each other. Then he connected us and he did my first mixtape in 2001. After that he was my DJ. Then "Toot It and Boot It" blew up in 2010. After than it was on with Mustard.

"Toot It and Boot It" was a big turning point in your career?
It got me to different places I was never in. That was my first national song ever, so it did do a lot for me.

You were probably real young when you met Mustard?
I was 17 when I met Mustard, then I turned 18.

When I listen to your lyrics you seem to have a very poetic feel, the way you put the words together. Do you write your lyrics down?
I write the shit most of the time, but sometimes you can catch me just in the booth rappin shit. Most of the time I write it though.

NWA was happening almost 30 years ago. What were you listening to growing up in Compton?
Me growin up? I was born in Compton, then my parents moved us out to the next city over to try to keep us out of the hood and that typa shit. Then when I was 16 my pops went to jail. That's when I started really doin shit in the streets. I got into crime, and I started gang bangin around that time. At that time I was listening to a lotta The Game and Lil Wayne and Jeezy. Before that I grew up on the West Coast shit, Snoop Dogg, The Chronic, Dr. Dre, all that shit. I grew up on that off top. Me being young and bein from the West Coast, that was the music we grew up on. But when I started doin my own thing in the streets I was listening to The Game and a lotta Lil Wayne and Young Jeezy and Jules Santana. There was a lot goin on around me. I started gang bangin, was ditching school, going to parties and shit. That was my life, ya feel me? That's really where my typa music comes from, that house party scene. I was breakin into a lotta houses, doin shit. That's where my music comes from.

In your music you talk about the streets and all the Compton culture. I mean you come across as someone hard, but also you come across as a cool person. You're a very likeable person; people like you.
Yeah, people like me and that's what's helpin me in my career. My music is hard, but then people love me. So they just accept it. That was like Eazy E. People always say Eazy E was nice and a cool guy, but he had the Gangsta Rap music. That's why all the people like that music more, cause Eazy E was cool.

I see you kind of like an Eazy E. It's like some people make music, but only a few people are stars. Eazy E was a star, you're like that. We've been waiting for you! How did you first meet Young Jeezy?
Young Jeezy came to LA a couple of years ago, and we was all in the same club at a show. When they played the YG shit the club went crazy, they was playin my record. He seen that. And he had a couple of niggaz with him and he was askin them like, who was I? They told him, "That's YG." He started askin more people about me and they said I was signed to Def Jam, and he was signed to Def Jam too. After that he started askin at Def Jam about me. About that time I was putting out my mixtapes and shit. He told Def Jam like, "OK, tell him I wanna fuck with him." So they connected us. When they connected us Jeezy came out to LA for the Grammy's in 2011 or 12. We had a little meeting; he told me what he was tryin to do and he fuck with what I was doing and he wanna see me win. He come from the same typa lifestyle, the same typa come-up, same typa grind and environment. From that day we was goin back and forth. He was flyin to LA doing little studio sessions, hoppin on my songs. I was going to Miami and Atlanta, hoppin on his songs. I was like, "Fuck that shit; let's make this shit official." Then we made it official. I came out with "My Nigga", and that shit just blew up. It's gonna go gold like next week.

That video is so hot with Jeezy and Rich Homie Quan! How did that video come about?
Me and Mustard collabed on the idea for the video. I told him I wanted to shoot the video in Atlanta but I wanted to be ridin around in a red low rider. And they came out with the little jail scene and that shit. We just put it together and made that shit.
It's funny that it was made in Atlanta, because it's got a real LA feel.
Exactly! It's got an LA feel, but we shot it in Atlanta to make Atlanta fuck with us.

I have people in Africa and they say you're real big out there. They're listening to YG right now.
Really? Yeah? Hell, yeah.

People might think you came out just yesterday, but you have a lot of history. You've released a lot of mixtapes.
For sure. I had mixtapes out in 2008 and 2009. I got the "4Fingaz" mixtape droppin in 2009. Then 2010 "The Real 4 Fingaz" came out. Then 2011 "Just Re'd Up" came out. In 2012 "4 Hunnid Degreez" came out. In January of 2013, top of this year, I dropped "Just Re'd Up 2". I've got five mixtapes to my name, and off the mixtapes I had a lotta hit singles. Off the first "Just Re'd Up" I had the "Bitches Ain't Shit" record. I had the "Up Good" record; I had the "The Up Record". Off the "4 Hunnid Degreez" I had the "I'ma Thug" record and the "Cali Livin" record. Then on "Just Re'd Up 2" I had the "You Broke" record and "I'm a Real One" record. You feel me? I have a lotta records. On all them mixtapes I have like 21 to 28 songs. That's around like 70 or 80 songs in the last 2 years.

What about the production on this new album?
DJ Mustard produced like 90% of it. There's 12 tracks on the album and he did like 7 of them. I've got Drake on a song. It's really like a day in the life type of piece, from the top of the morning to the end of the night. It's like a day in the life of YG. I'm taking you through different situations I've been through. I'm showing you where I come from and the culture of the West Coast.

I like that you worked with one producer for most of the tracks. That way there's a consistent feel throughout.
Exactly. You gonna feel YG on this muthafucka.

What motivates you to do what you're doing?
I just feel like people are loving this shit, so I'm gonna keep on doing it. I been listening to a lotta old school classic albums like Snoop Dogg "Doggy Style" and that kinda shit. I'm basically doin the same thing they did, but I'm doin it my way. I'm workin with my producer and we're gonna put it together like it's a book or a movie. When you get done with the CD you're gonna like it and respect it. Even if you ain't living the same lifestyle I'm living, you gonna understand it and get it. You're probably gonna wanna live that lifestyle too.

You say you listened to Snoop and classic West Coast Rap, but you don't sound anything like them. I feel like you're creating a new sound for the West Coast. It's like when NWA first came out, you're starting something new.
Hell yeah! That's something, you feeling like that. I feel like I'm bringing that same typa energy and that same lifestyle. For me to say I'm doing something big like NWA, I can't say that. But for you to say that, that's what's up! That means that you're looking at what I'm doing and it's reminding you of what they did. That's big.

How did you develop your lyrical style? You are an amazing writer.
I don't even think about it. I just write off of the shit I go through. And the flow is just real, that shit just be coming. When I hear a beat, the flow just comes.

When you were growing up, how was it? Did you have a big family?
Growing up for me until I was 16 was like normal. My mama didn't start off with money, but she started her own business and she was getting money. So I had whatever I damn near wanted. My mom was from the hood. My pops, he's from the country up in Atlanta. I was living that lifestyle, and my pops was all in my head about being in the streets and all that. So before he went to jail, I was doin shit but I was doin it on the low. When he went to jail when I was 16, my mama lost her house and she lost all her money. We moved in with my granddaddy, and after that we moved into an apartment. That's when I started doing shit in the streets, like breakin into houses, gang bangin and all that. From 16 to 19 that's what I was doin. Then I got signed at the age of 19, but I was still in the streets because my life really ain't changed. I just had a popular song, so I was going outa town a lot doing shows. But when I came back to the city I was still in the streets, up in the hood gang bangin, partying, doin all that shit.

The streets love you and the females love you, then you've also got the crossover crowd. It's not easy to get such a wide audience. Do you see that at your shows?
Yeah. My shows is like mixed crowd. They buy my albums and support.

If you could work with any artists, who would you choose to do songs with?
I wish I could do a record with Tupac (rest in peace). I wanna do a record with Lil Boosie; I hear he's getting outa jail soon. I wanna do a record with Aaliyah (rest in peace too). But really, I've got records with everybody that's important right now. Everybody that I fuck with is good too. I think I'm doing everything that I wanna do. It would be amazing if you did a record with M.I.A. or with Nikki Minaj.
I fuck with M.I.A. too. Hey, I fuck with that shit! Nikki Minaj—yeah, I wanna work with her too. I fuck with Nikki too.

At this point your doors are open. Just keep putting out the good quality music and don't sell out.
Oh yeah, no, bro! I ain't sellin out! Hell no. I'm givin 'em the raw shit! I finna go hard. Once

you hear my album you're gonna fuck with it. I'm goin hard, bro!

I thought this album was going to come out earlier. What happened?
I had just put out an early date to get everybody talkin and ready for a YG album. Cause I had already put out a lotta mixtapes, but I hadn't dropped an album. I felt like I had to start conditioning people, get 'em ready to buy an album from me. So I put the November date out to get people ready. Now people are gonna be ready. I'm gonna drop the official date soon, so be on the lookout for that.

Right now what are you doing?
I'm in fuckin Hawaii right now! I got a show tonight. I just got off the Yo Gotti tour; it was like a 40-city tour. That was successful. That helped my record, got me all over the South. But I'm in Hawaii now, chillin before we do the show tonight. Then I finna go back to the "Shitty" to do a little thing I gotta do to finish the album. I'm doin everything right now—I'm tourin, I'm chillin, I'm workin on my album.

Does your appeal to a lot of females or is it more of a male audience?
I make a lotta thug records, and then my music, how I'm comin, is hard. I'm comin hard. Females like hard, and when you got records for them then they fuck with you even more.

Do you feel like West Coast Gangsta Rap is coming back?
Sure, it's going on already! Labels are lookin for West Coast artists right now, and I think we did a lot for that. That's from the work we're putting in. Like we got strip clubs up in Hollywood and shit now. We ain't used to have that. But our music and what we was doing, that gets played in strip clubs. The shit is back poppin. Artists is getting deals. People droppin music, and it's all good.

What inspires you to write your lyrics?
My life inspires my lyrics, all the shit I do. All the females I fucked with, all the relationships I had, all the shit I done did, all that shit inspires me.

When I listen to your music I feel that what you're talking about is real. That tension is in your songs.
Yeah. It's emotional.

What sounds do you look for when you're picking tracks?
I like the heavy bass, and I like the little bell sounds and all the little synth. My thing I like the most is the 808's. That's what I love, the bass line.

When you were touring which towns did you have your best shows?
I fuck with San Francisco. I fuck with Oakland. I fuck with Arizona. I fuck with Milwaukee. I fuck with Grand Rapids, Michigan. I fuck with Seattle. I fuck with Denver, Colorado heavy. And DC and St. Louis, Missouri. I fuck with all that shit.

I really like your videos? How do you come up with the concepts for your videos?
All my videos you see, the ones you probably like the most are the ones I did the whole setup for. All my videos I'm the executive producer for.

Is there anything else you want to say to your fans?
I want my fans to know that I'd never be where I'm at without the fans. I wanna show my fans love. That's why we come out and do the tours, we fuck with the fans. I put a lotta time and thought into this shit so that when they see this shit they can live that life and enjoy this shit. For real, my album's gonna be way better than my mixtapes. I want my fans to know that I put a lot of time into this shit.

Compton was the original home to Gangsta Rap. Compton Rap has influenced music all over the world.
I think about that. Compton, LA, and California in general, we've influenced a lotta people in the world. Just the West Coast culture—

the beaches and the palm trees, the movies and actors, the Lakers, the Dodgers—we've influenced the world in so many way. Everybody likes hard shit, like action movies; people always like to see the bad shit. So when the OG homies came out with Gangsta shit—Dre, Eazy E, Ice Cube, Tupac, Snoop Dogg—when they came with that hard Gangsta Rap everybody loved it because it was hardcore. And then it's comin from muthafuckin LA. It was showing how the people was really living, and everybody loved that shit. A lotta people started living their life like that. There started to be gangs in places that there was never gangs at before. That's what the OG homies did with this music. We had a lotta influence on the world. That's why I take this serious, because I'm coming with this hard shit.

It's not just showing bad shit. It's real shit.
Yeah, the real shit! It's real, but on top of that it's hard. It is bad shit. People don't always wanna show the bad shit, but this is real. When peoples saw that they felt it and they was onto this shit. This is how we living and we don't give a fuck! They respect that.

Tech N9ne's first cover was Murder Dog. The Game's first cover was on Murder Dog. Is this the first cover story you're doing?
This is my first cover. Murder Dog! Turn the fuck up! I appreciate you reaching out. •

www.ingramcontent.com/pod-product-compliance
Lightning Source LLC
Chambersburg PA
CBHW041514220426
43668CB00002B/22